SCRIPTURAL TRACES:
CRITICAL PERSPECTIVES ON THE RECEPTION AND
INFLUENCE OF THE BIBLE

33

Editors
Matthew A. Collins, University of Chester
Michelle Fletcher, King's College London, UK
Andrew Mein, Durham University, UK

Editorial board
Michael J. Gilmour, David Gunn, James Harding, Jorunn Økland

Published under

LIBRARY OF NEW TESTAMENT STUDIES

673

Formerly the Journal for the Study of the New Testament Supplement series

Editor
Chris Keith

Editorial Board
Dale C. Allison, Lynn H. Cohick, Kylie Crabbe, R. Alan Culpepper,
Craig A. Evans, Jennifer Eyl, Robert Fowler, Juan Hernández Jr., John S.
Kloppenborg, Michael Labahn, Matthew V. Novenson, Love L. Sechrest,
Robert Wall, Catrin H. Williams, Brittany E. Wilson

FAN FICTION AND EARLY CHRISTIAN WRITINGS

Apocrypha, Pseudepigrapha and Canon

Tom de Bruin

LONDON • NEW YORK • OXFORD • NEW DELHI • SYDNEY

T&T CLARK

Bloomsbury Publishing Plc, 50 Bedford Square, London, WC1B 3DP, UK
Bloomsbury Publishing Inc, 1359 Broadway, New York, NY 10018, USA
Bloomsbury Publishing Ireland, 29 Earlsfort Terrace, Dublin 2, D02 AY28, Ireland

BLOOMSBURY, T&T CLARK and the T&T Clark logo are trademarks of
Bloomsbury Publishing Plc

First published in Great Britain 2024
Paperback edition published 2026

Copyright © Tom de Bruin, 2024

Tom de Bruin has asserted their right under the Copyright, Designs and Patents Act, 1988, to be identified as Author of this work.

For legal purposes the Acknowledgements on p.vii constitute an extension of this copyright page.

Cover image: 'Miracle during the flight: Jesus is taming a dragon'
© The Picture Art Collection / Alamy

All rights reserved. No part of this publication may be: i) reproduced or transmitted in any form, electronic or mechanical, including photocopying, recording or by means of any information storage or retrieval system without prior permission in writing from the publishers; or ii) used or reproduced in any way for the training, development or operation of artificial intelligence (AI) technologies, including generative AI technologies. The rights holders expressly reserve this publication from the text and data mining exception as per Article 4(3) of the Digital Single Market Directive (EU) 2019/790.

Bloomsbury Publishing Plc does not have any control over, or responsibility for, any third-party websites referred to or in this book. All internet addresses given in this book were correct at the time of going to press. The author and publisher regret any inconvenience caused if addresses have changed or sites have ceased to exist, but can accept no responsibility for any such changes.

A catalogue record for this book is available from the British Library.
A catalog record for this book is available form the Library of Congress.

ISBN: HB: 978-0-5677-0663-8
PB: 978-0-5677-0667-6
ePDF: 978-0-5677-0664-5
eBook: 978-0-5677-0666-9

Series: Library of New Testament Studies, volume 673
Scriptural Traces, 33, ISSN 2513-8790

Typeset by RefineCatch Limited, Bungay, Suffolk

For product safety related questions contact productsafety@bloomsbury.com.

To find out more about our authors and books visit www.bloomsbury.com
and sign up for our newsletters.

CONTENTS

Acknowledgements	vii
Introduction	
'I AM A JESUS FANFIC WRITER': ANCIENT FANS, EARLY CHRISTIAN DERIVATIVE WORKS, AND ANNE RICE	1
Fans	7
Ancient Fans	10
An Introduction to Fan Fiction	13
Defining Fan Fiction	15
Key Terms, Language, and Contexts	22
This Book	26
Chapter 1	
FASCINATION, FRUSTRATION, AND FIXING THE GOSPEL OF MARK: WHY WRITE A DERIVATIVE WORK?	29
Fascination and Frustration	30
The Endings of Mark	35
Fixing Mark and Fix-it Fic	38
Harmonization and the Gospel Harmonies	40
Refocalization and Mary Magdalene	42
Personalization and Snakes	47
Recontextualization and the Freer Logion	51
Conclusions and Significance	54
Chapter 2	
NOSTALGIA, NOVELTY, AND TEXTUAL AUTHORITY IN THE TESTAMENTS OF THE TWELVE PATRIARCHS: WHAT POWER DOES A DERIVATIVE WORK HAVE?	59
Fan Play and Fan Economies	61
Author's Notes and Paratextual Engagement in Authority	66
Nostalgic Fan Fiction	71
Novel Fan Fiction	78
Conclusions	83
Chapter 3	
CANONICITY AND THE POLITICS OF CANON: HOW DO PEOPLE (DE-)AUTHORIZE DERIVATIVE WORKS?	87
Christian Apocrypha	90
Canon, Canonicity and Tiers of Canon	93

Canon Debates and Fan Works	102
Debating Canon	107
Conclusions	113

Chapter 4
GATEKEEPING, HERESY, INFANTILIZATION, AND FEMINIZATION: HOW DO PEOPLE POLICE DERIVATIVE WORKS? — 115

Creating Canon, Creating Heresy	116
Heretics, Gatekeeping and Bad Fans	123
Infantilizing Fans	126
Feminizing Fans	130
Conclusions	135

Chapter 5
HEADCANON, FANON, AND THE CHRISTIAN TRANSMEDIA STORYWORLD: WHY DO DERIVATIVE WORKS MATTER? — 137

The Power of Headcanon	139
World Building is Political	143
Inhabiting the Early Christian Storyworld	150
Storyworld Influences Readings	155
Conclusions and Significance	166

Epilogue
'I COULDN'T GET THESE LEGENDS OUT OF MY MIND' — 169

Bibliography	175
Index	195

ACKNOWLEDGEMENTS

This book, like any, has been a journey. It exists thanks to so many people and despite many others. Not knowing where to start, let me begin with my partner in British New Testament crime, Michelle Fletcher. Her constant optimism and desperate attempts to keep in me in academia have kept me sane. She also let me constantly bounce ideas off her, to see what works and what doesn't. If it wasn't for Sara Parks I would also have left academia years ago. She has been a constant cheerleader and friend, and I'm still upset that she left the UK. The third member of this holy trinity is Meredith Warren, for her unconditional belief in me, her tireless letter-writing when I applied for *yet another* job, and her tactful avoidance in asking if I ever heard anything back.

This project has been long, and many people contributed to it. I must start by thanking Kelsie Rodenbiker for reading drafts of most of this book and giving me highly constructive feedback! And, Aulikki Nahkola proofread all my references, and apparently enjoyed the task. But, as in all academic projects, most of the labour remains invisible. Throughout this work, I have tried to make it visible by naming those that contributed (see the footnotes), but scores still remain nameless. I cannot, for instance, remember who asked the amazing question at the *British New Testament Society* that spawned the epilogue to this book. I also no longer have any idea who suggested the Christmas stable for Chapter 5 at the *Tracing Global Christianity in Late Antiquity* conference. And, of course I must thank my anonymous peer reviewer, who really went out of their way to make this book much better. The list goes on. Thank you all! Hopefully you know who you are.

I want to thank my many communities. The editorial team at the *Journal for Interdisciplinary Biblical Studies* has been a constant source of joy and support. I've taken so much from the frequent chats with Meredith Warren (again!) and Eric Vanden Eykel. I treasure the messages of support, the teamwork and the covering for each other when life invariably happened.

Thank you to the people taking part in the Bible, Critical Theory and Reception seminars, and to James Crossley and John Lyons for organizing these. You risked bodily harm by allowing me to present on *My Little Pony* fans in a Birmingham pub. More importantly, you gave me many good and supportive contributions that helped me shape this project.

To my queer friends at Seventh-day Adventist Kinship, who welcomed a scholar rejected by their church into a warm community when I needed it most: Catherine Taylor, Ruud Kieboom, Floyd Poenitz, Kees Meiling, Frieder & Ingrid Schmid, and the other new friends I made there – I love you guys! We all matter, even if the Adventist church doesn't seem to think so.

Diolch to my colleagues at Pride Cymru, who let me join in their fight for LGBTQ+ rights in Wales for an (all too) little while. I'm sad to have left you, especially my 'workfriend' Emma Jones, and the best boss you'll ever have, Cath Harrison; my newer colleagues, Felicity McKee, always sharing amazing insights into histories of disability, and Patsy Hudson. Remember, dear reader, that trans rights are human rights.

Thanks to my former roommates from Cardiff who are now spread out over the world: Marija Grech, Chris Muller, Megen Molé. Playing *Pandemic* over Zoom is still the best way to spend a Sunday morning. I still don't know what y'all mean with critical posthumanism.

To my former colleagues at Newbold who, like me, became disenfranchised while I was writing this book: I am glad that three years later, our WhatsApp group is still called 'Workers unite!' Aulikki Nahkola (who went from former teacher, to colleague, to a treasured friend), one day I will join you birding. Julian Thompson, I wish we had worked together longer, and I want to talk a lot more about orality and folklore with you. *Bedankt* to my new colleagues at Radboud University who have made me feel extremely welcome as I joined them in the final stages of this project: Justine Bakker, Seth Bledsoe, Carly Crouch, Matthijs den Dulk, Mike Kochenash, Annet den Haan.

I've had far too many amazing students to name them all here, but you know who you are. You welcomed me into your life and trusted me to help you find your voice and your fight. In return, you pushed me to reconsider my opinions, my voice and my privilege. Keep shouting loud, your voices are important.

My family grew during this project: my absolute bestest sibling-in-law Kaity married the amazing Dan Stewart. Stupid COVID kept me from the wedding, but their queer love and quirky texts kept me going through some dark days. My family also shrank: I can no longer thank my fabulous cousin Mark who passed away last year. Of course, family always stays the same-ish. I am always thankful to my extremely supportive parents, who get very angry with people who are horrible to me and who seem to think everything I do is absolutely amazing. Both of those things are highly necessary.

Finally, there's the insanely supportive community of friends in and outside scholarship. Thanks to y'all: Esther Brownsmith, Reinder Bruinsma, Jeremiah Coogan, Cristian Cardozo, Wayne Erasmus, Kimberly Fowler, Stefan Höschele, Siobhán Jolley, Lydia Lijkendijk, Luca Marulli, Keisha E. McKenzie, Sarah Parkhouse, Shailey Patel, Hans Ponte, Isaac Soon, Janet Spittler, Katie Turner, Nelske Verbaas, Taylor Weaver. I am sure I am forgetting many more people who I should thank – by all means send me an angry message and I'll take you out to dinner to apologize.

There are also some things and people to unthank. As a project, this work also exists *despite* many things. Here the Marxist words of the Salvage Editorial Collective come to mind:

Sometimes it seems hopeless, and yet, and yet. We go on, despite that.

As well as that preposition – in spite of, regardless of, in the face of – the word 'despite' has an older meaning as a noun. Contempt; disdain; spite itself; an outrage committed.[1]

---

1. Salvage Editorial Collective, 'Salvage Perspectives #2: Awaiting the Furies', *Salvage*, 9 November 2015, https://salvage.zone/in-print/salvage-perspectives-2-awaiting-the-furies/.

I know many who go on, even when it seems hopeless. They go on *despite*. Despite capitalism. Despite the state of higher education. Despite the Tories and right-wing politics. Despite homophobia and transphobia. Despite the impending climate apocalypse. Despite precarity. Despite racism. Despite unfair labour practices. Despite discrimination. Despite it all.

I see this work as a work of spite. It exists, in spite of all these things. I hope it can also inspire others towards utopian spite. Despise these inequalities and injustices with everything you have. And if you have anything left, desire community, kinship and equity.

And then, finally, to end on a higher note, I cannot but thank Megen. I think she knows why.

Nijmegen, July 2023

Introduction

'I AM A JESUS FANFIC WRITER': ANCIENT FANS, EARLY CHRISTIAN DERIVATIVE WORKS, AND ANNE RICE

In 2005 famous vampire novelist Anne Rice published the first book of a planned trilogy on the life of Jesus Christ. In her concluding 37-page 'Author's Note' she goes into extreme detail about her motivations and preparations for writing this novel. Detailing a long spiritual journey, she tells that in 2002 she was 'ready to do violence to [her] career' and that she 'consecrated' herself and her work to Christ.[1] Rice, apparently driven by pious rather than economic reasons, wrote this book, *Christ the Lord, Out of Egypt*, in order to:

> take the Jesus of the Gospels, the Gospels which were becoming ever more coherent to me, the Gospels which appealed to me as elegant first-person witness, dictated to scribes no doubt, but definitely early, the Gospels produced before Jerusalem fell – to take the Jesus of the Gospels, and try to get inside him and imagine what he felt.[2]

Rice, wishing to detail the emotional world of Jesus, decided to write a first-person novel. Key for her is that she is not writing about the historical Jesus, or 'a liberal Jesus, a married Jesus, a gay Jesus, a Jesus who was a rebel', but 'the Jesus of the Gospels'.[3]

Christ the Lord, Out of Egypt is an apt introduction to this monograph on fan fiction because it is modern-day example of how a pious person views their creativity within a religious realm, and feels the need to write a secondary work. Like the millions of fans worldwide, writing texts based on their fandom, Rice wishes to creatively contribute to *her* fandom: Christianity. Admittedly, Anne Rice would not wish her book to be called fan fiction. Rice's dislike of, and litigation against, fan fiction about her own books is infamous.[4] Indeed, her disdain of fan

---

1. Anne Rice, *Christ the Lord: Out of Egypt* (London: Arrow, 2007), 435.
2. Rice, *Christ the Lord*, 2007, 451.
3. Rice, *Christ the Lord*, 2007, 450.
4. 'Anne Rice', *Fanlore*, https://fanlore.org/wiki/Anne_Rice.

fiction is so well-known that science fiction news site Tor.com devoted its 2009 April Fool's spoof article to the topic:

> Long-time opponent of fanfiction and author of at least two readable books, Anne Rice has reluctantly changed her tune about the genre she so strongly dislikes. 'I am a Jesus fanfic writer,' she admitted in a recent restatement of the headline.... Asked why she opposed material derived from her own work, but felt no compunction borrowing Jesus, she commented, 'I don't want people reworking my imagination. I invented bisexual vampirism, after all. And creepy children. I invented them too. As for Jesus, I just filled in the blanks.'[5]

Here Tor.com is playing with the irony of the fact that someone so against fan fiction wrote a book that so many people see as Jesus fan fiction.[6] This is not how Rice sees it. Reflecting on her own work, Rice explains that it was a decision in 2002 'to use any talent I had acquired as a writer, as a storyteller, as a novelist – for Him and for Him alone'.[7] Rice, wishing 'to be more than a scribe',[8] writes this book to 'serve Our Blessed Lord'.[9] She decides, in essence, to become a Jesus fan fiction writer, though refuses to frame it that way.

Looking at how Rice reflects on and reacts to *Christ the Lord*, raises an important issue: how do fiction and historical fact relate when it comes to her book? In the original 2005 publication, including the 'Author's Note', Rice does not address the issue of fiction(ality) in her book, yet she repeatedly emphasizes how much historical research she did, and that the work 'chronicles the life of Jesus Christ' and is 'based on the Gospels and on the most respected New Testament scholarship'.[10] Yet in the 2007 paperback edition, a new introduction and a new, additional 10-page Author's Note, both emphasize the fictionality of the work.[11] Her book

---

5. 'Anne Rice Admits to Writing Jesus Fan Fiction', *Tor.com*, 1 April 2009, https://www.tor.com/2009/04/01/april-fooanne-rice-admits-to-writing-jesus-fan-fiction/.

6. See, for example, Aspree, 'The Young "Messiah": Christians Delight in Really Bad Fanfiction', *The Aquila Report*, 14 March 2016, https://theaquilareport.com/the-young-messiah-christians-delight-in-really-bad-fanfiction/. Rice's book might not be identified as fan fiction in the strictest sense. Key identifiers of fan fiction (which I will discuss below) may be less applicable to her work. For example, her book was not written outside the marketplace – it was always meant to be sold. And, it was not written to standards of a fan community. At the same time, as she considers writing the book doing 'violence to her career' and she is exceedingly careful to toe the line of traditional catholic theological orthodoxy, even these two identifiers are applicable to her work.

7. Anne Rice, 'Anne's Profession of Faith', *AnneRice.com: The Official Site*, 11 June 2008, http://annerice.com/ChristTheLord-Profession.html.

8. Rice, *Christ the Lord*, 2007, 465.

9. Rice, 'Anne's Profession of Faith'.

10. Anne Rice, *Christ the Lord: Out of Egypt: A Novel* (New York: Knopf, 2005), back cover.

11. Rice, *Christ the Lord*, 2007, ix, 461.

now begins with the words: 'This book seeks to present a realistic fictional portrait of Our Lord in Time'.[12] In this account, the book is framed as fiction that *could* be true. In the subsequently published 'Anne's Profession of Faith', Rice extends this dichotomy between fact and fiction:

> Please understand: they are fiction, but they are fiction that seeks to bring the reader closer to the Lord in whom my life belongs. You will find no watering down of the gospels in these novels. You will find no modern twists. I am a believer in every word of Matthew, Mark, Luke and John.[13]

Rice attempts to walk a fine line between fiction and truth in her own work, strongly arguing that her fictional book is true to the canonical gospels. At the same time, from this introduction, it is clear that there is another level to this dichotomy between fact and fiction: Rice's fictional book also serves to reinforce the historical accuracy of the canonical gospels themselves. Rice sees the gospels, as Margaret Ramey argues, to be 'accurate depictions of history' and she 'aims at defending both the historical and theological truth of their stories'.[14] By creating a historical world that is both plausible and informed by scholarship, Rice creates a realistic milieu for the gospel accounts, and thus she 'enhances for her readers a sense of historicity of these events'.[15] These issues, dichotomies and inconsistencies are precisely the kind of things I am interested in exploring in this book on derivative texts in early Christianity.

Though accuracy to the gospels is Rice's stated goal, her book begins with a tale of seven-year-old Jesus killing a young boy, a narrative that does not exist in any canonical gospel, but is famously part of the non-canonical Infancy Gospel of Thomas.[16] Rice explains that she became enamoured with the apocryphal gospels, leading her to include these 'legends' in her book.[17] This means that her 'accurate retelling' of the 'Jesus of the Gospels' includes accounts from outside the four canonical gospels, including Jesus making clay doves and bringing them to life (Infancy Gospel of Thomas 2–3) and details about Mary's parents (Protoevangelium of James 1–10). This was an intentional step, as she credits these narratives in her original Author's Note:

---

12. Rice, *Christ the Lord*, 2007, ix.
13. Rice, 'Anne's Profession of Faith'.
14. Margaret E. Ramey, *The Quest for the Fictional Jesus: Gospel Rewrites, Gospel (Re)Interpretation, and Christological Portraits within Jesus Novels* (Cambridge: Lutterworth Press, 2017), 30.
15. Ramey, *The Quest for the Fictional Jesus*, 30.
16. Throughout this book, I have not italicized the titles of ancient texts, as this is the common practice in biblical studies. The capitalization should hopefully be sufficient to recognize these as titles.
17. Rice, *Christ the Lord*, 2007, 451.

then there were the legends – the Apocrypha – including the tantalizing tales in the Infancy Gospel of Thomas. I'd stumbled on them very early in my research, in multiple editions, and never forgotten them. And neither had the world. They were fanciful, some of them humorous, extreme to be sure.... I couldn't get these legends out of my mind.[18]

These narratives, 'legends' as Rice calls them, speak to her on a fundamental level. She sees a 'deep truth' in them and argues that these stories are also 'true to the declaration of the Council of Chalcedon' and 'true to Paul'.[19] She then, again, concludes with a pious note. The novel is dedicated to various groups including the readers of her vampire novels:

in the hope that Jesus will be as real to you as any other character I've ever launched into the world we share. After all, is Christ Our Lord not the ultimate supernatural hero, the ultimate outsider, the ultimate immortal of them all?[20]

In his analysis of Anne Rice's motives, Tony Burke argues that they are twofold: (1) she feels the need to fill the gaps in the canonical texts with apocryphal and novel narratives; and (2) she expanded the canonical narratives for pious reasons.[21] These motives also guided ancient authors, something Burke immediately claims. Tobias Nicklas also sees these two forces at work in ancient writings. He argues:

it becomes clear that even if apocryphal infancy stories contain many details and dates that we do not find in the texts which came to be part of the New Testament, some of them at least were not developed simply out of sheer delight for telling crude and strange stories, but rather out of theological motives.[22]

Similarly to Rice, ancient authors were interested in filling the gaps but also had theological motives. This example illustrates some of the forces at play in the production and consumption of derivative writings more generally. Rice writes because she feels the need, but also does this for pious reasons. The Apocrypha themselves shaped her reading of the canonical gospels, affecting her understanding

---

18. Rice, *Christ the Lord*, 2005, 451.
19. Rice, *Christ the Lord*, 2005, 452.
20. Rice, *Christ the Lord*, 2005, 452.
21. Tony Burke, 'Early Christian Apocrypha in Popular Culture', in *The Oxford Handbook of Early Christian Apocrypha*, ed. Andrew F. Gregory et al., Oxford Handbooks (Oxford: Oxford University Press, 2015), 433, doi:10.1093/oxfordhb/9780199644117.013.29.
22. Tobias Nicklas, 'The Influence of Jewish Scriptures on Early Christian Apocrypha', in *The Oxford Handbook of Early Christian Apocrypha*, ed. Andrew F. Gregory and C. M. Tuckett, Oxford Handbooks (Oxford: Oxford University Press, 2015), 144, doi:10.1093/oxfordhb/9780199644117.013.8.

of Jesus fundamentally. In her writing she likewise hopes to fundamentally influence her reading community, and readers and non-readers alike reacted very strongly – though not always positively – to the book. The reactions were so strong that Rice felt she needed to again elucidate her pious reasons and defend her choice to include apocryphal narratives in the second Author's Note, added to the paperback edition just one year later.[23] Rice's interaction with canon and non-canon demonstrates some of the aspects that I wish to explore in this monograph. Looking at works similar to Rice's – that is works that are derivative of existing narratives – I will examine four key questions.

But first, a short note is necessary on the term 'derivative text' or 'derivative work'. I have chosen to use the term throughout this book, as is common practice among fan scholars, though the term is not without weaknesses or detractors. Admittedly, the term is rather broad and unspecific: all texts are intertextual and thus in some way derivative of other texts.[24] Additionally, it contains a certain stigma about originality and artistry.[25] And even if a text is the worst kind of derivative – as we will see in this book – it still can matter immensely. Though alternatives exist to the term,[26] none of these are without issues themselves, and for the purposes of this monograph, the term 'derivative text' remains the least problematic way to refer to a text that derives specific, important aspects from another pre-existing text created by another person.

Returning to the questions I wish to ask about derivative works, the first revolves around the 'why'. In my example, why did Anne Rice write her book? She already had access to the four gospels, as well as centuries of scholarship and many fictional retellings of Jesus's life. What compelled her to create a new derivative text? In the

23. Rice, *Christ the Lord*, 2005, 462.

24. See for a discussion of intertextuality in the context of fan fiction, Paul Booth, *Digital Fandom 2.0: New Media Studies*, 2nd ed., Digital Formations 114 (New York: Peter Lang, 2017), 59–63.

25. I discuss the stigma associated with the term 'derivative' on pp. 30–34. See also the discussion in Abigail Derecho, 'Archontic Literature: A Definition, a History, and Several Theories of Fan Fiction', in *Fan Fiction and Fan Communities in the Age of the Internet: New Essays*, ed. Karen Hellekson and Kristina Busse (Jefferson, NC: McFarland, 2006), 64.

26. Examples include, 'transformative works' or 'text in the second degree'. See, for some discussion of these terms Gerard Genette, *Palimpsests: Literature in the Second Degree*, trans. C. Newman and C. Doubinsky (Lincoln, NE: University of Nebraska Press, 1997), 5; Suzanne Scott, *Fake Geek Girls: Fandom, Gender, and the Convergence Culture Industry*, Critical Cultural Communication (New York: New York University Press, 2019), 37–39; Karen Hellekson and Kristina Busse, 'Introduction: Why a Fan Fiction Studies Reader Now?', in *The Fan Fiction Studies Reader*, ed. Karen Hellekson and Kristina Busse (Iowa City, IA: University of Iowa Press, 2014), 5; Judith Fathallah, *Fanfiction and the Author: How Fanfic Changes Popular Cultural Texts*, Transmedia: Participatory Culture and Media Convergence (Amsterdam: Amsterdam University Press, 2017), 9.

context of early Christianity, we can ask very similar questions: why did Matthew write his gospel, knowing that he already had Mark? What drove later copyists to extend Mark's gospel, writing numerous *different* endings to it? Why write a new book, the Acts of Paul and Thecla, decades after Paul's death? I will explore these questions in Chapter 1.

Anne Rice's work also raises a second question: 'what does the author hope to achieve?' In her case she seems to want to reinforce the authority of the canonical gospels, as well as introduce Jesus to her current audience. Though she does not mention it, she also fortifies traditional Catholic interpretations of the gospels. She attempts to achieve this in her book by interweaving traditional elements with completely novel inventions. Early Christian derivative texts have a similar interplay of existing and imaginative elements. Why add a donkey, an ox, and even a dragon to the story of the birth of Christ? Why reimagine the apostle Thomas as the twin brother of Jesus? And more importantly, what kinds of power does such imagination have? This is the topic of Chapter 2.

The third and fourth questions revolve around how audiences react to derivative works. Anne Rice had pious reasons and goals for writing her novel, yet it is not clear that she achieved her goals. Audiences reacted in various ways to this book, and certainly many felt that her book was more fiction than fact, more heresy than orthodoxy. In early Christianity, we see similar concerns. Some authors called other Christians heretics. Some Christians designated certain derivative texts as 'not to be read', others wholeheartedly embraced these. Chapters 3 and 4 explore how communities react to texts, agreeing canons, forming communities and gatekeeping them.

The final question that Rice's example raises is how reading a new work affects the reception of an older one. Anne Rice could not resist including non-canonical narratives into her story of 'Jesus of the Gospels'. Her consumption of the Apocrypha fundamentally changed her view of the canonical gospels, even though she sees the Apocrypha as 'legends' and the gospels as 'truth'. Early Christians experienced the world of Christianity through much more than just the books that became canonical – besides the non-canonical writings, there was other work such as art, liturgies, and hymns. How did seeing images on sarcophagi, lamps, and glasses of the apostle Peter baptizing his jailers influence how early Christians imagined Peter's imprisonment? What influence did seeing the ass and the ox in the Christmas stable have on how Christians viewed non-Christians? I will examine the effect of the expanded world of Christianity on earlier texts in Chapter 5.

For the purposes of this book, I will examine these questions in the context of fan studies and the study of derivative writings authored by fans, usually called fan fiction or fanfic. The key thesis to this book is that there are important and illuminating similarities between (what we now call) the 'fannish' creation of fiction, based on the object of one's fandom, and the writings created by early Christ-followers. Furthermore, these similarities allow us to apply the critical tools developed by fan scholars to ancient texts, which will contribute to long-standing biblical studies discussions on authorship, pseudepigraphy, traditions, canonicity, diversity, and the notion of 'text' itself. My argument here is one of similarities not equivalences. My aim is *not* to argue that ancient Christians were fans, or that Christian writings are fan fiction. I instead aim to explore the world of early Christian literature through the lens of contemporary fandom, fan studies and fan fiction, elucidating obscurities, highlighting tensions and hypothesizing similarities. In the rest of this Introduction, I will briefly outline the field of fan studies in general, and argue why this seemingly anachronistic endeavour is a methodologically legitimate approach for biblical studies. I will split this discussion into two parts: the first on fans and the study thereof, the second specifically on the nature of fan fiction. I'll end with an overview of this book and set out to define some key terms.

Fans

The term 'fan', coined as an abbreviation of (religious) fanatic, entered English in the seventeenth century. Mark Duffett traces the use of the term in its modern sense to describe baseball supporters a century later, and film and music enthusiasts after that.[27] This *late* – at least from the perspective of early Christianity – invention of the term does not mean fans didn't exist earlier. Duffett reminds us not to 'mistake the invention of the label for the beginning of phenomenon'[28] and points to existing research on ancient celebrity fandom including Caesar and early Christianity.[29]

It seems, at first glance, easy enough to define a fan. Matt Hills's first sentence to his book *Fan Cultures*, introduces the (assumed) simplicity: 'Everybody knows what a "fan" is'.[30] His following summary of what 'everybody knows' spans seven lines, and includes obsession, encyclopedic knowledge, interpretative action, and communal participation. Hills, thus, points to a common knowledge that both consumption and production are part of fandom. Yet this second part of fandom, production, is not necessarily always included. Consider these two other definitions:

> I define fandom as the regular, emotionally involved consumption of a given popular narrative or text in the form of books ... as well as popular texts in a broader sense such as sports teams and popular icons and stars.[31]

---

27. Mark Duffett, *Understanding Fandom: An Introduction to the Study of Media Fan Culture* (London: Bloomsbury, 2013), 5.
28. Duffett, *Understanding Fandom*, 5.
29. Leo Braudy, *The Frenzy of Renown: Fame & Its History* (Oxford: Oxford University Press, 1986).
30. Matt Hills, *Fan Cultures* (London: Routledge, 2002), ix.
31. Cornel Sandvoss, *Fans: The Mirror of Consumption* (Cambridge: Polity Press, 2005), 8.

> A fan is a person with a relatively deep, positive emotional conviction about someone or something famous, usually expressed through recognition of style or creativity. He/she is also a person driven to explore and participate in fannish practices.[32]

Cornel Sandvoss and Mark Duffett give different definitions to both one another and Hills, demonstrating the diversity that there is in defining fandom. These three definitions highlight several issues that I will discuss in more detail: emotional connection/obsession, production, and fannish practice/performance.

All three authors put a key characteristic first: an emotional bond with the object of fandom. Hills uses the popular term 'obsession', the other two talk of emotional conviction or emotional consumption. This commitment to the object of fandom can be seen, according to Sandvoss, 'in the regularity with which they visit and revisit their object of fandom'.[33] The difficulty in defining fandom lies not in this connection, but rather in deciding when this emotional connection becomes an 'obsession', 'deep', or 'regular'. Kristina Busse points to this difficulty:

> fan studies scholars identify fans as a particular group of people; ... they create a spectrum of behavior in which fans are merely on an extreme end of a fandom continuum. Fans are thus either described as simply a more extreme version of viewers ... or regarded as engaging media with a different intensity and investment that resembles particular forms of identity politics.[34]

Fans are seen as the group of people with an emotional connection that is either above average or whose identity becomes inherently intertwined with the fandom. When we place these definitions in the context of early Christianity, the difficulty in definition does not disappear. Yet it would not be reductionist to claim that early Christians found their identity in their 'fandom' of the Christian faith. In fact, the group noun they identify with is based on their fandom, just like contemporary fans.[35] When it comes to the gradation of emotional connection, a similar grading should be easy to see in Christian contexts. Not every ancient Christian engaged with Christianity with the same intensity and investment as the apostle Paul or the Christian teacher Clement of Alexandria did. Indeed, passages such as the letter to the Laodiceans – 'you are neither cold nor hot' (Revelation 3:14–22) – or Hebrews' likening of the author's audience to infants (Hebrews 5:11–14) demonstrate exactly this continuum. Thus, this aspect of a fan's emotional conviction readily applies to early Christians.

---

32. Duffett, *Understanding Fandom*, 18.
33. Sandvoss, *Fans*, 8.
34. Kristina Busse, *Framing Fan Fiction: Literary and Social Practices in Fan Fiction Communities* (Iowa City, IA: University of Iowa Press, 2017), 9.
35. Many *Doctor Who* fans identify as Whovians, *My Little Pony* fans identify as Bronies, *Hannibal* fans identify as Fannibals, the list is infinite.

Moving on to the object of fandom, I will consider how we could place early Christians' affective relationship with Christianity within the context of fan studies. Lynn Zubernis and Katherine Larsen's statement that 'fandom, much like religion, involves an intensely affective experience' should come as no surprise.[36] There is a long tradition of likening fandom itself to religion, from calling Elvis a god and Elvis fandom a cult[37] to envisioning *Star Trek* as a religion,[38] to name just two. There are clearly similarities between religion and fandom, and as Matt Hills points out, it 'has a certain appeal' as it allows the linking of a 'new' phenomenon fandom to tropes of the ancient world such as the Bacchantes and Maenads.[39] Yet, Hills is rightly wary of trivializing fans and fandom by taking these similarities too far. More recently, the equation has sometimes been reversed – as I am doing in this book – to examine religion in the context of fandom. As Zubernis and Larsen argue:

> This is not meant to take away from the value of religion, but instead to focus on the ways in which religious practices ... align with our understanding of the affective power of imaginary worlds and arise, perhaps, from the same impetus – to create and refine narratives that help us to understand our place in the world, that provide guidelines for living our lives and connect us to something beyond ourselves and to connect to the 'sacred'.[40]

The analogies between fandom and religion have thus been explored and are significant. Going forward I will remain careful not to become too reductionist by equating religion with fandom or vice versa. Yet, this 'affective relationship' between a fan and the object of their fandom exists both in fandom and religion.

In our context of early Christianity, the object of fandom is not easy to define. Let me begin by noting that while fandom revolves around the consumption of popular narratives, this does not in any way require an actual written text to exist. Sandvoss explains that 'whether we find our object of fandom in Britney Spears, *Buffy the Vampire Slayer*, or the Boston Red Sox, these are all read and negotiated

---

36. Lynn Zubernis and Katherine Larsen, 'Make Space for Us! Fandom in the Real World', in *A Companion to Media Fandom and Fan Studies*, ed. Paul Booth, Wiley Blackwell Companions in Cultural Studies (Hoboken, NJ: Wiley Blackwell, 2018), 151.

37. John Frow, 'Is Elvis a God?: Cult, Culture, Questions of Method', *International Journal of Cultural Studies* 1 (1998): 197–210.

38. Michael Jindra, '*Star Trek* Fandom as Religious Phenomenon', *Sociology of Religion* 55 (1994): 27–51; Michael Jindra, 'It's about Faith in Our Future: *Star Trek* Fandom as Cultural Religion', in *Religion and Popular Culture in America*, ed. Bruce David Forbes and Jeffrey H. Mahan (Berkeley, CA: University of California Press, 2000), 165–80.

39. Matt Hills, 'Sacralising Fandom? From the "Loss Hypothesis" to Fan's Media Rituals', *Kinephanos* 4 (2013): 8–16.

40. Zubernis and Larsen, 'Make Space for Us! Fandom in the Real World', 155.

as (mediated) texts by their fans'.[41] Taking these three examples and applying them to our context we could see that early Christians could have been fans of the historical figure of Jesus (cf. Britney Spears)[42] or the Christ of faith that developed in the teachings, writings and oral traditions of or adopted by the early church (cf. *Buffy the Vampire Slayer*). Additionally, there is no reason to assume that early Christians were not fans of characters in these writings and traditions, like Moses, Abraham, Paul, the apostles, or Mary.[43] Finally, early Christians could have been fans, not of the characters, but of the group itself: their church or indeed Christianity (cf. the Red Sox). Each of these objects are different and would lead to different ways of consuming and interacting with the fandom; I could explore these in detail, as Sandvoss does for contemporary fandoms, but that discussion is not strictly necessary for what this book aims to achieve. In other words, the best conclusion for my purposes is that there *is* no simple object of early Christian fandom. This varies from Jesus to Christ to other characters, from oral traditions to writings, to the church itself.

Early Christians resemble fans in many meaningful ways. They have strong emotional attachment to Christianity, including regular consumption of Christian texts – writings, art, liturgies, hymns. They take part in fannish practices; they go to church, read texts, pray. And they are productive, as fans are, creating thousands upon thousands of pieces of fan art.

Ancient Fans

My book is by no means the first academic work to read fans, fandom, and fan fiction into a much earlier place in history.[44] In 2016 fan studies journal *Transformative Works and Cultures* published a special edition which focussed on the classical canon as an object of fandom. Guest editor Ika Willis sets the stage in her editorial, outlining that edition's contribution to fan studies, when she claims that the articles 'widen the historical scope of our enquiry beyond industrial modernity back through the Renaissance, the Middle Ages, and the Roman Empire, all the way to the oral culture of Homer and archaic Greece'.[45] She notes that

---

41. Sandvoss, *Fans*, 8.

42. Cf. DC Talk's relatively popular Christian Rock single *Jesus Freak* (1995).

43. As Eva Mroczek suggests for David in the Psalms. Eva Mroczek, *The Literary Imagination in Jewish Antiquity* (New York: Oxford University Press, 2016), 58, 205.

44. Anna Wilson, for example, calls it 'cliché of any introduction to fan fiction to claim its precursors in canonical authors, including Virgil, Shakespeare, Dante, Chaucer, and Milton'. Anna Wilson, 'Fan Fiction and Premodern Literature: Methods and Definitions', *Transformative Works and Cultures* 36 (2021): para. 0.1, doi:10.3983/twc.2021.2037.

45. Ika Willis, 'The Classical Canon and/as Transformative Work', *Transformative Works and Cultures* 21 (2016): para. 1.2, doi:10.3983/twc.2016.0807.

widening is legitimate as there are striking similarities between classical literature and fan fiction: 'both are undeniably transformative modes of writing, whose authors use the techniques of allusion, appropriation, and transvaluation to expand on and/or to critique existing works; both address a highly knowledgeable and engaged audience'.[46] She suggests that there is a shared practice and aesthetic between these two corpora that are culturally valued very differently: classical literature is extremely highbrow, and fan fiction the exact opposite. We thus see that these two groups, while sharing a similar aesthetic, are valued very differently *from an aesthetic point-of-view*. This demonstrates the importance of context: 'historical, cultural, social, linguistic, material and technological',[47] which is immediately the counter side to any examination of fan fiction outside of the contemporary, late-capitalist environment.

Building on Willis's conceptualization and qualification of fan fiction as a heuristic tool for the study of classical literature, a few more qualifications need to be added when it comes to early Christian literature. Most significantly we need to address cultural and aesthetic value. Whereas some Christian literature is widely seen as significantly culturally relevant for much of Western society (e.g. the gospels, the writings of Paul, or the book of Revelation), others have had much less influence (e.g. many Old Testament Pseudepigrapha, Christian Apocrypha, or the findings in Nag Hammadi or Oxyrhynchus). Aesthetically there is similarly a popular difference seen between, for example, the canonical Acts of the Apostles and the apocryphal Acts of John. Janet Spittler's analysis of the miracle traditions in the apocryphal acts shows just this. She demonstrates that academic analyses of these acts see them as 'more fanciful' and 'weirder', having 'free rein to the fantastic', 'galloping towards a bizarre and absurd horizon'.[48] This means, ultimately, that early Christian writings have a different aesthetic relationship with fan fiction than classical literature. Whereas with classical literature we have the potential to nuance cultural valuations of both classical literature and fan fiction, enabling us 'to invert and displace the high/low binary',[49] when it comes to early Christianity that binary is already present in the reception of the corpus itself. Fan fiction as a heuristic tool in biblical studies, then, doesn't serve to revalue contemporary derivative works, but rather to revalue the ancient ones. It allows us, as I will regularly discuss in this book, to displace both the (historically dubious) canonical/non-canonical binary but also the real/fake or authentic/forgery one.

---

46. Willis, 'The Classical Canon and/as Transformative Work', para. 1.3.
47. Willis, 'The Classical Canon and/as Transformative Work', para. 1.5.
48. Janet Spittler, 'The Development of Miracle Traditions in the Apocryphal Acts of the Apostles', in *Between Canonical and Apocryphal Texts: Processes of Reception, Rewriting and Interpretation in Early Judaism and Early Christianity*, ed. Jörg Frey, Tobias Nicklas, and Claire Clivaz (Mohr Siebeck, 2019), 360, doi:10.1628/978-3-16-155232-8.
49. Willis, 'The Classical Canon and/as Transformative Work', para. 1.3.

Though in popular media a link is often made between (specifically extra-canonical) Christian writings and fan fiction,[50] very little academic work has been published on the topic of early Christianity and fan studies or fan fiction. This is a lacuna this monograph attempts to address. Publications on biblical studies and fan fiction can be counted on both hands, most of which were published in the last five years. In 2006 Meredith Warren explored the way fan fiction could help understand the relationship between canon and pseudepigrapha.[51] In the 2010s, Rachel Barenblat examined similarities between ancient Midrash and fan fiction.[52] More recently, Kasper Bro Larsen has been exploring fan fiction in relation to Christian Apocrypha, hypothesizing the literary strategies and functions of these Apocrypha in Christian communities.[53] Hugo Lundhaug examined the Coptic *Investiture of the Archangel Michael* as a form of monastic fan fiction.[54] In 2019, *Transformative Works and Cultures* also published a special edition on 'ancient scribal cultures', which had a strong focus on biblical studies. The edition included articles on the Apocryphon of John,[55] the Testaments of the Twelve

---

50. Examples abound. On Reddit, in the r/atheism subreddit, there are more than 300 comments in reply to 'Did you know there's bible fanfiction.' https://www.reddit.com/r/atheism/ [accessed 15 September 2023]. News website Vice, posted an article on the Apocrypha as Bible fan fiction. Rick Paulas, 'The Bible Is Nothing but Fan Fiction for Jesus', *Vice*, 1 April 2014, https://www.vice.com/en/article/8gvpj5/the-bible-is-nothing-but-jesus-fan-fiction. Biblical scholars, such as Isaac Soon, regularly tweet on the usefulness of fan studies for the field of biblical studies, see e.g. https://twitter.com/isaacsoon2/status/1575656148803366915 [accessed 15 September 2023]. YouTube channel Religion for Breakfast has a 5-minute video using *Star Wars* fan fiction to explain early Christian Apocrypha. Religion for Breakfast, 'Star Wars Fan Fiction Explains Early Christian Apocrypha', *YouTube*, 22 August 2018, https://www.youtube.com/watch?v=rTTRIA_YWIA. Bible Podcast Apocrypals regularly refer to extra-canonical texts as Bible fan fiction, e.g. Apocrypals, 'Biblerella (The Acts of Paul and Thecla)', 21, https://apocrypals.libsyn.com/21-biblerella-the-acts-of-paul-and-thecla [accessed 15 September 2023].

51. Meredith Warren, 'My OTP: Harry Potter Fanfiction and the Old Testament Pseudepigrapha', *Scriptura* 8 (2006): 53–66.

52. Rachel Barenblat, 'Fan Fiction and Midrash: Making Meaning', *Transformative Works and Cultures* 17 (2014), doi:10.3983/twc.2014.0596; Rachel Barenblat, 'Transformative Work: Midrash and Fanfiction', *Religion & Literature* 43 (2011): 171–77.

53. Kasper Bro Larsen, 'Fan Fiction and Early Christian Apocrypha: Comparing Hypertextual Practices', *Studia Theologica – Nordic Journal of Theology* 73 (2019): 43–59, doi:10.1080/0039338X.2018.1552894.

54. Hugo Lundhaug, 'Textual Fluidity and Monastic Fanfiction: The Case of the *Investiture of the Archangel Michael* in Coptic Egypt', in *The Archangel Michael in Africa: History, Cult, and Persona*, ed. Ingvild Sælid Gilhus, Alexandros Tsakos, and Marta Camilla Wright (London: Bloomsbury Academic, 2019), 59–74, doi:10.5040/9781350084742.

55. Kristine Toft Rosland, 'Reading the "Apocryphon of John" as Genesis Fan Fiction', *Transformative Works and Cultures* 31 (2019), doi:10.3983/twc.2019.1559.

Patriarchs,[56] the Babylonian Talmud,[57] ancient martyrs,[58] and Midrash Bereshit Rabbah.[59] In 2020 Nicholas Elder argued that Joseph and Aseneth can be characterized as fan fiction,[60] and in 2021 Rebecca Raphael published on *Star Trek*'s ship 'Enterprise' and the temple in Ezekiel.[61] All of these works test the water on this topic in interesting ways, but usually exploring single texts from a very specific point of view. This monograph is the first broader, sustained analysis of early Christianity and its writings through the lens of Fan Studies.

An Introduction to Fan Fiction

If you go online and search for 'fan fiction', you will discover millions of texts created by fans. There are websites dedicated to fans' short stories, novellas and even books based on and in the storyworlds of *Game of Thrones*, *My Little Pony*, *Twilight*, *Star Trek*, *Supernatural*, and *Star Wars*, to name just a few. The key element to this book is the thesis that various early Christian writings can be considered analogous to these fan fictions. I will begin with a basic understanding of fan fiction and how it relates to Christian texts, before problematizing the definition and exploring ways contemporary fan fiction relates to these ancient religious writings. *Fanlore*, an online, semi-authoritative, multi-authored fan site, defines fan fiction as 'a work of fiction written by fans for other fans, taking a source text or a famous person as a point of departure'.[62] This definition has a number of key points: (1) fan fiction is written by fans, (2) fans are the audience, (3) fan fiction is a work of fiction, and (4) fan fiction is based on a source text or famous person.

The fourth characteristic is the easiest and most obvious to apply to early Christian writings. Many Christian texts, and indeed every text that I will consider

---

56. Tom de Bruin, 'Nostalgia, Novelty, and the Subversion of Authority in "The Testaments of the Twelve Patriarchs"', *Transformative Works and Cultures* 31 (2019), doi:10.3983/twc.2019.1553.

57. Monika Amsler, 'The Making of Ḥanina Ben Dosa: Fan Fiction in the Babylonian Talmud', *Transformative Works and Cultures* 31 (15 December 2019), doi:10.3983/twc.2019.1647.

58. Monika Amsler, 'Martyrs, Athletes, and Transmedia Storytelling in Late Antiquity', *Transformative Works and Cultures* 31 (2019), doi:10.3983/twc.2019.1645.

59. Rachel Barenblat, 'Gender, Voice, and Canon', *Transformative Works and Cultures* 31 (15 December 2019), doi:10.3983/twc.2019.1589.

60. Nicholas A. Elder, 'Joseph and Aseneth: An Entertaining Tale', *Journal for the Study of Judaism* 51 (2020): 19–42, doi:10.1163/15700631-12511267.

61. Rebecca Raphael, 'Sacred Schematics, or Ships and Sanctuaries', *Journal for Interdisciplinary Biblical Studies* 3, no. 2 (2021): 41–62, doi:10.17613/wnc7-8w05.

62. 'Fanfiction', *Fanlore*, https://fanlore.org/wiki/Fanfiction [accessed 15 September 2023].

in this book, are based on the lives of people important to Judaism and Christianity (from the patriarchs of Israel to the first-century apostles), on earlier texts (canonical and non-canonical alike), or most commonly on both.

As far as authorship is concerned, at this point it is important to note that early Christianity grew out of Judaism and over a number of centuries developed a separate identity to Judaism. Many writers we might now call 'early Christians' would probably not have self-identified as such. Yet, as established in the previous section, a case can be made that these people are, in a sense, fans. It seems almost inescapable that what we now think of as early Christian texts, be those canonical, non-canonical, apocryphal, or theological writings, were written by people with an affective relationship towards Judaism and/or Christianity. Indeed, who else would write a text treating themes important to Christianity? As such, it is simple enough to meet the first key characteristic of fan fiction: texts written by fans. The second characteristic also might seem clear-cut, but is decidedly less so than the first: the texts were written for fans. Here we meet some larger problems. When discussing some texts, such as Paul's letters to his churches, the catholic epistles, and the Gospel of Luke (cf. Luke 1:4), it is easy enough to assume that the audience were Christ-followers. But other texts, for example the Gospel of John (cf. John 20:31), might assume an audience that are not Christ-followers. Thus, it would appear that when considering the audience, some early Christian texts fit this definition of fan fiction and others do not. This difficulty will have to be taken into account in my further discussion.

The third characteristic, that these writings are works of fiction, is difficult to apply to early Christianity. The concepts fiction and non-fiction do not easily map onto ancient texts, and attempting to decide whether an ancient text is fiction or not is a highly anachronistic endeavour. The title of Tony Burke's recent edited collection *Fakes, Forgeries, Fictions: Writing Ancient and Modern Christian Apocrypha*[63] immediately sets the tone for these Christian writings. Although in this study I am trying to specifically move outside the fake/forgery debate, Burke's introduction does shed some light on how we can see many of these texts as fiction:

> Forgery and Christian apocrypha are old, constant friends. By their very nature (i.e., they contain false attributions), most Christian apocrypha *are* forgeries, created to satisfy the ever-changing needs of Christian communities. Throughout the Middle ages, ecclesiastical voices tried to discredit noncanonical texts by declaring them false. When enlightenment historians in the West were introduced to new texts from the east, Christian apocrypha were found among them; and when some of these same scholars created texts to fill in the gaps of history, Christian apocrypha were created also. When fiction writers took up the

---

63. Tony Burke, ed., *Fakes, Forgeries, and Fictions: Writing Ancient and Modern Christian Apocrypha: Proceedings from the 2015 York University Christian Apocrypha Symposium* (Eugene, OR: Cascade Books, 2017).

age-old motif of presenting their work as if it were from a lost text found in a newly discovered manuscript, new, fictional gospels also came to light.[64]

Burke's three terms – fake, forgery, and fiction – are all strongly related, yet slightly different. The difference between a forgery and a fiction is the intentionality of the author, which is hard to determine for a millennia-old text; and the difference between a fake and a fiction relates to reception (did the audience receive it as factual or fictional?) and presentation (did the author or publisher attempt to pass it off as factual?).[65] But, no matter if a derivative text is a fake or a forgery, it is also fictional, at least in some regard. Thus, when it comes to the fictional aspect of fan fiction, clearly there are many early Christian texts – especially overtly derivative texts like the Old Testament Pseudepigrapha, and Christian Apocrypha – that are works of fiction.

All in all, taking a simplistic definition of fan fiction, it is evident that many, but maybe not all, early Christian writings can meet common characteristics of fan fiction. Early Christian writings are writing by fans, most often for fans. They are very readily works of fiction, or at least contain fictional aspects, and are based on famous people or source texts. I will now examine fan fiction in more detail to better ascertain the similarities and differences with the corpus of early Christianity.

Defining Fan Fiction

Fan fiction, just like fandom itself, remains notoriously difficult to define. *Fanlore*'s definition above is necessarily simplistic and reductive, but the same is true for every definition. Francesca Coppa begins her introduction to fan fiction by pointing out that there are many ways to define fan fiction, 'each slightly different and none of them correct or exclusive'.[66] She then continues to give a list of five definitions of fan fiction (these too are not 'correct or exclusive'[67]) which I will use to explore early Christian literature as fan fiction in more detail.

The first definition that Coppa gives is that 'fanfiction is fiction created outside the literary marketplace'.[68] While this characteristic reflects fan fiction's historical existence as a nonprofessional counterpart to professional fiction, it also allows fan fiction certain liberties. As fan fiction functions outside the consumerist

---

64. Burke, *Fakes, Forgeries, and Fictions*, 'Introduction', 15.
65. See, for a useful discussion of these issues as they relate to ancient Greco-Roman texts, Irene Peirano, *The Rhetoric of the Roman Fake: Latin* Pseudepigrapha *in Context* (Cambridge: Cambridge University Press, 2012), 1–7.
66. Francesca Coppa, 'Introduction: Five Things That Fanfiction Is, and One Thing It Isn't', in *The Fanfiction Reader: Folk Tales for the Digital Age*, ed. Francesca Coppa (Ann Arbor, MI: University of Michigan Press, 2017), 1.
67. Coppa, 'Introduction: Five Things', 2.
68. Coppa, 'Introduction: Five Things', 2–3.

metanarrative of monetary value, profitability is not the issue that it often is in the creation of products. Fan fiction's market-less existence allows the creation of works that would normally not exist, either because they are too experimental, or go against the majority's prevailing tastes. In this comparison of professional/nonprofessional, it is key to note that quality is not the issue – many fan fiction authors are also professional authors.[69] The medium of fan fiction allows amateurs and professionals alike opportunities that are not available elsewhere, but it also defines that creator's relationship to the work itself. The creator is not a professional doing work for remuneration, but an amateur, following the words Latin root *amare*, working for love itself. They do not wish to accept the limitations and restrictions that come with doing the same work in a marketplace.

This aspect of fan fiction is rather difficult to examine with regards to early Christian writings. The difficulty arises not in whether these ancient writers were professional scribes (or trained to be professional scribes) as the skill and training of the authors of fan fiction is not the point Coppa is making. Rather, we need to understand whether these writers partook in a marketplace, where certain financial aspects would have defined what and how they wrote what they wrote. The ancient practice most similar to the contemporary audience-driven marketplace would be formal patronage. We could imagine that some Christian works were written by an author-client for their patron, and thus are required to meet the expectations of their patron. Yet this is hardly the case for the overwhelming majority of texts produced in early Christianity. The ancient world didn't work along the consumerist metanarrative of monetary value engendered by late-stage capitalism. Ancient writers did not take part in a marketplace that is at all comparable to the contemporary ones.

Coppa's second definition of fan fiction is that it 'rewrites and transforms other stories'.[70] Fan fiction functions as an outlet of sorts, giving fans the opportunity to engage with existing texts, to take control of existing characters or settings and tell their own stories about them. Fan fiction allows fans to expand existing material, building on it, even tweaking and optimizing it. As such fan fiction ends up functioning like a traditional campfire, it gives us the opportunity to 'pass the time by telling stories to each other'.[71] In this context, originality or marketability are not important, the sharing of the story itself is enough. Ultimately, this emphasis on the storytelling aspect leads to a love for well-known types and tropes, rather than fully developed and unique characters.

A very useful example of this aspect of fan fiction in the context of early Christianity can be seen in many of the apocryphal acts. Jennifer Eyl outlines a common narrative that many of these writings contain:

---

69. See, for example, the Lawrence Public Library's list of 21 professional fan authors. Centi Clogston, '21 Authors Who Write Fanfiction', *Lawrence Public Library*, 17 May 2019, https://lplks.org/blogs/post/21-published-authors-who-write-fanfiction/.
70. Coppa, 'Introduction: Five Things', 4.
71. Coppa, 'Introduction: Five Things', 4.

a celibate traveling apostle comes to town.... He attracts a number of followers, including the wife ... of a local elite male [who] decides to become a Christian and renounce sexuality, and her romantic rejection of her powerful husband/fiancé instigates conflict and tension.[72]

This trope of the chaste female convert and the sexually frustrated husband may be used to 'dislodge ethical nature from biological sex'[73] or to demonstrate a Christian adaptation of the Roman imperial rule,[74] or might simply reflect sociological reality.[75] Whatever the specific narratological outcomes of the trope, it occurs frequently in the apocryphal acts, and can be found – with minor variations – in the Acts of Andrew, the Acts of Peter, the Acts of John, and the Acts of Paul and Thecla, to name but a few.[76] The traditional critical examination of this trope in these writings, which attempts to find the original source and later copies, has been plagued by difficulties of provenance and date, rendering any source-critical hypothesis highly speculative. This is further complicated by the transmission of these texts, where there was 'cross-contamination'.[77] But, leaving attempts to find the original narrative behind, and focussing on fan fiction's love for rewriting and transforming characters, we note the way all of these acts engage with these apostolic characters. Just as the legends of King Arthur are hard to imagine without the Arthur/Lancelot/Guinevere love triangle – though it is in fact a twelfth-century French invention of Chrétien de Troyes[78] – compilations of the adventures of an apostle often include the conversion of an elite woman and her upset spouse.[79] This

---

72. Jennifer Eyl, 'Apocryphal Acts of the Apostles', in *The Oxford Handbook of New Testament, Gender, and Sexuality*, ed. Benjamin H. Dunning, Oxford Handbooks (Oxford University Press, 2019), 387, doi:10.1093/oxfordhb/9780190213398.013.18.

73. Eyl, 'Apocryphal Acts of the Apostles', 400.

74. John W. Marshall, 'Trophy Wives of Christ: Tropes of Seduction and Conquest in the Aprocryphal Acts', in *Reading and Teaching Ancient Fiction Jewish, Christian, and Greco-Roman Narratives*, ed. Sara Raup Johnson, Rubén R. Dupertuis, and Christine Rita Shea, Writings from the Greco-Roman World Supplement Series 11 (Atlanta, GA: SBL Press, 2018), 43–70.

75. Francois Bovon, 'Canonical and Apocryphal Acts of Apostles', *Journal of Early Christian Studies* 11 (2003): 184.

76. Other examples of common tropes in the acts could be the friendly lion (Acts of Paul and Thecla and Life and Conduct of the Holy Women Xanthippe, Polyxena, and Rebecca) or a shipwreck (Found in Acts of John, Acts of Peter, and Acts of Paul).

77. Marshall, 'Trophy Wives of Christ', 46.

78. Lori J. Walters, 'Introduction', in *Lancelot and Guinevere: A Casebook*, ed. Lori J. Walters, Arthurian Characters and Themes 4 (New York: Routledge, 2000), xiii.

79. And the apostle will often also be shipwrecked, meet a friendly lion, perform a large public healing, and have a showdown with a priest of a foreign god.

constant retelling of what is essentially the same narrative is a 'process by which these characters are expanded and made epic, loved by their fans into greatness'.[80] This aspect of fan fiction is surely present in various early Christian texts.

Coppa's third definition of fan fiction is potentially the hardest to apply to early Christianity, as it is again specifically related to late capitalism and mass media. Fan fiction, in this context, is the fictional rewriting and transformation of stories that are *owned* by others.[81] This concept of ownership is important to fan fiction, as Coppa concludes:

> It is only in such a system – where storytelling has been industrialized to the point that our shared culture is owned by others – that a category like 'fanfiction' makes sense. Everyone's always surprised by how huge the world of fanfiction is; I'm not. Fanfiction is what happened to folk culture: to the appropriation of fables and the retellings of local legends, to the elaborations of tall tales and drinking songs and ghost stories told round the campfire. Fanfiction is the bastard child; the disavowed heir; outlawed.[82]

Fan fiction as the late-capitalist fate of folk culture and fables makes little sense in an ancient culture of myth and fable. Additionally, the simple idea that a story can be owned is a recent invention, and builds on the Romantic ideal of a genius author[83] and contemporary conceptions of copyright and intellectual property.[84] Applying this definition of fan fiction to early Christian writings is further confused by the fact that so many early Christian texts are anonymous and pseudonymous: we could argue that the character 'Onesimus' is owned by the apostle Paul (Philemon 1:10), but who owns Thecla from the anonymous Acts of Paul and Thecla? Nevertheless, there are essential aspects of this definition that do apply to many early Christian writings. The first regards marginalization of fan authors. The legal aspects of ownership 'has marginalized a group of (mostly female) writers and their literary practices'.[85] The second aspect of ownership is specifically important for ancient *Christian* writings, and relates to how stories are more and more owned by a 'small handful of multinational media conglomerates'.[86]

---

80. Coppa, 'Introduction: Five Things', 5.
81. Coppa, 'Introduction: Five Things', 6.
82. Coppa, 'Introduction: Five Things', 7.
83. See Kristina Busse, 'The Return of the Author: Ethos and Identity Politics', in *A Companion to Media Authorship*, ed. Jonathan Gray and Derek Johnson (Malden, MA: Wiley Blackwell, 2013), 48–68.
84. Matthew H. Birkhold, *Characters before Copyright: The Rise and Regulation of Fan Fiction in Eighteenth-Century Germany*, Law and Literature (Oxford: Oxford University Press, 2019), 15–17.
85. Coppa, 'Introduction: Five Things', 6.
86. Henry Jenkins, 'The Cultural Logic of Media Convergence', *International Journal of Cultural Studies* 7, no. 1 (March 2004): 33, doi:10.1177/1367877904040603.

Contemporary fan authors, creating what is considered to be a legally, intellectually, and creatively derivative work, are automatically cast in a negative light: many claim that the work is not original or creative, and thus less aesthetically valuable. Added to this is that fan production is historically gendered female, which has led to further 'cultural devaluation and marginalization of fan fiction because it is written largely by women for women'.[87] This marginalization and devaluation or certain works is also present in early Christianity. A useful example can be found when we consider the Acts of Paul and Thecla. Shelly Matthews examines the reception of the Acts of Paul and Thecla as representative of exactly that what fan fiction is often seen as: 'stories told by women'.[88] In her analysis of both recent and ancient authors, she notes how female authorship is widely marginalized, noting ancient dismissals of female 'hysteria' to contemporary ones of 'feminist fantasy'.[89] Take for example the highly influential second century Christian writer Tertullian, who famously marginalizes the Acts of Paul and Thecla in his work *On Baptism*. In arguing that women should not be ministers he writes:

> But if certain Acts of Paul [and Thecla], which are falsely so named, claim the example of Thecla for allowing women to teach and to baptize, let men know that in Asia the presbyter who compiled that document, thinking to add of his own to Paul's reputation, was found out, and though he professed he had done it for love of Paul, was deposed of his position. (*On Baptism* 17.5)[90]

Tertullian, here, writes polemically against the Acts of Paul and Thecla in a way that is extremely similar to how fan fiction is often dismissed: it as derivative, unoriginal, and un*authorized*. By calling the book 'false', by pointing out that the author 'was found out', by referring to the work as an addition, he engages with it as a work that rewrites something owned by another. Though the apostle Paul had no copyright, there was still a sense of ownership when it came to his biography, his reputation. Tertullian also engages, potentially, with the second aspect of this ownership, that media conglomerates own stories. When Tertullian talks about ownership in this context, more than a century after Paul's life, Paul is no longer the owner of 'Paul.' Ownership has moved on to, as represented by Tertullian, the church as an institution itself. Indeed, Tertullian's meaning is clear, the presbyter was deposed for letting his love of Paul lead him to write 'folk tales'

---

87. Allison McCracken, 'Fic: Why Fanfiction Is Taking Over the World by Anne Jamison', *Cinema Journal* 54 (2015): 172, doi:10.1353/cj.2015.0023.

88. Shelly Matthews, 'Thinking of Thecla: Issues in Feminist Historiography', *Journal of Feminist Studies in Religion* 17 (2001): 40.

89. Matthews, 'Thinking of Thecla', 42–43.

90. Translation from Ernest Evans, *Tertullian's Homily on Baptism: The Text Edited with an Introduction, Translation, and Commentary* (Eugene, OR: Wipf & Stock, 2016).

about Paul[91] – a perfect definition of fan fiction if there ever was one – tales that were not authorized by the church. This is extremely similar to Coppa's description of contemporary culture 'where storytelling has been industrialized to the point that our shared culture is owned by others'.[92]

Coppa's fourth definition of fan fiction serves to differentiate fan fiction from other derivative works. Fan fiction is written in a community and to the standards of that community. In essence fans and fan fiction make up a community that further shapes fans and fan fiction. This community is essential for Coppa, who further defines fan fiction as 'networked creative work produced within and for a community of fans'.[93] Thus, a fan-made derivative work that is produced outside of this network (e.g. Gregory McGuire's *Wicked*),[94] or even a fan-made derivative work that is removed from its network (e.g. E. L. James's *Fifty Shades of Grey*),[95] is not fan fiction. Unfortunately, historical distance makes it impossible to ascertain how early Christian texts were written. Surely some, for example homilies given by church leaders, were written in and for communities, as the leader would present these to the church on a regular basis. Others may have been created through a more collaborative effort. Scholarship has often used the contents of specific texts to imagine a community for them. 'This kind of 'mirror reading', writes Larry Hurtado, 'has often generated proposals that this or that kind of reader or 'community' is reflected in, and lay behind, a given text'.[96] This methodology has become increasingly criticized in recent years, and Hurtado lists several 'dubious assumptions' that underlie this thinking.[97]

Yet, even though history significantly obscures the reality of early Christian communities, we can still sense some of the influences that the community may have had on early Christian texts. Coppa argues that the influence of the fan community in shaping fan fiction is high:

---

91. Laura Salah Nasrallah, '"Out of Love for Paul": History and Fiction and the Afterlife of the Apostle Paul', in *Early Christian and Jewish Narrative: The Role of Religion in Shaping Narrative Forms*, ed. Ilaria Ramelli and Judith Perkins, Wissenschaftliche Untersuchungen zum Neuen Testament 348 (Tübingen: Mohr Siebeck, 2015), 73–96.

92. Coppa, 'Introduction: Five Things', 7.

93. Coppa, 'Introduction: Five Things', 8.

94. *Wicked: The Life and Times of the Wicked Witch of the West* (1985), written by Gregory Macguire, is a revisionist retelling based in the world of Oz, as first created by L. Frank Baum in 1900 and extended in later novels and the 1939 film *The Wizard of Oz*.

95. *Fifty Shades of Grey* (2011) is an erotic novel by E. L. James, that began as *Twilight* fan fiction. It was first published episodically online under the title 'Master of the Universe', under James's penname Snowqueen's Icedragon.

96. Larry W. Hurtado, 'Who Read Early Christian Apocrypha?', in *The Oxford Handbook of Early Christian Apocrypha*, ed. Andrew Gregory et al., Oxford Handbooks (Oxford: Oxford University Press, 2015), 154, doi:10.1093/oxfordhb/9780199644117.013.1.

97. Hurtado, 'Who Read Early Christian Apocrypha?', 155.

This isn't a simple matter of fandom being the audience or the marketplace for the work; rather, the key point is that fanfiction is shaped to the literary conventions, expectations, and desires of that community, and is written in genres developed by and in community.[98]

Without stretching the point too far, many early Christian documents resemble one another when it comes to genre. This close resemblance is arguably attributable to a similar process as that in fan communities. Allow me to take the genre of the gospels as an example to illustrate this point. The genre of the four canonical gospels (Matthew, Mark, Luke, and John) has been a point of debate for centuries.[99] Recent suggestions range from a Greco-Roman *bios*, a unique mixing of Jewish and Greco-Roman genres, historiography, to the more radical suggestion that Mark was 'the first of its kind, and was really the beginning of the unique genre of a "gospel"'.[100] Whether Mark invented the genre when he wrote the first gospel, or whether it was a common genre among early Jesus traditions, or it was an adaptation of existing genres, it seems that quickly the 'genre' gospel was adopted within Christian circles. Matthew and Luke, who include parts of Mark in their text, strongly resemble Mark. Even John, who does not copy the others, resembles them. Gospels that did not end up in the canon engage with these and other narratives of Jesus's life. As Christine Jacobi argues, 'as a variety of "gospels" came into circulation, there arose in early Christianity a consciousness of a "gospel" genre differentiated from other genres'.[101] This consciousness, I would argue, is analogous to the influence of the fan community. Early Christians let their community shape their products, when writing about the life of Jesus Christ they wrote *gospels*, a genre – to quote Coppa – 'developed by and in community'.[102] The differences between local Christian communities also further shaped each individual book, as François Bovon has argued for the various acts,[103] in the same way different fan communities shape their fan products.[104]

Coppa's final definition of fan fiction regards the type of fiction that fan works are: they speculate about characters, not about the world or ideas.[105] Fan fiction, unlike for example science fiction, is specifically interested in characters. Applying

---

98. Coppa, 'Introduction: Five Things', 9.

99. See, for an overview of the discussion, Judith A. Diehl, 'What Is a "Gospel"? Recent Studies in the Gospel Genre', *Currents in Research* 9 (2011): 171–99, doi:10.1177/1476993X10361307.

100. Diehl, 'What Is a "Gospel"?', 196.

101. Christine Jacobi, 'Jesus' Body: Christology and Soteriology in the Body-Metaphors of the *Gospel of Philip*', in *Connecting Gospels: Beyond the Canonical/Non-Canonical Divide*, ed. Sarah Parkhouse and Francis Watson (Oxford: Oxford University Press, 2018), 78.

102. Coppa, 'Introduction: Five Things', 9.

103. Bovon, 'Canonical and Apocryphal Acts of Apostles'.

104. See Busse, *Framing Fan Fiction*, 108–17.

105. Coppa, 'Introduction: Five Things', 12.

the definition to the writings of early Christianity would imply that, in general terms, Christian Apocrypha or Old Testament Pseudepigrapha have much more in common with contemporary fan fiction than the writings of the Church Fathers or Paul. The first two usually revolve around characters from the Hebrew Bible and New Testament, whereas the last focus more on the theological and philosophical. In this book I will, therefore, look much more closely at texts that explore character, than those that explore theology.

Having looked at Coppa's five definitions of fan fiction, we can conclude that early Christian writings and fan fiction have many comparable characteristics. Both rewrite and transform texts that are 'owned' by others according to the standards of a community. Both exist outside of a capitalist marketplace, though for the early Christian writings this is mostly true because it predates capitalism. Coppa's fifth definition helps narrow down the potential texts of early Christianity to those that focus on characters rather than on the world or ideas.

Naturally there are also a number of differences that should be kept in mind going forward. Fan fiction assumes an authorized canon, while it is unclear exactly how set that canon was when many of the stories collected in early Christian writings were composed. Fan fiction is written as fiction and received as fiction, whereas this varies greatly for early Christian writings. Furthermore, significant economic, philosophical, and sociological differences between the context that spawned early Christian writings and fan fiction cannot be glossed over. These, and other, complications to seeing early Christian writings as fan fiction will be taken into account throughout the rest of this book.

Key Terms, Language, and Contexts

Writing an interdisciplinary book presents a challenge. Many completely self-evident terms from one discipline are incomprehensible jargon for another. As I wish this book to be accessible to fan scholars and biblical scholars alike, I have attempted to err on the side of caution throughout the work, explaining more rather than less. I have avoided abbreviations wherever possible, even for common ancient books, as readers outside of biblical studies may not recognize them. I have also taken the liberty to extend any abbreviations in secondary sources, following that work's list of abbreviations. Inversely, I have supplied the first mention of fandoms with footnotes, explaining what, for example, *Star Wars* or *Lost* are for those less immersed in twenty-first-century culture. Ancient authors and characters are likewise introduced, even if it's only by supplying an adjective to elucidate who that person is. It is my hope that these steps make the research accessible to more readers. Despite these running clarifications, three key terms still need to be discussed in more detail here, to remove any potential confusion going forward: parabiblical, canon, and non-canon.

The first word, parabiblical, is the primary focus of this book: the many writings from early Christianity that are derivative of other, earlier works. I call these writings 'parabiblical' building on the more common usage of this word in biblical studies, such as that given by Kelsie Rodenbiker:

> I use the term 'parabiblical' in order to recognize not that these canon-extending texts were *originally* penned with reference to a closed canon of biblical texts, but rather to acknowledge that they are *now* situated alongside, but not within, the biblical canon.... To label a text parabiblical is thus not a derogatory description, but rather one that recognizes the role of creative exegesis[106] that supplements, rather than supplants, what has become the canonical biblical text.[107]

My usage extends Rodenbiker's ever so slightly to recognize that the canon itself also contains parabiblical texts. Many canonical texts do exactly the same thing as these non-canonical texts, the only difference is that at a later stage in history they were included in the canon whereas others were not. In other words, I am rejecting as a-historic the usual distinction of calling canonical derivative texts 'biblical' and non-canonical derivative texts 'parabiblical', for the simple reason that in the first centuries of Christianity – that is before a canon existed – this distinction would not have made sense.

Going forward, I will refer to texts derivative of biblical ones as parabiblical, whether they were included in the canon or not. These could be texts based on earlier oral traditions or written manuscripts, on works of art or hymns sung in churches. I use the term parabiblical, as I am not aware of a single term to refer to these texts which include many texts that were not included in the canon (e.g. the Christian Apocrypha and Old Testament Pseudepigrapha) but also many that were included (e.g. Chronicles, Luke). In essence, I am looking at the early Christian texts that are specifically secondary, obviously derivative. These are texts that take earlier traditions and works and create new ones, by writing, editing, collating, and so on. Examples are texts like the apocryphal acts that create new narratives of apostles from the canonical gospels and acts; or the infancy gospels that give new narratives of Jesus's life; works like the gospels of Matthew or Luke, that derive much from others sources like the Gospel of Mark; the pseudonymous epistles attributed to Paul, be those canonical or non-canonical; and the less obvious, like the various endings to Mark that were added at a later date. I will be using the term

---

106. Exegesis is a common term in biblical studies to refer to the (critical) interpretation of texts, usually religious ones.

107. See Kelsie Rodenbiker, 'Disputing with the Devil: Jude, Michael the Archangel, and the Boundaries of Canon', in *Antike Kanonisierungsprozesse und Identitätsbildung in Zeiten des Umbruchs: Tagungsband zur Internationalen Nachwuchstagung in Münster (26.-27. Mai 2017)*, ed. Marcel Friesen and Christoph Leonard Hesse, Wissenschaftliche Schriften der WWU Münster Reihe 10 28 (Antike Kanonisierungsprozesse und Identitätsbildung in Zeiten des Umbruchs, Münster: ULB Münster, 2019), 272.

parabiblical texts to denote this contemporary group of ancient texts that are related to the writings that we have come to collect in the Christian canon.

The second term, canon, is a term that has a long history in both biblical studies and fan studies. Fans appropriated this term from Christianity, but in this process a significant shift of meaning occurred. In biblical studies, the term canon is usually used to refer to the list of books that are authoritative for a community. In this field you will often find definitions such as 'a fixed standard or collection of acknowledged Scriptures that defines the faith and identity of a particular religious community and functions authoritatively in the church'.[108] The idea that there could or should be a canon gained weight in the second and third centuries, and this canonization process in Christianity took several centuries to find any kind of general consensus. Yet, it is clear that there was and is a plurality of canons. Canon, for scholars of early Christianity, only concerns the actual texts that are considered authoritative, not the interpretation of these texts.

In fan studies, on the other hand, canon refers to both the list of texts *and* their interpretation. To illustrate this conflation of, what for biblical scholars are, two separate concepts, consider this discussion of canon by Kristina Busse and Karen Hellekson:

> Complete agreement on what comprises canon is rarely possible, even with repeated viewings of the primary source, because of the range of individual interpretation. Furthermore, what comprises canon can be called into question: for *Lord of the Rings*, for example, the canon may include any combination of the books (including or excluding Tolkien's supplementary work such as *The Silmarillion*), the animated movie directed by Ralph Bakshi released in 1978, and the 2001-2003 blockbuster Peter Jackson films. For *Star Trek* fandom, usually any of the four TV series and any of the movies, but not the animated TV show or the novelizations, may be considered canon. An understanding of canon is particularly important for the creators of fan texts because they are judged on how well they stick to or depart from canon.[109]

At first this discussion sees canon as the interpretation of a primary source. The authors quickly pivot to discussion of 'what comprises canon', giving some examples of where communities include or exclude certain texts from their canon. The final sentence, however, returns to the original meaning of canon in fandom – the generally agreed-upon interpretation of the authoritative texts. The ambiguity of the term canon is ubiquitous in fan circles, and needs to be constantly foregrounded for those coming from the study of early Christianity.

---

108. Lee Martin McDonald, *The Formation of the Biblical Canon: Volume I: The Old Testament: Its Authority and Canonicity*, 4th ed. (London: Bloomsbury T&T Clark, 2017), 98.

109. Kristina Busse and Karen Hellekson, 'Introduction: Work in Progress', in *Fan Fiction and Fan Communities in the Age of the Internet: New Essays*, ed. Karen Hellekson and Kristina Busse (Jefferson, NC: McFarland, 2006), 9–10.

Going forward, I will attempt to be clear which meaning is used where, but often – especially in fan scholarship – both meanings will overlap.

The final term I need to discuss concerns the Jewish and Christian texts that are *not* included in the biblical canon.[110] These are the focus of this book, yet there is no generally accepted term for them in biblical studies. To make the book slightly more readable, I will continue to use the anachronistic terms 'canon'/'canonical' and 'non-canon'/'non-canonical', where appropriate, as shorthand for 'texts that came to be included in the canon' and 'texts that did *not* come to be included in the canon'. Non-canonical texts abound from the era of early Christianity. Contemporary scholars usually gather these texts into collections. It is key to note that these collections are modern-day constructions, based in many cases on outdated and incorrectly applied criteria.[111] Often these collections obscure more than they illuminate,[112] yet it is still common practice to work with these collections, if only for reasons of publication and easy identification. Examples of these collections of non-canonical books are the Deuterocanonical books (sometimes called the [Old Testament] Apocrypha), which are supplements to the Greek Old Testament; the Dead Sea Scrolls, a collection of ancient Jewish texts found near the Dead Sea; the Old Testament Pseudepigrapha, parabiblical books related to figures from the Hebrew Bible/Old Testament; and the Christian Apocrypha (often called New Testament Apocrypha), parabiblical books relating to the New Testament. I will continue to refer to these collections for identification purposes, and will remind the reader from time to time how tenuous these collections are.

Finally, a few words on the ancient texts I will be examining, and how I will try to deal with them accessibly. The ancient Jewish and Christian texts that I discuss in this book are never the original texts as written by the ancient author. At best we have ancient copies in the original language, sometimes from 'only' a few centuries after the text was penned. More commonly the texts we read are (re)constructed from many ancient manuscripts, full of missing sections and contradictions, or we only have the text in a later translation into another language. Some texts, especially the canonical ones, exist in thousands of manuscripts, others only in a few, or even one. Usually, when we have many manuscripts, we create a 'critical edition' of the

---

110. Here is it important to note that the 'biblical canon' does not exist, different religious groups have different canons and it is more correct to speak of 'canons'. Or the purposes of my argument this is not terribly important, but certainly worth noting.

111. Annette Yoshiko Reed, 'The Modern Invention of "Old Testament Pseudepigrapha"', *The Journal of Theological Studies* 60, no. 2 (2009): 403–36, doi:10.1093/jts/flp033.

112. Tom de Bruin, *The Great Controversy: The Individual's Struggle between Good and Evil in the Testaments of the Twelve Patriarchs and in Their Jewish and Christian Contexts*, Novum Testamentum et Orbis Antiquus 106 (Göttingen: Vandenhoeck & Ruprecht, 2015), 27–28; Peter Tóth, 'Way Out of the Tunnel? Three Hundred Years of Research on the Apocrypha: A Preliminary Approach', in *Retelling the Bible: Literary, Historical, and Social Contexts*, ed. Lucie Doležalová and Tamás Visi (Frankfurt am Main: Lang, 2011), 47–86.

text, which is an attempt to create the most 'original' version possible, from the many manuscripts we have.

The texts I work with are written in Hebrew, Aramaic, Greek, Latin or Coptic, but I will cite them in English translation. Whenever I refer to an ancient text, I will supply a footnote to help you understand whose translation I am using (often my own). I will also share information on where to find other translations, and the text in the original language.

Finally, ancient texts are – confusingly – referred to by a variety of systems for historical reasons. We cannot, as we can for contemporary printed texts, use page numbers, as these vary wildly from (handwritten) manuscript to manuscript. In this book, I follow the guidelines of the Society of Biblical Literature's *Handbook of Style*.[113] The gist of this system is relatively simple to understand. The title of a text is followed by a series of numbers, separated by commas, dots, or colons. These numbers help the reader find the reference in the original text, just like a page number would. Most often there are two numbers (e.g. 3:5 or 6.4). The first number gives the chapter or the column, and the second gives the verse, line number or paragraph number – which of these options it gives depends on the source. Sometimes there are three numbers (e.g. 3.12.4): this is because a work has multiple books or consists of multiple fragments. In this case, the first number indicates the book number or fragment, the second the chapter/column, and the third the verse/line/paragraph. With this information and with the original text in hand, readers should be able to locate the original citations.

This Book

The main aim of the chapters following this Introduction is to explore what early Christian literary production, consumption, and transmission looks like if reimagined as fan practice. I will put insights from contemporary research on fan communities into conversation with aspects of early Christian literature, showing new or different insights and points of view on traditional questions.

In Chapter 1, 'Fascination, Frustration, and Fixing the Gospel of Mark: Why Write a Derivative Work?', I will start my exploration of parabiblical texts in conversation with fan scholarship. Taking as example the various endings to the Gospel of Mark, I will use introductory theory from fan studies to analyse the production of alternate endings to an existing text. I will discuss how the fannish forces of fascination with a text (and frustration that a text does not meet all of one's expectations) drive the creation of derivative and transformative texts.

Having highlighted some forces that lead to the creation of derivative texts, in Chapter 2, 'Nostalgia, Novelty, and Textual Authority in the Testaments of the Twelve Patriarchs: What Power Does a Derivative Work Have?' I will explore how

---

113. Billie Jean Collins, ed., *The SBL Handbook of Style: For Biblical Studies and Related Disciplines*, 2nd ed. (Atlanta, GA: SBL Press, 2014).

writers actually create these texts. I will do this by examining the way the writer of the parabiblical text the Testaments of the Twelve Patriarchs expands on existing narratives. Utilizing the concept of fan play, I will demonstrate that ancient writers create texts based on both a nostalgia for the original narratives and a desire for novel experiences.

In Chapter 3, 'Canonicity and the Politics of Canon: How Do People (De-) Authorize Derivative Works?' I examine the way that fan communities and early Christians deal with diverging information in texts. Using a range of examples from early Christian leaders, I explore processes of canonization in fandom and early Christianity and how hierarchies of texts are created and enforced. Closely related is Chapter 4, 'Gatekeeping, Heresy, Infantilization, and Feminization: How Do People Police Derivative Works?'. Here I focus not on the texts, but the people deemed undesirable to the community. I examine how interpretative communities gatekeep their communities and how they stigmatize certain people to keep them out of their social and interpretative groups.

Finally, in Chapter 5, I explore the key question of why we should study derivative texts. In 'Headcanon, Fanon, and the Christian Transmedia Storyworld: Why Do Derivative Works Matter?' I explore how consuming this vast collection of texts influences people and meaning. Examining how fans develop their own lists of authoritative texts to rival canon, I will look at how this non-canon influences canon itself through the example of the Christmas stable. Comparing ancient Christianity to contemporary transmedia storyworlds, I investigate how the storyworld influences the perception and reception of earlier narratives.

My conclusion, entitled 'Epilogue: "I couldn't get these legends out of my mind"', reflects on the implications of fan studies for the field of biblical studies. Moving from analysis to meta-analysis, I reflect on how discussions on fan studies scholarship might shed further light on issues in biblical studies scholarship.

As we embark on this journey into ancient fandom, I would like to allude to my own personal fandom, *The Hitch Hiker's Guide to the Galaxy*.[114] Like the eponymous Guide, I am sure that this book 'has many omissions and contains much that is apocryphal, or at least wildly inaccurate'.[115] A novel and interdisciplinary project such as this one is highly complex, fraught with danger, and easily criticized. This book will be full of discontinuities and anachronisms and methods that feel strange to biblical scholars and fan scholars alike. Yet, I hope that the ground tilled in this book is productive for the study of biblical texts and early Christianity, as well as for fan studies. In this book I make the first steps into systematically putting early Christianity in conversation with fandom and fan studies, and I hope it can be a point of embarkation for future discussions, conversations, and research.

---

114. The *Hitch Hiker's Guide to the Galaxy* started as a BBC Radio 4 play in 1978, authored by Douglas Adams. The storyworld currently includes several books, a TV show, a film, two video games, illustrated novels, and comic books.

115. Douglas Adams, *The Hitch Hiker's Guide to the Galaxy*, Pan Original (London: Pan Books, 1979), 4.

Chapter 1

FASCINATION, FRUSTRATION, AND FIXING THE GOSPEL OF MARK: WHY WRITE A DERIVATIVE WORK?[1]

Rather than jumping straight into what is, for many, the obscure depths of pseudepigraphic, parabiblical, or apocryphal writings, in this chapter I will explore an example a bit closer to home. It is commonly known, and evident in almost every Bible translation, that the Gospel of Mark has a complex history. There are multiple endings to the gospel, and the ending most commonly found in Bibles and manuscripts is probably not the original. In this chapter I will explore these slightly better known, yet murky, waters of Mark's endings in the context of fan studies and fan fiction. After introducing Henry Jenkins's important work on fan studies,[2] I will use the theories he pioneered to engage with Mark's endings.

In the Introduction I discussed Anne Rice's book about the life of Jesus.[3] She included apocryphal narratives in her book, because, as she recounts, 'I couldn't get these legends out of my mind'.[4] To quote Tony Burke, she was '*fascinated* also by the infancy gospels'.[5] This fascination drove her writing, but at the same time another force was at play. 'Somewhere during my journey', she reflects after naming scores of books on the life of Jesus, 'I became disillusioned.... The "Quest for the Historical

---

1. Drafts of this chapter were presented at the *British New Testament Society Conference*, and at research seminars at the University of Wales, Trinity Saint David and the University of Sheffield. Heartfelt thanks to the organizers of these events for the opportunity to share my developing thoughts. The feedback received from attendees has improved this chapter vastly. I'm also highly indebted to Kelsie Rodenbiker for her extensive feedback on a draft of this chapter!

2. Henry Jenkins, *Textual Poachers: Television Fans & Participatory Culture* (London: Routledge, 1992).

3. Anne Rice, *Christ the Lord: Out of Egypt: A Novel* (New York: Knopf, 2005).

4. Rice, *Christ the Lord*, 451.

5. Tony Burke, 'Early Christian Apocrypha in Popular Culture', in *The Oxford Handbook of Early Christian Apocrypha*, ed. Andrew F. Gregory et al., Oxford Handbooks (Oxford: Oxford University Press, 2015), 432, doi:10.1093/oxfordhb/9780199644117.013.29, emphasis mine.

Jesus" had become a joke'.[6] She had a growing frustration with other interactions with the life of Jesus. Two poles drive her work: fascination and frustration.

Mark's gospel was clearly a fascinating work. Chris Keith argues, in his *The Gospel as Manuscript*, that Mark lay at the heart of an 'explosion of Jesus tradition in the first and second centuries'.[7] He sees Mark as a media innovation, arguing that the other gospels 'mimic Mark's media form', and that they 'do so self-consciously'.[8] At the same time Mark is a frustrating text. 'The good news of Jesus Christ' (Mark 1:1) ends with only three women – not the most authoritative witnesses in the ancient world – to witness to the empty tomb, and they are too afraid to tell anyone. In this chapter I will explore these two poles of fascination and frustration – in fan studies and in Mark.

Fascination and Frustration

Henry Jenkins's *Textual Poachers: Television Fans & Participatory Culture* is often taken as the starting point of academic fan studies.[9] Whereas before this foundational work fans were generally negatively stereotyped, Jenkins 'represented fans as thoughtful, productive and creative people'.[10] Indeed, Jenkins's book is so important that Mark Duffett refers to it as 'a bible for fan researchers', which even has 'its own fan following'.[11] In this book Jenkins borrows the metaphor of the poacher, who operates 'from a position of cultural marginality and social weakness'.[12] Having no direct access to what they desire (in the case of fans to cultural production), they poach texts. Jenkins speaks of fans as fascinated by these texts and by borrowing these media. They create a cultural and social identity. Furthermore, he claims that fans are resistant readers who appropriate, or 'poach', texts, asserting their own authority over them.[13] This resistance to the texts and the need to assert authority over them shows the other side of fan engagement: 'frustration and antagonism'.[14] The narratives do not fully satisfy the needs of the fans, yet as they are so fundamentally fascinating, fans cannot simply let them fade into non-existence. They 'must struggle with them,

---

6. Rice, *Christ the Lord*, 450.
7. Chris Keith, *The Gospel as Manuscript: An Early History of the Jesus Tradition as Material Artifact* (Oxford: Oxford University Press, 2020), 73–74.
8. Keith, *The Gospel as Manuscript*, 14.
9. Judith Fathallah, *Fanfiction and the Author: How Fanfic Changes Popular Cultural Texts*, Transmedia: Participatory Culture and Media Convergence (Amsterdam: Amsterdam University Press, 2017), 21.
10. Mark Duffett, *Understanding Fandom: An Introduction to the Study of Media Fan Culture* (London: Bloomsbury, 2013), 15.
11. Duffett, *Understanding Fandom*, 16.
12. Jenkins, *Textual Poachers*, 27.
13. Jenkins, *Textual Poachers*, 24–28.
14. Jenkins, *Textual Poachers*, 24.

to try to articulate to themselves and others unrealized possibilities within the original works'.[15] Fan engagement with texts thus has these two poles: fascination and frustration. This frustration could be because the narrative ended, but it can equally easily be due to frustration with events in the narrative itself. Either perceived problem can be solved by fan production.

Communal fan production is key. Unlike nomadic poachers, the community of fans produce lasting artefacts. As fans read texts, 'individual interpretations are shaped and reinforced through ongoing discussions with other readers'.[16] The interpretations are by no means personal experiences, but involve creating a new text – a manuscript, to borrow language from biblical studies. Each of these poached texts 'provide a foundation for future encounters with the fiction, shaping how it will be perceived, defining how it will be used'.[17] In this way, Jenkins argues that fans are more than a passive audience: they actively participate in the arena of media production.

Judith Fathallah discusses the reception of Jenkins's book. She points to two tendencies following his work. First, it caused a 'celebration of fanfiction as a political resistance'.[18] Casting fans as poachers caused them to be seen as countercultural.[19] Reflecting on this, Jenkins writes:

> Like all metaphors, 'poaching' enabled us to see certain things about fandom, offering a powerful counterimage to prevailing stereotypes of fans as passive consumers and cultural dupes; yet it also masked or distorted some significant aspects of the phenomenon, focusing on the frustration more than the fascination, encouraging academics to read fan fiction primarily in political terms, and constructing a world in which producers and consumers remain locked in permanent opposition.[20]

Jenkins attributes this over-politicization of fan fiction to an overemphasis on the frustration of fans, eliding the fascination that brings fans and media together. Fathallah terms the second tendency 'the opposite extreme', where fan fiction becomes seen as art, the latest postmodern step in a long literary tradition.[21] This privileges a small subset of fan fiction that 'exhibit[s] literary cultural capital in a scholastic context. That is, texts that are polished, stylish, complete, conform to Standard English', etm.[22] Less 'literary' texts are easily thrown by the wayside. In

---

15. Jenkins, *Textual Poachers*, 24.
16. Jenkins, *Textual Poachers*, 46.
17. Jenkins, *Textual Poachers*, 46.
18. Fathallah, *Fanfiction and the Author*, 21.
19. Duffett, *Understanding Fandom*, 67.
20. Henry Jenkins, *Fans, Bloggers, and Gamers: Exploring Participatory Culture* (New York: New York University Press, 2006), 37.
21. Fathallah, *Fanfiction and the Author*, 23.
22. Fathallah, *Fanfiction and the Author*, 25.

this trend I would also place Abigail Derecho's often-cited article 'Archontic Literature: A Definition, a History, and Several Theories of Fan Fiction'.[23]

Derecho borrows Derrida's term 'archontic' in her attempt 'to develop a theoretical vocabulary if we are to think seriously about fan fiction as art'.[24] The emphasis on legitimizing fan fiction as a form of art is immediately apparent. She argues against the generally used terms 'derivative' and 'appropriative'. The first as it implies a poor copy of an original work, the second as it suggests 'thieving' or 'stealing'.[25] Archontic, on the other hand, implies an archive, which is always expanding. As an example, Derecho gives the *Pride and Prejudice* archive, which includes (1) Jane Austen's novel, (2) 'artifacts' such as characters, locations and tropes from the novel, and (3) 'new creations' based on the archive.[26] While Derrida's conceptualization of the ever-growing archive is a useful one, Derecho conveniently leaves out key parts of how Derrida talks of archives. He links archive to the Greek *archē*, which he defines as both 'commencement' and 'commandment'.[27] The first, just like 'appropriation', still suggests an original: Austen's novel; without which there would be no *Pride and Prejudice* archive. The second implies for him that archives are ontologically linked to power, law, and government. He emphasizes the place the archive is kept (*archeion*) and the ruler (*archōn*) who control it. Or, in simpler terms, every archive has an archivist who decides what is stored in the archive itself. For Derrida, fundamental to archontic literature are 'both of the law which begins by inscribing itself there and of the right which authorizes it.'[28] Thus, while Derecho may well be correct that 'archontic texts are always open and have the potential for infinite expansion,'[29] issues remain. Though she dislikes the term derivative, the elements in the archive are still derivative of the original element that started the archive. Derecho's argument falls apart further when she sees archontic literature as 'the writing of subordinated groups,'[30] which is hard to reconcile with Derrida's nomological archive kept by rulers.[31] Fathallah potentially alludes to the power of the archivist – whatever form that function may take in contemporary fan communities – when she reiterates that 'different statements in

---

23. Abigail Derecho, 'Archontic Literature: A Definition, a History, and Several Theories of Fan Fiction', in *Fan Fiction and Fan Communities in the Age of the Internet: New Essays*, ed. Karen Hellekson and Kristina Busse (Jefferson, NC: McFarland, 2006), 61–78.
24. Derecho, 'Archontic Literature', 63.
25. Derecho, 'Archontic Literature', 63.
26. Derecho, 'Archontic Literature', 65.
27. Jacques Derrida, *Archive Fever: A Freudian Impression*, Religion and Postmodernism (Chicago, IL: University of Chicago Press, 1996), 1.
28. Derrida, *Archive Fever*, 4.
29. Derecho, 'Archontic Literature', 65.
30. Derecho, 'Archontic Literature', 72.
31. See, for a useful examination of how the concept of the archive is useful to analyse fan wikis, Paul Booth, *Digital Fandom 2.0: New Media Studies*, 2nd ed., Digital Formations 114 (New York: Peter Lang, 2017), 94–97.

fanfic make different levels of impact on fandom and canon, and some make no impact at all'.[32] I will explore these topics of impact and authorities in Chapters 3 and 4.

Despite these issues, Derecho's suggestion remains useful in that it 'turns questions of ownership and hierarchies on their heads'.[33] Surely, the archive metaphor problematizes a hierarchical view, though archives do have an order, sort, and rank to their contents.[34] The underlying attraction remains, however, in linking fan fiction to a long tradition of 'archontic literature', starting with *Medea* in the fifth century BCE. This is a method of legitimization, which I feel is probably more productively done with by engaging with concepts of canon in ancient Greece,[35] especially in the context of oral performance,[36] rather than coining a new term. In biblical studies, Nicholas Elder's article on the ancient Jewish text Joseph and Aseneth as fan fiction relies strongly on the concept of archontic literature.[37] Elder uses the theory of archontic literature to legitimize the anachronistic endeavour of reading Joseph and Aseneth as fan fiction: 'both Joseph and Aseneth and fan fiction are archontic, and therefore fan fiction theory can inform the narrative'.[38] As should be clear from the Introduction, my methodological defence is based on other grounds.

Indeed, it is this literary undertaking itself that resonates strongly with the study of parabiblical[39] literature – that is literature that supplements other biblical narratives – for two reasons. The first relates to the attempt to elevate fan fiction into the realm of art. It is common for people to describe parabiblical literatures as less-than: 'many modern writers' writes Tony Burke, 'consider them inferior – whether theologically or stylistically – to their canonical counterparts'.[40] And, Stephen Shoemaker argues that 'scholars have laboured to remove the early

---

32. Fathallah, *Fanfiction and the Author*, 25.

33. Maria Lindgren Leavenworth and Malin Isaksson, *Fanged Fan Fiction: Variations on Twilight, True Blood and The Vampire Diaries* (Jefferson, NC: McFarland, 2013), 111.

34. Paul Booth sees Derrida's concept of archontic literature as more useful for analysing how fan communities inscribe their existence, especially in online wikis. Booth, *Digital Fandom 2.0*, 94–97.

35. Ika Willis, 'The Classical Canon and/as Transformative Work', *Transformative Works and Cultures* 21 (2016), doi:10.3983/twc.2016.0807.

36. Ahuvia Kahane, 'Fan Fiction, Early Greece, and the Historicity of Canon', *Transformative Works and Cultures* 21 (2016), doi:10.3983/twc.2016.0681.

37. Nicholas A. Elder, 'Joseph and Aseneth: An Entertaining Tale', *Journal for the Study of Judaism* 51 (2020): 19–42, doi:10.1163/15700631-12511267.

38. Elder, 'Joseph and Aseneth', 23.

39. See my discussion and definition of parabiblical literature in the Introduction, on pp. 22–24.

40. Tony Burke, 'Introduction', in *Fakes, Forgeries, and Fictions: Writing Ancient and Modern Christian Apocrypha: Proceedings from the 2015 York University Christian Apocrypha Symposium*, ed. Tony Burke (Eugene, OR: Cascade Books, 2017), 1.

Christian apocrypha from the shadow of the New Testament writings'.[41] Though Burke and Shoemaker are specifically discussing Christian Apocrypha, the same argument can easily be made for any other non-canonical text. I will examine this view of parabiblical literature in more detail in Chapter 4. The second way this literary undertaking resonates, is very specific: through the term 'archive'. Eva Mroczek's *The Literary Imagination in Jewish Antiquity* is a landmark study in decentring modern conceptions of the book and book culture in ancient Judaism.[42] Arguing that the term 'book' is not useful to describe the literature of the time, she grasps for better metaphors:

> Alternative metaphors, like projects or archives, suggest new ways to visualize the sources spatially, unbinding them from anachronistic bookish constraints and making it possible to see new ways in which texts might go together.[43]

She suggests considering projects, archives, or – as she suggests elsewhere – databases as conceptual analogues for understanding the way texts functioned in antiquity. This is, for her, a much more useful concept than a once-written, bound and closed book.

> The language of archive or database may indeed be helpful, as it allows us to see processes of expansion, rearrangement, variance, and incompleteness not as problems requiring explanation, but as basic aspects of the way textual collections were formed.[44]

There is thus a surprising amount of overlap between Mroczek's description of how texts function in antiquity and conceptualization of fan fiction. Mroczek does not argue for a single new metaphor to replace book, instead suggesting a few options with strengths and weaknesses. For both fan fiction and parabiblical texts, the archive might not be an entirely satisfactory metaphor either – both space and the archivist throw spanners in the works. Yet, the intent is clear: for contemporary fans *and* ancient scribes a text was never finished. It lies waiting to be expanded.

---

41. Stephen J. Shoemaker, 'Early Christian Apocryphal Literature', in *The Oxford Handbook of Early Christian Studies*, ed. Susan Ashbrook Harvey and David G. Hunter, Oxford Handbooks (Oxford: Oxford University Press, 2008), 521, doi:10.1093/oxfordhb/9780199271566.003.0026.

42. Eva Mroczek, *The Literary Imagination in Jewish Antiquity* (New York: Oxford University Press, 2016).

43. Mroczek, *Literary Imagination*, 121.

44. Mroczek, *Literary Imagination*, 42.

The Endings of Mark

Manuscripts of the Gospel of Mark contain four variant endings. The final chapter of Mark tells the story of Mary of Magdalene, Mary the mother of James, and Salome going to Jesus's tomb to anoint his body. Arriving, they see that the tomb has been opened and a young man in white sitting next to it. He tells them to not be afraid, that Jesus has risen from the dead. He commands them to return to the eleven disciples to tell them to go to Galilee to meet Jesus, where Jesus has gone ahead.[45] 'So they went out and fled from the tomb, for terror and amazement had seized them; and they said nothing to anyone, for they were afraid' (Mark 16:8).[46] The oldest two manuscripts of Mark – amongst many others – end the gospel here.[47] This is, in all probability, the original ending to Mark.[48]

In the following centuries three additions were made to the text. Most well-known of these is the so-called Longer Ending. This version is also in the so-called Textus Receptus, and thus in many foundational translations in modern European languages.[49] The Longer Ending is by far the most common ending in the manuscripts of Mark.[50] Here the story continues for another twelve verses (Mark 16:9–20). Mary Magdalene tells Jesus's followers that he is risen, but they do not believe her. Jesus subsequently appears to two other disciples who tell the news. They too are not believed. Finally, Jesus appears to the eleven disciples at a meal, he chastises them for their unbelief. He commands them to go and share the good news, promising salvation for all believers. He also promises signs of faith: power over demons, speaking in tongues, snake-handling, immunity to poison, and healing. After this, Jesus is taken up to God's right hand, and the eleven disciples share the good news. The Lord supports them and confirms their message with the promised signs. Bruce Metzger, in his *Textual Commentary on the Greek New Testaments*, claims that 'the section was added by someone who knew a form of

---

45. The twelfth disciple, Judas Iscariot the betrayer of Jesus, is dead by this time, leaving eleven of the original twelve.

46. The translation of Mark is an edited version of the New Revised Standard Version. The Greek, including the variants I discuss, can be found in Eberhard Nestle and Barbara Aland, *Novum Testamentum Graece*, 28th ed. (Stuttgart: Deutsche Bibelgesellschaft, 2012).

47. Bruce M. Metzger, *A Textual Commentary on the Greek New Testament, Second Edition*, 4th ed. (London: United Bible Societies, 1994), 102.

48. R. T. France, *The Gospel of Mark: A Commentary on the Greek Text*, New International Greek Testament Commentary (Grand Rapids, MI: Eerdmans, 2002), 685.

49. The Textus Receptus (Received Text) refers to a collection of editions of the Greek New Testament. The first one was published by Erasmus in 1516, with later editions by himself and other scholars. These editions were the basis for the first European translations into the vernacular, including Luther's German Bible and the King James Version.

50. Metzger, *Textual Commentary*, 103.

Mark that ended abruptly with verse 8 and who wished to supply a more appropriate conclusion'.[51]

Besides the Longer Ending, there is also a Shorter Ending, which is but one verse:

> And all that had been commanded them they told briefly to those around Peter. And afterward Jesus himself sent out through them, from east to west, the sacred and imperishable proclamation of eternal salvation.

Most manuscripts that have this Shorter Ending, continue with the Longer Ending,[52] thus creating another option for the ending. Finally, one manuscript (though according to Jerome there were more) includes the 'Freer Logion' in its ending, immediately after Jesus's rebuke of the eleven disciples. In this these disciples excuse themselves, blaming Satan's rulership of the age. Jesus explains that Satan's power has passed, and promises salvation. This addition appears to soften Jesus's words, and give a better transition from rebuke to commission. About the Freer Logion, Metzger writes, that it 'has about it an unmistakable apocryphal flavor', though gives no indication what he means with that.[53]

All in all, we thus have the following five variations of endings to Mark in antiquity: (1) ending in verse 8; (2) just the Shorter Ending (with the last six words of verse 8 removed); (3) just the Longer Ending; (4) the Shorter Ending *and* some or all of the Longer Ending; and (5) the Longer Ending with the Freer Logion.[54] Scholarship has debated the reasons for the existence of these endings for centuries, as well as the originality of each variant. A 'virtually unanimous' agreement has been reached that Mark 16:8 (i.e. with no additions) is the most historically accurate ending.[55] Thus it appears that in the first centuries at least three additions were written to the gospel, one of which is an addition to an addition. Though I am taking the ending of Mark as an example here, the New Testament contains hundreds of such examples, where a later scribe added minor or major details to an existing text. Perhaps most commonly known are the additions of 'for thine is the kingdom, the power, and the glory, forever. Amen' to the Lord's Prayer (Matthew 6:13); the story of Jesus forgiving the woman found in adultery (John 7:53–8:11); and the single reference to the Trinity in the New Testament (1 John 5:7–8).

---

51. Metzger, *Textual Commentary*, 105.
52. Metzger, *Textual Commentary*, 103.
53. Metzger, *Textual Commentary*, 104. See Chapter 3 for a discussion of the common association of apocrypha with low aesthetic value.
54. Most contemporary commentaries will list these five options, see, for examples, France, *The Gospel of Mark*, 686–87; Adela Yarbro Collins, *Mark: A Commentary*, Hermeneia: A Critical and Historical Commentary on the Bible (Minneapolis, MN: Fortress, 2007), 804–7.
55. France, *The Gospel of Mark*, 685.

While the ending in Mark 16:8 may be the original, it remains to be seen if that ending is the 'best'. Though, generally, historical scholarship is interested in accessing the most original or earliest version of a text, many of the other readers of Mark are interested in something else altogether. The earliest ending of Mark feels abrupt, especially as the book would then end in the word 'because'. Bruce Metzger and Bart Ehrman, in *The Text of the New Testament*, witness to this feeling: 'it is difficult to believe that the note of fear would have been regarded as an appropriate conclusion to an account of the Evangel, or Good News'.[56] There is a long scholarly tradition that there is a lost ending to Mark,[57] or even the suggestion that Mark 'was forced to stop at 16:8'.[58] Robert Stein, for example, tries to differentiate between the authentic and the intended ending: 'Mark 16:8 is clearly the most authentic ending of Mark that we possess. ... But is it the original and intended ending of Mark?'[59] Stein argues that the text of Mark sets the reader up for a different ending, one including a resurrection narrative in Galilee, which may have been 'lost or intentionally mutilated or ... Mark was never able to write his intended ending (perhaps because of martyrdom or persecution or some other reason)'.[60] Additionally, in recent years more and more scholars are arguing that the ending does not fit in the first-century literary context, though others also argue the exact opposite.[61] The scholarly debate surrounding this issue is messy, complicated and nowhere near a consensus, thus Metzger and Ehrman's conclusion is most apt: 'all that is known is that more than one person in the early Church sensed that the Gospel is a torso and tried in various ways to provide a more or less appropriate conclusion'.[62] It is with exactly these attempts to provide a 'better' conclusion to Mark that I would like to engage. In the following pages I will explore how the fan forces of frustration and fascination inform the creation of these endings.

---

56. Bruce M. Metzger and Bart D. Ehrman, *The Text of the New Testament: Its Transmission, Corruption, and Restoration*, 4th ed. (Oxford: Oxford University Press, 2005), 326.

57. See, for example, Robert Oliver Kevin, 'The Lost Ending of the Gospel According to Mark: A Criticism and a Reconstruction', *Journal of Biblical Literature* 45, no. 1/2 (1926): 81, doi:10.2307/3260167.

58. Maurice Robinson, 'Amid Perfect Contempt, a Place for the Genuine: The Long Ending of Mark as Canonical Verity', in *Perspectives on the Ending of Mark: Four Views*, ed. David Adam Black (Nashville, TN: Broadman & Holman, 2008), 41.

59. Robert H. Stein, 'The Ending of Mark', *Bulletin for Biblical Research* 18 (2008): 85.

60. Stein, 'The Ending of Mark', 98.

61. See, for example, Elizabeth E. Shively, 'Recognizing Penguins: Audience Expectation, Cognitive Genre Theory, and the Ending of Mark's Gospel', *The Catholic Biblical Quarterly* 80 (2018): 273–92, doi:10.1353/cbq.2018.0051; J. Lee Magness, *Marking the End: Sense and Absence in the Gospel of Mark* (Wipf & Stock, 2002).

62. Metzger and Ehrman, *The Text of the New Testament*, 326.

Fixing Mark and Fix-it Fic

There is a common assumption that the Longer Ending functions to solve the unsatisfying ending in Mark 16:8. Yet, few have analysed whether the Longer Ending actually does that.[63] Surely the Longer Ending does solve the problem of the lack of a resurrection narrative, redeems the three women who were too afraid to spread the news of the resurrection, and does some work to harmonize the gospels. But at the same time, it also introduces other potential issues, and has innovations of its own. Bridget Gilfillan Upton has argued that 'oddities, from a narrative point of view, abound',[64] highlighting innovations such as the peculiar reintroduction of Mary Magdalene. Kara Lyons-Pardue's analysis of the Long Ending as an ending to Mark, highlights two important (and often overlooked) aspects to it.[65] First, Jesus appears to Mary Magdalene alone, and she is portrayed in an extremely positive light. Second, as the eleven disciples repeatedly disbelieve, the Longer Ending puts their already dubious actions from the passion into an even more negative light. Lyons-Pardue argues that the Longer Ending 'conflicts with ancient gender stereotypes in ways that are likely to be intentional'.[66]

Whereas in the original ending Mary Magdalene and the other two woman are portrayed as too fearful to share the news, in the Longer Ending she becomes the first witness to the resurrected Jesus:

> Now after he rose early on the first day of the week, he appeared first to Mary Magdalene, from whom he had cast out seven demons. She went out and told those who had been with him, while they were mourning and weeping. But when they heard that he was alive and had been seen by her, they disbelieved it. (Mark 16:9–11)

Though Jesus does not command her to, she immediately goes and tells Jesus's other followers, 'certainly the Eleven [disciples], likely others'.[67] This narrative reflects Jesus's first appearance to only Mary in John 20:11–18, yet does not contain any of the emotions of that Johannine narrative, and much less detail. In this way, the Longer Ending and John elevate Mary's position as compared to Matthew and Luke, where she is not alone. Additionally, Mary is framed as living proof of Jesus's power and authority, as she was formerly demon possessed. Though the reference to Mary is short, Lyons-Pardue claims that 'the fact that Mary Magdalene reappears

---

63. Kara Lyons-Pardue, *Gospel Women and the Long Ending of Mark*, The Library of New Testament Studies 614 (London: T&T Clark, 2020), 23.

64. Bridget Gilfillan Upton, *Hearing Mark's Endings: Listening to Ancient Popular Texts through Speech Act Theory*, Biblical Interpretation Series 79 (Leiden: Brill, 2006), 158–59.

65. Lyons-Pardue, *Gospel Women*.

66. Lyons-Pardue, *Gospel Women*, 2.

67. Lyons-Pardue, *Gospel Women*, 120.

in the narrative expansion *at all* suggests that her role is more than perfunctory'.[68] Mary's role as first witness becomes the pattern, most obviously for the two *anonymous* disciples who meet Jesus on a road (Mark 16:12-13, cf. Luke 24:13-43), but also in a sense for the other disciples preaching the good news of the risen Christ. The eleven disciples are commanded by Jesus to 'go and preach', just as Mary 'goes and reports'. The importance of Mary's testimony is emphasized when Jesus appears to the eleven disciples to rebuke them:

> Later he appeared to the eleven themselves as they were sitting at the table; and he upbraided them for their disbelief and stubbornness, because they had not believed who saw him after he had risen. (Mark 16:14)

These eleven disciples stand in stark contrast to Mary Magdalene. Throughout the Gospel they have been 'dense . . ., blundering . . ., defiant . . ., and fearful, the Twelve [disciples] have been called failures, blind, inept, fallible and other uncomplimentary things'.[69] The Longer Ending does little to redeem their faith and character, and the insertion of doubt puts Mark back in line with the other gospels (Matthew 28:17, Luke 24:11, John 20:24-25). Indeed, though it might be expected that the eleven disciples now, finally, take up the mantle of discipleship, they 'once again have their response, and therefore perhaps their authority, undermined'.[70] Furthermore, whereas there is no mention of emotions when it comes to Mary, the eleven disciples are portrayed as mourning and weeping, emotions that were generally seen as unmanly and evidence of weakness;[71] emotions that often are ascribed to Mary Magdalene to undermine her reliability (e.g. Origen's *Against Celsus* 2.59).[72] Yet, it is the eleven disciples and not Mary, that Jesus then commissions for the spread of the gospel.

Returning to fan studies, let me explore some of the forces that may underlie the writing of Mark's Longer Ending. As discussed above, 'fans relate to favorite texts with a mixture of fascination and frustration, attracted to them because they offer the best resources for exploring certain issues, frustrated because these fictions never fully conform to audience desires'.[73] In the case of Mark's ending, it appears that the ending did not conform to the desires of the audience. On the one hand this desire can be seen in the context of harmonization: all the other Gospels

---

68. Lyons-Pardue, *Gospel Women*, 50.
69. Lyons-Pardue, *Gospel Women*, 89.
70. Gilfillan Upton, *Hearing Mark's Endings*, 161.
71. Brittany E. Wilson, *Unmanly Men: Refigurations of Masculinity in Luke-Acts* (Oxford: Oxford University Press, 2015), 65–66.
72. Origen claims that Celsus calls Mary Magdalene a hysterical woman (*Against Celsus* 2.59).
73. Henry Jenkins, 'Reception Theory and Audience Research: The Mystery of the Vampire's Kiss', in *Reinventing Film Studies*, ed. Christine Gledhill and Linda Williams (London: Arnold, 2000), 175.

have resurrection narratives, why doesn't Mark? Allied to this is the silence of Mary, which goes against other Gospel accounts. This notion of desire is not an innocent consideration; indeed, as James Kelhoffer argues, 'one can wonder whether the Gospel of Mark would ultimately have been included in the New Testament canon without the addition(s) of the Longer Ending'.[74] Yet the surprising way that both Mary and the eleven disciples are depicted, shows that there might well be more to the ending than simply the need for witnesses of the risen Christ or Gospel harmonization. I will discuss both in turn.

Harmonization and the Gospel Harmonies

In contemporary fan fiction, there is a genre known as fix fic or fix-it fic. Such a fan product rewrites 'canonical events the fan dislikes, paradoxically exerting its power over the text it is sourced from'.[75] An angry fan, frustrated with the canonical source, attempts 'to make right what the source text made "wrong"'.[76]

In the context of biblical studies, this genre is well-demonstrated with Frauke Uhlenbruch and Sonja Ammann's example:

> By filling Jerusalem with the blood of the innocent and promoting abominable idolatrous cults, King Manasse definitely was the worst of all rulers, according to 2 Kings 21:1–18. How can it be, then, that he, of all kings of Jerusalem, ruled for fifty-five prosperous and peaceful years – the longest rule of a king in the entire history of the kingdom? The biblical book of Chronicles, which is a later work based on the book of Kings, rectifies this gap between Manasse's behavior and his success as a king. According to 2 Chronicles 33:1–20, Manasse was indeed the worst of kings, but he came to regret his evil deeds and became a pious king, and he therefore eventually merited his long and peaceful reign. Readers familiar with the genres and techniques of fan fiction will not be surprised by this rewriting of Manasse's story in Chronicles and probably consider it as a piece of fix-it fic.[77]

Fix-it fic attempts to solve issues in the source text, appropriating the source, claiming authority over it, and creating a new fan text without the original's

---

74. James A. Kelhoffer, *Miracle and Mission: The Authentication of Missionaries and Their Message in the Longer Ending of Mark*, Wissenschaftliche Untersuchungen zum Neuen Testament 2. Reihe 112 (Tübingen: Mohr Siebeck, 2000), 480.

75. Judith Fathallah, 'Statements and Silence: Fanfic Paratexts for *ASOIAF/Game of Thrones*', *Continuum* 30, no. 1 (2016): 84, doi:10.1080/10304312.2015.1099150.

76. Lesley Goodman, 'Disappointing Fans: Fandom, Fictional Theory, and the Death of the Author', *The Journal of Popular Culture* 48, no. 4 (August 2015): 663, doi:10.1111/jpcu.12223.

77. Frauke Uhlenbruch and Sonja Ammann, 'Fan Fiction and Ancient Scribal Cultures', *Transformative Works and Cultures* 31 (2019): para. 1.1, doi:10.3983/twc.2019.1887.

deficiencies. Two seemingly opposed forces interact here. The value of the text is elevated and its authority reinforced, while at the same time the text itself is degraded and its authority usurped. As in Uhlenbruch and Ammann's example, the issues that a fan has with the text can often relate to perceived inaccuracies: how can Manasse be *both* bad and blessed? Lesley Goodman examines this tendency in fan authors, and demonstrates that underlying it are three authoritative discourses, which we can call (1) the universe, (2) canon, and (3) fandom.[78] In the context of fictional narratives, when an author creates a work they also create a fictional universe. This first work is both the entire canon *and* the universe. As an author creates more works in the universe, both of these expand. With this expansion, 'there is now room for contradiction and inaccuracy, room for other differences between one of the texts and the fictional universe. The text can now be evaluated with respect to the fictional universe'.[79] Indeed, even before a second work is added to a canon, there is room for contradiction and inaccuracy – as demonstrated in the example of Manasse. Fandom, as the third source of authority, now can intervene and 'fix' the contradiction, by rewriting (a part of) the narrative – as the Chronicler did. Admittedly, unlike in Goodman's theorization, both Manasse and Mark should not necessarily be seen as fictional, and the universe that we are looking for is not one created by the author, but is an attempt to reflect reality.[80]

Applying Goodman's three discourses to Mark, we can see how they reflect the harmonization process evident in the Longer Ending. The universe that early Christians expect is based on their 'canon' of Gospel endings, which – in all probability – was the endings to Matthew, Luke, and John. Fandom, in our case Christ-followers, knows that Jesus appeared to many people after his resurrection and that Mary Magdalene did not remain silent from fear. Though they know that Mark ends with the unsatisfying phrase 'for they were afraid', 'fans, then, feel free to disregard the authority of the author'.[81] In the eyes of fans, and presumably early readers of Mark, the author has 'failed' and is a 'disappointment'.[82] Within fandom the 'fannish impulse is to maintain the integrity of the fictional universe at the expense of the integrity of the creator(s) and the text itself',[83] just as Mark's Longer Ending puts more emphasis on maintaining the integrity of a harmonized gospel over the authentic ending to Mark. This elevation of the fan above the creator is a peculiar process, which implies 'emotional, aesthetic, and moral superiority' of the fan.[84] The same can be said for the Longer Ending of Mark, where some scribe decided they had superiority over the evangelist themself. Being frustrated by

---

78. Goodman, 'Disappointing Fans', 665–66.
79. Goodman, 'Disappointing Fans', 665.
80. For a further nuancing and extension of this discussion, see pp. 75–76, 155–66.
81. Goodman, 'Disappointing Fans', 668.
82. Goodman, 'Disappointing Fans', 668–69.
83. Goodman, 'Disappointing Fans', 669.
84. Goodman, 'Disappointing Fans', 669.

Mark's ending, realizing that Mark had failed, this Christian fan decided to fix it. By borrowing from other Gospels and – as we shall see shortly – adding some of their own innovations, this tradition-bearer changed the face of Mark forever. The aesthetic value of the fan creation is evident in its ongoing ubiquitous reception. The frustrated fan did indeed write a better ending than the evangelist themself did.

It may be tempting to see the work of the author of the Longer Ending simply as an attempt to make Mark fit better with the other gospels, potentially relating this to the appearance of texts containing gospel harmonies from around the same time. Yet the contents of the Longer Ending are not representative of a simple desire to bring Mark in line with Matthew, Luke and John. As discussed, the Longer Ending contains innovations of its own. In other words, the force of harmonization does not appear to be a detail-oriented 'fixing' of various details in Mark, but rather a broader process. A process which seems to be, at least, not much more than the addition of a resurrection narrative; potentially because the absence of such a narrative troubles the entire notion of gospel. This is a curious conclusion, considering that Mark is the first text that could be called a gospel, and indeed 'Mark's textualization of the Jesus tradition was a watershed act that was soon copied, and to great effect'.[85] Though the other gospels were based on Mark's textual innovation, it appears that these later documents became the benchmark for the original. This demonstrates, once again, that for many, Christians and fans alike, original does not mean best.

Refocalization and Mary Magdalene

Turning from the force of harmonization, let me examine the trends that Lyons-Pardue has highlighted in the Longer Ending, where the portrayals of Mary and the eleven disciples intentionally subvert gender stereotypes. This too can be related to fans who respond to texts with frustration and fascination. Jenkins argues that:

> Fan writing brings the duality of that response into sharp focus: fan writers do not so much reproduce the primary text as they rework and rewrite it, repairing or dismissing unsatisfying aspects, developing interests not sufficiently explored.[86]

This means that in the creation of the Longer Ending, there were more forces at work than simply reproducing the work. The ancient scribe also reworked and – quite literally – rewrote it. As they repaired the unsatisfying ending, we can see that

---

85. Keith, *The Gospel as Manuscript*, 102.
86. Jenkins, *Textual Poachers*, 165.

they also developed an interest in Mary Magdalene's role as follower of Jesus. To some extent one could argue that much of Mary's portrayal is a harmonization with the other three gospels – she is alone (cf. John 20:1–14, *contra* Luke 24:10, Matthew 28.1), she is first (cf. Matthew 28:1, Luke 24:1, John 20:1), she had seven demons (cf. Luke 8:2), she told the eleven disciples (cf. Matthew 28:8, Luke 24:10, John 20:18), and the disciples didn't believe her (cf. Luke 24:11). This process of adding 'missing' elements to Mark, by fixing the narrative falls under the forces discussed above, and this is surely part of the process leading to the production of the Longer Ending. Yet it is noticeable that when other gospels give varying accounts, the most positive option is reliably chosen. Added to this should be the negative way that the eleven disciples are portrayed: overcome by weak, unmanly weeping and under rebuke by Jesus – both unique to the Longer Ending. Thus, the Longer Ending does more than simply harmonize the Marys of the other gospels, or simply vindicate Mary Magdalene from fearful silence. It elevates her to 'the basic pattern of discipleship commissioned by Jesus (16:15) and fulfilled by the disciples (16:20)'.[87]

The way the Longer Ending focusses on Mary Magdalene and elevates her role in the narrative resonates with a common trend in fan fiction called 'refocalization'. Here, an author moves the narrative away from the original protagonists towards secondary figures.[88] Refocalization allows authors to explore less prominent characters, and to allow these characters to reach their 'full potential'.[89] In early Christian literature there are many examples of this approach, for example in apocryphal acts, where suddenly disciples like Thomas and Andrew have protagonist roles, which they did not have in earlier writings. These characters, who are part of the very select group of apostles, have little chance to show themselves as apostles in the earliest narratives: they do no miracles and are mostly or entirely silent. Furthermore, as Marvin Meyer has argued, various early Christian texts can be seen as attempts to redeem 'maligned and marginalized' characters such as Thomas, the doubting apostle, Judas, who betrayed Jesus, and Mary Magdalene.[90]

Within fannish refocalization there is often an emphasis on 'women and minorities, who receive limited screen time'.[91] 'Fan writers', Jenkins argues, 'reclaim female experiences from the margins of male-centered texts, offering readers the kinds of heroic women still rarely available elsewhere in popular culture'.[92] While, in the context of contemporary fan fiction feminism surely underlies some of this focus on female voices and characters, this can hardly be argued for early

87. Lyons-Pardue, *Gospel Women*, 120.
88. Jenkins, *Textual Poachers*, 169.
89. Jenkins, *Textual Poachers*, 171.
90. Marvin W. Meyer, *The Gospels of the Marginalized: The Redemption of Doubting Thomas, Mary Magdalene, and Judas Iscariot in Early Christian Literature* (Eugene, OR: Cascade Books, 2012).
91. Jenkins, *Textual Poachers*, 169.
92. Jenkins, *Textual Poachers*, 171.

Christianity. As Lyons-Pardue points out, 'the author of Mark's Longer Ending and the copyists and churchpersons who secured its place in the Gospel tradition almost certainly did not champion its place within canonical Mark at the behest of latent, proto-feminist impulses'.[93] Yet, at the same time, there are significant similarities in the forces at play. It is a common argument that the role and standing of women in early Christianity was diminished in the first centuries, as Sara Parks concludes in her analysis of gender in the sayings of Jesus and the first century world:[94]

> There was a strong push to force women back into socially acceptable roles by the time of the Pastoral Epistles in the second century, and these countertrends had developed in directions that denigrated womanhood quite drastically by the time of the so-called Church Fathers.[95]

This denigration of womanhood is surely also evident in the portrayal of Mary Magdalene in early Christianity. Ann Graham Brock argues that 'some corners of early Christianity diminished the memory of Mary Magdalene's leadership role in several ways'.[96] Her analysis demonstrates that already in Luke there is evidence of Mary's role being diminished. In this gospel, she is portrayed as formerly demon-possessed by *seven* demons, she is anonymized at the cross, loyal *men* are added to the crucifixion scene besides the loyal women, Mary's witness is put in the mouth of other disciples, and Mary is not commissioned as a witness. Later her identity is conflated with other women in the gospels to make her a penitent sinner (cf. Luke 7:37–50) and eventually she is seen to be a prostitute, which certainly was a concern in second-century Christianity (cf. Origen's *Against Celsus* 2.59–60). Thus, there remains a tension in early Christianity between Mary the prostitute and Mary the first witness to the resurrected Christ. Bas van Os rightly wonders, 'why would Christians discredit their major witness to the resurrection?'[97]

---

93. Lyons-Pardue, *Gospel Women*, 2.

94. See, besides Sara Parks, Amy Richlin, 'Sexuality in the Roman Empire', in *A Companion to the Roman Empire*, ed. David S. Potter, Blackwell Companions to the Ancient World (Malden, MA: Blackwell, 2006), 327–53, doi:10.1002/9780470996942.ch18; Blossom Stefaniw, 'Feminist Historiography and Uses of the Past', *Studies in Late Antiquity* 4, no. 3 (2020): 260–83, doi:10.1525/sla.2020.4.3.260; Blossom Stefaniw, 'Masculinity, Historiography, and Uses of the Past: An Introduction', *Journal of Early Christian History* 11, no. 1 (2021): 1–14, doi:10.1080/2222582X.2021.1931903.

95. Sara Parks, *Gender in the Rhetoric of Jesus: Women in Q* (Lanham, MD: Lexington Books, 2019), 155.

96. Ann Graham Brock, 'Mary Magdalene', in *The Oxford Handbook of New Testament, Gender, and Sexuality*, ed. Benjamin H. Dunning, Oxford Handbooks (Oxford: Oxford University Press, 2019), 436.

97. Bas van Os, 'A Whore from Bethany? A Note on Mary Magdalene in Early Non-Christian Sources', in *Mary Magdalene from the New Testament to the New Age and Beyond*, ed. Edmondo F. Lupieri (Leiden: Brill, 2020), 131, doi:10.1163/9789004411067_008.

Discrediting Mary is, however, only one side of the picture. In *The Gendered Palimpsest*, Kim Haines-Eitzen examines women, books and writing in Early Christianity.[98] In her analysis of Mary Magdalene, she too argues that there is more to this extension of Mary's role in Mark than simply gospel harmonization, noting that 'these various endings to Mark, along with the textual variants within them, betray a central issue in the depiction of Mary Magdalene in early Christian literature'.[99] It simply won't do for Mary to have a role that disciple Peter does not. Despite Mary Magdalene's rather minor role in the gospels, her role is key in gospel accounts of the empty tomb. Haines-Eitzen talks of this leading to a 'controversy about her role as witness to the resurrection and, in particular, her role in comparison to that of Peter'.[100] Brock, similarly, sees that there is 'evidence of Mary Magdalene's strong leadership role' in early Christianity.[101] They both point to other second- and third-century texts where the role of Mary Magdalene is discussed. In these texts there is a tendency to focus on Mary, refocalizing a male-oriented narrative on a female follower of Jesus. In the final part of the Gospel of Thomas, the disciple Peter suggests to Jesus that Mary Magdalene should go away, as women are not worthy of life. He attempts to marginalize Mary more, but Jesus replies: 'Look, I shall lead her so that I will make her male in order that she may also become a living spirit, resembling you males' (Gospel of Thomas 111).[102] Though this is not the most positive portrayal of gender, it does show an attempt to reclaim Mary Magdalene as an apostle. Other apocryphal gospels speak more highly of her. The Gospel of Philip names three Marys who always walked with Jesus, and names Mary Magdalene his companion (Gospel of Philip 59). Famously this text also includes a reference to Jesus frequently kissing her on her ... – infuriatingly the final word of that sentence is not legible in the Gospel of Philip. The missing body part has led to much speculation of a possible romance, but as platonic 'holy kisses' were common in early Christianity (cf. Romans 16:16, 1 Corinthians 16:20, 2 Corinthians 13:12), this needn't be the case.[103] Later the disciples ask Jesus why he loves Mary more than them, and 'clearly voiced their discomfort with or resentment of Mary Magdalene's special position and preferred status'.[104]

---

98. Kim Haines-Eitzen, *The Gendered Palimpsest: Women, Writing, and Representation in Early Christianity* (Oxford: Oxford University Press, 2012).

99. Haines-Eitzen, *The Gendered Palimpsest*, 85.

100. Haines-Eitzen, *The Gendered Palimpsest*, 85.

101. Brock, 'Mary Magdalene', 431.

102. Translation from J. K. Elliott, *The Apocryphal New Testament: A Collection of Apocryphal Christian Literature in an English Translation* (Oxford: Clarendon Press, 1993). The original text can be found in André Gagné, trans., *The Gospel According to Thomas: Introduction, Translation and Commentary*, Apocryphes 16 (Turnhout: Brepols, 2019), doi:10.1484/M.APOCR-EB.5.117535.

103. Brock, 'Mary Magdalene', 432.

104. Brock, 'Mary Magdalene', 433.

A final example of refocalization of Mary Magdalene in early Christianity can be found in the Gospel of Mary: a Gospel that, according to Sarah Parkhouse, 'looked to fill in the gaps of what happened after the resurrection'.[105] Though there is still some debate whether this Mary is Magdalene or the mother of Jesus,[106] it is rather clear that the role of Mary in this text is that of the Magdalene in the gospels.[107] For our discussion it is noticeable that, as Parkhouse argues, the Gospel of Mary has 'four particular similarities' with the Longer Ending of Mark: (1) Jesus appears to Mary Magdalene first and alone, (2) Mary tells the others, (3) the disciples are weeping and grieving, and (4) the disciples doubt her words.[108] These same four are only found together in the Longer Ending of Mark.[109] In this apocryphal gospel, Mary teaches the other disciples hidden knowledge, and sees visions of the resurrected Jesus. This special role for a female disciple does not go undiscussed. Andrew complains that the hidden teachings did not come from Jesus, calling them 'alien' (Gospel of Mary 17.15), Peter doubts that Jesus chose a woman over them (Gospel of Mary 17.20–22), and Mary Magdalene's authority is also further undermined by her overemotional state.[110] Thus, as Parkhouse argues, 'Mary is presented within the cultural gender dynamics of her time; by trying to overcome them, the author reinscribes them. Certainly the evangelist has egalitarian intentions yet cannot prevent a fetishization of her gender'.[111] Ultimately, the underlying gender politic is subverted yet reinscribed, allowing the marginal Mary Magdalene to become a major figure, even superseding the male disciples in knowledge, yet maybe not in acceptance.

Within this context of early Christianity, it is apparent that to some extent the Longer Ending functions to establish Mary Magdalene as a reliable witness. As such it stands counter to 'cultural commonplaces [and] is not the kind of textual modification that modern interpreters have conditioned themselves to expect'.[112] Jenkins argues that often 'fan appropriations' are seen as a form of '"resistance" to dominant ideology', and that while this is certainly part of the issue, the issue is more complex.[113] These early Christians are not simply going against dominant, hegemonic gender roles, but also exploring the storytelling potential of the 'most

---

105. Sarah Parkhouse, *Eschatology and the Saviour: The Gospel of Mary among Early Christian Dialogue Gospels*, Society for New Testament Studies Monograph Series 176 (Cambridge: Cambridge University Press, 2019), 136.

106. Brock, 'Mary Magdalene', 433–34.

107. Parkhouse, *Eschatology and the Saviour*, 133–35.

108. Parkhouse, *Eschatology and the Saviour*, 135.

109. The Gospel of Mary also has similarities with the text of the Gospel of John: her witness is almost exactly the same and both talk of Jesus's ascension to heaven.

110. Sarah Parkhouse, 'The Fetishization of Female *Exempla* : Mary, Thecla, Perpetua and Felicitas', *New Testament Studies* 63, no. 4 (2017): 572–73, doi:10.1017/S0028688517000157.

111. Parkhouse, 'The Fetishization of Female *Exempla*', 574.

112. Lyons-Pardue, *Gospel Women*, 143.

113. Jenkins, 'Reception Theory', 175.

well-known female figure of the New Testament' – after Mary the mother of Jesus, of course.[114] Mary Magdalene's position is strengthened at the cost of the other disciples. She is given a unique relationship to Jesus, and given access to hidden knowledge, that even the twelve disciples did not receive. Mary Magdalene is allowed, to borrow Jenkins's words, 'to achieve their full potential'.[115]

Personalization and Snakes

Besides the addition of Mary and the doubting apostles, the Longer Ending of Mark includes a list of signs that will accompany Christians: believers will be able to handle snakes and drink poison with no ill effect. These signs are not found in the three other canonical gospels. The text reads:

> And these signs will accompany those who believe: by using my name they will cast out demons; they will speak in new tongues; they will pick up snakes in their hands, and if they drink any deadly thing, it will not hurt them; they will lay their hands on the sick, and they will recover. (Mark 16:17-18)

This part of the Longer Ending has garnered far more attention than Mary Magdalene's portrayal has. Though, as James Kelhoffer gives as the reason for his monograph, this section too 'has yet to receive an adequate explanation'.[116] There are several aspects of this section that should be noticed. First, the list details five miracles: driving out demons in Jesus's name, speaking in tongues, picking up snakes, drinking poison without consequence, and healing the sick by laying on hands. While in many canonical (Isaiah 35:5-7, Matthew 15:31) and non-canonical (Acts of Andrew and Matthias 10, Sibylline Oracles 6:13-16) miracle lists the phrasing of the miracles is very similar, there isn't a direct source to be found for these five miracles. Second, of these five miracles, Jesus performs only two in early Christian literature.[117] Third, these miracles should occur *after* Jesus's ascension, presumably up to and even beyond the time of the writer of the Longer Ending. The text implies that contemporary readers of the Longer Ending can expect to witness these miracles, unlike, for example, the healings in the gospels. Finally, those performing the miracles are the believers, not Jesus or the apostles. The only two possible canonical connections for this statement are Jesus's words that 'very truly, I tell you, the one who believes in me will also do the works that I do and, in fact, will do greater works than these, because I am going to the Father' (John 14:12) and the apostle Paul surviving a snake bite on Malta (Acts 28:1-6).

James Kelhoffer's *Miracle and Mission: The Authentication of Missionaries and Their Message in the Longer Ending of Mark* is a broad survey of the themes in the

---

114. Brock, 'Mary Magdalene', 429.
115. Jenkins, *Textual Poachers*, 171.
116. Kelhoffer, *Miracle and Mission*, 47.
117. Kelhoffer, *Miracle and Mission*, 211.

Longer Ending in Jewish, Christian, and Greco-Roman contexts. In his survey he demonstrates that when early Christians give miracle lists, they almost always refer to miracles in the past, not the present day. Usually they refer to miracles Jesus could do, and sometimes such a list is about the miracles that Jesus's first followers, the apostles, could do.[118] He notes only two sources that have miracle lists, expecting *current* miracles from believers: Against Heresies by Irenaeus of Smyrna (c. 130–202) and the third- or fourth-century text Pistis Sophia. Indeed, even outside of the miracle lists, it is exceptional to see a non-apostle performing a miracle. Usually, whenever a non-apostle performs a miracle, it is at the command of an apostle, who authorizes the miracle.[119] The only context where Kelhoffer found a consistent emphasis on believers doing miracles were five Christian apologists of the second and third century: Justin Martyr, Theophilus of Antioch, Irenaeus of Smyrna, Tertullian, and Origen of Alexandria.[120] Kelhoffer uses this analogy as a basis for his argument for a second-century provenance of the Longer Ending. Building on Kelhoffer's analysis, I will explore how these miracles are inserted into Mark in more detail. Though it is productive to see these apologists as a context for the Longer Ending, there is a difference between claiming that believers can do miracles and adding believers' miracles to an existing text. The apologists make the claim, and that claim is fittingly an apologetical step. The writer of the Longer Ending adds miracles to Mark. This involves completely different hermeneutics that that of the apologists. It is this adding of miracles that I will explore in the context of fan fiction.

The eighth of Jenkins's ten dominant approaches in fan fiction is 'personalization'.[121] Here there is an attempt by the fan writer to bridge the gap between their world and the one of the text. Jenkins explains: 'fan writers also work to efface the gap that separates the realm of their own experience and the fictional space of their favorite programs'.[122] This often takes the form of inserting oneself into the fictional world, often called 'self-insertion fic'.[123] Self-insertion of the author into their work, as a literary trope, goes back millennia.[124] A specific and controversial type of this is the

---

118. Kelhoffer, *Miracle and Mission*, 210.

119. Kelhoffer, *Miracle and Mission*, 338. Acts 19:11–20 is an interesting example of unauthorized miracles. The narrative starts by recounting how Paul's handkerchiefs and aprons were used to heal the sick. Seven men, the sons of Sceva, decided to try using Jesus's and Paul's names in their exorcisms, apparently without Paul's approval. The demon replies 'Jesus I know, and Paul I know; but who are you?'. It then overpowers them and causes them to leave the house naked and wounded.

120. Kelhoffer, *Miracle and Mission*, 310–38.

121. Jenkins, *Textual Poachers*, 176–78.

122. Jenkins, *Textual Poachers*, 176.

123. Kristina Busse, 'Beyond Mary Sue: Fan Representation and the Complex Negotiation of Gendered Identity', in *Seeing Fans: Representations of Fandom in Media and Popular Culture*, ed. Lucy Kathryn Bennett and Paul Booth (London: Bloomsbury Academic, 2016), 159.

124. Ika Willis, '"Writers Who Put Themselves in the Story": Dante Alghieri, Roland Barthes, Lieutenant Mary-Sue and Me' (Desiring the Text, Touching the Past: Towards an Erotics of Reception Conference, Bristol, 2010).

so-called 'Mary Sue', which, originating from *Star Trek* fandom in 1973, refers to the insertion of 'idealized images of the writers as young, pretty, intelligent' characters into the story.[125] These ideal characters often sideline canonical characters by making Mary Sue more important to the narrative than the canonical (male) figures.[126] Though Mary Sues were originally gendered female, male Mary Sues exist as well. As 'there is no single often-used term for the male version',[127] male Marys are referred to as Gary, Marty, Murry, or Larry to name a few.

Potentially a case could be made that the portrayal of Mary Magdalene, as discussed above, is a Mary Sue; and surely the self-insertion of female characters into the passion narrative long predates fan fiction – for example, 'English Christian mystic Kempe visualizes herself speaking with the Virgin Mary after the death of Jesus and offering her a hot drink to comfort her'.[128] That Mary Magdalene was an existing character does not mean she cannot also be a self-insert: Karen Hellekson and Kristina Busse argue that 'instead of creating a Mary Sue self-insertion character, fan writers might co-opt existing female characters'.[129] Indeed, as discussed above based on Lyons-Pardue's analysis, the character of Mary Magdalene is idealized in the Longer Ending: she becomes the apostle *par excellence*, over and above the male disciples. These canonical apostles, which are much more central to the narrative of Mark, are sidelined and emasculated: the 'character denies other characters the right to be central in their own stories'.[130] And if we keep the extension of Mary's role in other early Christian works, as discussed above, this tendency is even more evident. At the same time, it is unlikely (but not implausible!)[131] that the writer of the Longer Ending was female, so Mary (Sue) Magdalene may not be a self-insertion in the traditional sense.

A more likely self-insertion are, what we might call, the 'second century miracles' in the Longer Ending of Mark. These 'Gary Stu' miracles allow the second-century author to do what any Mary Sue fic does: insert '"glorified versions" of themselves into the storyworld of an existing and usually beloved media text'.[132] It is a common argument in early Christian scholarship that the miracles performed by believers

---

125. Jenkins, *Textual Poachers*, 176.

126. Busse, 'Beyond Mary Sue', 160.

127. Pat Pflieger, '"Too Good to Be True": 150 Years of Mary Sue', 2002, http://www.merrycoz.org/papers/MARYSUE.xhtml.

128. Anna Wilson, 'The Role of Affect in Fan Fiction', *Transformative Works and Cultures* 21 (2016): para. 2.1, doi:10.3983/twc.2016.0684. Wilson gives several more examples.

129. Karen Hellekson and Kristina Busse, eds., *The Fan Fiction Studies Reader* (Iowa City, IA: University of Iowa Press, 2014), 133.

130. Busse, 'Beyond Mary Sue', 161.

131. Haines-Eitzen, *The Gendered Palimpsest*, 25–34.

132. Beth E. Bonnstetter and Brian L. Ott, '(Re)Writing Mary Sue: *Écriture Féminine* and the Performance of Subjectivity', *Text and Performance Quarterly* 31 (2011): 344, doi:10.1080/10462937.2011.602706.

were a powerful weapon in the spread of Christianity. Indeed, Kelhoffer quotes church historians from Eusebius (*c.* 260–339) – who attributes conversions of entire crowds to strange miracles – to Adolf von Harnack (1851–1930), who called miracles very important means of mission and propaganda.[133] Second- and third-century apologists, in particular, detail miracles that they and their audience have witnessed. As by this time the original followers of Jesus, the apostles, are no longer alive, these miracles must have been performed by non-apostles – or to borrow the Longer Ending's term: 'believers'. Christian philosopher Justin Martyr (*c.* 100–165) repeatedly points to contemporary exorcisms (e.g. *Second Apology* 6.5–6; *Dialogue with Trypho* 30.3; 76.6; 85.1–2) and works of power (*Dialogue with Trypho* 35.5), which he uses as proof of Jesus's power and nature. Bishop Theophilus of Antioch (died *c.* 185) also discusses contemporary exorcisms (*To Autolycus* 2.8.8–9) to discuss the nature of inspiration. Bishop Irenaeus of Smyrna (*c.* 130–202) compares the miracles of heretics with those of believers, emphasizing how much better the church is, where people are regularly healed and even raised from the dead (*Against Heresies* 2.31.3). He also counters those who do not believe in the authenticity of Jesus's miracles by referring to contemporary ones as proof: exorcisms, foreknowledge, healings, and raising from the dead (*Against Heresies* 2.32.4). Prolific Christian author Tertullian (*c.* 155–230) similarly refers to contemporary exorcisms and healings (*Apology* 23, *Prescription against Heretics* 41; *To Scapula* 2.8–9), to opening prison doors, loosing bonds, raising the dead (*Prayer* 29.2) and even in passing to the power over snake bites (*Antidote for the Scorpion's Sting* 1.3–4). These signs are evidence of a Christ-follower's orthodoxy. Finally, the theologian Origen (*c.* 184–253) uses contemporary miracles – exorcisms, healings, foreknowledge – as a counterargument in his responses to Celsus (*Against Celsus* 1.6, 46; 3.24; 7.67). These five apologists thus all bear witness to believers performing miracles. Furthermore, as Kelhoffer summarizes, they 'typically do not emphasize the miracles of the twelve apostles. Moreover, when they do occasionally discuss the miraculous, they tend instead to relate feats performed by contemporary believers rather than by the apostles'.[134] While this might well be the context for the Longer Ending of Mark, in the writings of these early Christians the goal of the miracles is apologetic. They are used as evidence for Christianity. For the Longer Ending of Mark there appears to be other forces at work as well, let me explore those in detail.

The forces that drove the writer of the Longer Ending can be elucidated by Jenkins's concept of 'personalization'. This ancient Christ-follower, clearly fascinated enough by the Gospel of Mark to pen a more fulfilling ending, may well have been frustrated by more than just the silence of the women and the lack of a resurrection narrative. Besides a minor reference in John, no gospel refers to the ability of believers to do miracles. Yet, as evidenced by the five apologists, it appears that

---

133. Kelhoffer, *Miracle and Mission*, 310–11.
134. Kelhoffer, *Miracle and Mission*, 338.

second-century miracles were common enough. As quoted above, fans personalize texts 'to efface the gap that separates the realm of their own experience and the fictional space of their favorite programs'.[135] The gap between their own experience and the gospels can be bridged through insertion of a promise – 'I as a believer can do miracles *too*'. As Busse explains: insertion fic 'tends to be wish fulfilment, allowing the author (and, if successful, the reader) to enter the canon and participate in the action'.[136] The second-century writer can quite literally enter texts written a century earlier and put their words into the mouth of Jesus.[137] This is primarily a matter of identity, as self-insertion fic is 'an exemplary way in which fans explore and engage with their favourite media texts, their own identities and desires'.[138] The fundamentally different nature of being a second-century Christ-follower, without contemporary apostles or apostolic witness, drives a desire to recognize one's own identity in a foundational text. The writer wishes to 'address [their] own experiences and emotions within the worlds of [their] favorite texts'.[139] At the same time, by connecting the world of the canon with the world of the writer, they 'can address current and personal issues through their writings'.[140] The second-century concerns of the apologists are addressed in the Longer Ending of Mark. As contemporary miracles function as proof for the authenticity of Jesus and the apostle's miracles, as does Jesus's promise of future miracles authenticate these later works. Indeed, making post-resurrection Jesus promise future miracles further authenticates Jesus's resurrection itself.

Recontextualization and the Freer Logion

Leaving the majority text of the Longer Ending aside, let me move onto the Freer Logion. This saying attributed to Jesus is a single insertion into the Longer Ending between Jesus's rebuke and commission of the eleven disciples. It has survived in

---

135. Jenkins, *Textual Poachers*, 176.
136. Busse, 'Beyond Mary Sue', 160.
137. Naturally, all the gospel writers put words in Jesus's mouth, and an analysis of how the earliest Gospel writers do this – though extremely interesting – would go beyond the scope of this chapter. Useful examples in the context of self-insertion could be John's 'the disciple whom Jesus loved' (John 13:23, 19:26, 20:2, 21:7, 21:20) or Matthew 9:9, where the tax collector 'Levi' (Mark 2:14) is curiously renamed 'Matthew'. Indeed, Ulrich Luz argues that this change is the reason for the gospel being named after Matthew: 'the best suggestion is still that [Matthean authorship] was a conclusion that later readers drew based on Matt 9:9'. Ulrich Luz, *Matthew 8–20: A Commentary on Matthew 8–20*, Hermeneia: A Critical and Historical Commentary on the Bible (Minneapolis, MN: Fortress Press, 2001), 33.
138. Busse, 'Beyond Mary Sue', 159.
139. Busse, 'Beyond Mary Sue', 168.
140. Busse, 'Beyond Mary Sue', 168.

only one codex,[141] though it was also known to the famous Bible translator Jerome (c. 345–420).[142] The logion is as follows:

> And they excused themselves, saying, 'This age of lawlessness and unbelief is under Satan, who does not allow the truth and power of God to prevail over the unclean things of the spirits. Therefore reveal your righteousness now' – thus they spoke to Christ.
>
> And Christ replied to them, 'The term of years of Satan's power has been fulfilled, but other terrible things draw near. And for those who have sinned I was handed over to death, that they may return to the truth and sin no more, that they may inherit the spiritual and imperishable glory of righteousness that is in heaven.'

James Kelhoffer suggests that this section exists to 'smooth over this transition' from rebuke to commission.[143] This addition does make for a better transition, and it's quite plausible that this drove its creation. This reason, however, only justifies the existence of the addition, not the contents of the addition. The writer could have smoothed the narrative in a number of ways, and the actual contents are evidence of a common theme in fan fiction.

Above I have already discussed two of what Jenkins calls 'characteristic strategies of interpretation, appropriation, and reconstruction' by fans.[144] He defines a total of ten,[145] and the first of these strategies is 'Recontextualization'. Here writers fill 'in the gaps in the . . . material and provide additional explanations for the character's conduct'.[146] Key here is the character focus: these stories elucidate confusing behaviour of characters and give further background to help explain character's motivations and actions. This could well be the same strategy that some scholars identify in the writings commonly called 'rewritten' Bible. This is certainly a primary hermeneutical tool in James Kugel's 1000+ page *Traditions of the Bible: A Guide to the Bible As It Was at the Start of the Common Era*.[147] In it, Kugel explains that 'interpreters sometimes felt themselves obliged to explain why a particular person in a biblical story should have behaved the way that he or she did, or to find

---

141. A codex is basically an ancient book, consisting of a number of pages bound together by a variety of means.

142. Lyons-Pardue, *Gospel Women*, 151.

143. Kelhoffer, *Miracle and Mission*, 166.

144. Jenkins, *Textual Poachers*, 165.

145. The list of all ten are: Recontextualization, Expanding the Series Timeline, Refocalization, Moral Realignment, Genre Shifting, Cross Overs, Character Dislocation, Personalization, Emotional Intensification, and Eroticization. See Jenkins, *Textual Poachers*, 165–80.

146. Jenkins, *Textual Poachers*, 165.

147. James L. Kugel, *Traditions of the Bible: A Guide to the Bible As It Was at the Start of the Common Era* (Cambridge, MA: Harvard University Press, 1998).

some connection between what a particular prophet had predicted and some later event in history'.[148] It is vital to note here that the genre 'rewritten Bible' is a-historic. Both terms – rewritten *and* Bible – are highly problematic at the start of the common era.[149] There is little evidence to assume there was any concept of canon, and the term rewriting implies a textual hierarchy that did not exist yet.[150] But, if we move away from this canon-centred, hierarchical view of ancient traditions, the basic motivations that Kugel describes are still valid. Surely, ancient writers didn't see existing traditions as 'Bible' and what they were doing was probably not seen as 'rewriting', but they clearly are reacting to existing traditions. Rather than imagining this as a rewriting of a Bible, we could rather see these writers reacting to narratives that they knew.[151] In doing this they often appear to be trying to explain what led a specific character to do a certain thing.

Before looking at how the Freer Logion recontextualizes Mark's ending, let me shortly give some examples of this way to write fan fiction from the three Synoptic gospels (Matthew, Mark and Luke). Here it is generally assumed that both the gospel writers Matthew and Luke had access to the written Gospel of Mark. In Mark's Gospel, Jesus regularly commands people not to tell anyone about him or his miracles. This so-called Messianic Secret is a mysterious aspect of Mark's Jesus:[152] what on earth could drive Jesus to stop people spreading his good news? Matthew knows of Mark's theme of secrecy, and 'has no interest in most of the material'.[153] As such he usually leaves this aspect out of his Gospel. The following inclusion stands out:

> [Jesus] ordered them not to make him known. This was to fulfill what had been spoken through the prophet Isaiah: 'Here is my servant, whom I have chosen.... He will not wrangle or cry aloud, nor will anyone hear his voice in the streets.' (Matthew 12:16, 17, 19)

---

148. Kugel, *Traditions*, xvii.
149. Mroczek, *Literary Imagination*, 8–9.
150. See also Hindy Najman's emphasis on the 'vitality' of these texts. Hindy Najman, 'The Vitality of Scripture Within and Beyond the "Canon"', *Journal for the Study of Judaism* 43, no. 4–5 (2012): 497–518, doi:10.1163/15700631-12341237. See also Hindy Najman and Irene Peiran Garrison, 'Pseudepigraphy as an Interpretative Construct', in *The Old Testament Pseudepigrapha: Fifty Years of the Pseudepigrapha Section at the SBL*, ed. Matthias Henze and Liv Ingeborg Lied, Early Judaism and Its Literature 50 (Atlanta, GA: SBL Press, 2019), 331–58.
151. See also Najman, 'Vitality of Scripture'; Anders Klostergaard Petersen, 'The Riverrun of Rewriting Scripture: From Textual Cannibalism to Scriptural Completion', *Journal for the Study of Judaism* 43, no. 4–5 (2012): 475–96, doi:10.1163/15700631-12341236.
152. This term was first introduced by Wilhelm Wrede in 1901. For a good introduction see these two major English language reflections on the term: David E. Aune, 'The Problem of the Messianic Secret', *Novum Testamentum* 11, no. 1–2 (1969): 1–31, doi:10.1163/156853669X00010; James D. G. Dunn, 'The Messianic Secret in Mark', *Tyndale Bulletin* 21 (1970): 92–117.
153. Luz, *Matthew 8–20: A Commentary on Matthew 8–20*, 190.

Matthew attempts to give, to borrow Jenkins's words, 'additional explanations for the character's conduct'.[154] Matthew finds in another authoritative source (the prophet Isaiah) a (semi-)logical reason why Jesus would command silence. Another example could be how the Gospels deal with Judas's betrayal of Jesus. In Mark no reason is given why the apostle Judas betrays Jesus. He writes: 'Then Judas Iscariot, who was one of the twelve [disciples], went to the chief priests in order to betray him to them. When they heard it, they were greatly pleased, and promised to give him money. So he began to look for an opportunity to betray him' (Mark 14:10–11). Luke's retelling of this narrative clearly attempts to give a suitable explanation why one of Jesus's closest comrades would betray him. Luke's recontextualization of Judas adds Satan to the narrative (Luke 22:3). He claims that Satan possesses Judas, thus justifying Judas's actions.[155] These additions demonstrate how the fan strategy of recontextualization 'invites fans to reread ... episodes'[156] in a new light.

The introduction of Satan is also the solution that the Freer Logion chooses. The disciples justify their cowardly conduct by claiming that Satan rules the age, and Satan won't let good prevail over evil. In somewhat poetic language they are simply saying that they cannot believe the situation that they are in, where their Messiah, Saviour and master has been killed. As fans rely on 'meta-textual understanding of ... characters, their history, cultural backgrounds, motivations, and psychology to resolve questions posed' by the narrative,[157] the writer of the Freer Logion relied on the same. Borrowing from the parable of the sower earlier in Mark, the disciples are likened to the road, where the seed of the gospel is sowed. Satan had immediately come and taken away the word (Mark 4:15). Though we might have expected the disciples to realize they need to be more fertile soil for the seed of the gospel, they rather ask Jesus to end the dominion of Satan. Jesus admits that Satan's rule is over, but that other trials await. Promising salvation, he can then easily move on to the commission of the disciples. The Freer Logion smooths out the narrative, but also takes the opportunity to discuss the disciples' perplexing behaviour. Their disbelief and emotional state are recontextualized through the Freer Logion.

Conclusions and Significance

In this chapter I have looked at how fan studies can inform our analysis of the forces at work that led to the creation of additional endings to the Gospel of Mark. Allow me to place this analysis within a larger debate. Kelhoffer's significant

---

154. Jenkins, *Textual Poachers*, 165.

155. See, for an analysis of the role of Satan in Luke 22, Tom de Bruin, 'In Defence of New Testament Satanologies: A Response to Farrar and Williams', *Journal for the Study of the New Testament* 44, no. 3 (2022): 445–48, doi:10.1177/0142064X211045311.

156. Jenkins, *Textual Poachers*, 166.

157. Jenkins, 'Reception Theory', 166.

analysis of the Longer Ending of Mark ends with a contextualization. He refers to an argument that early Christian author Origen (c. 184–253) alludes to in *Against Celsus*:

> After this he says that some believers, as though from a drinking bout, go so far as to oppose themselves and alter the original text of the gospel three or four or several times over, and they change … its character to enable them to deny difficulties in face of criticism. (Origen *Against Celsus* 2.27)[158]

Taking the Longer Ending as a possible example of 'this very type of alteration', Kelhoffer sees this as a 'striking example of what Bart Ehrman has credibly termed the corruption and continual re-writing of biblical texts by proto-Orthodox believers'.[159] Lyons-Pardue is not convinced by this statement, and argues that 'alteration of New Testament texts does not automatically constitute "corruption"',[160] pointing out that the Longer Ending itself is hardly an orthodox 'panacea' – a miracle cure for all problematic elements of the original ending. Yet she does not discuss what this alteration is, if it is not to be termed a corruption. The usage of the term 'corruption' seems to lie at the heart of this discussion, and indeed cuts to the heart of this book. Is the Longer Ending, to borrow the terms from the Introduction, a fake, a fiction, a forgery? Is it a corruption?

Ehrman devotes three pages to the discussion of the term 'corruption'.[161] He explains that he borrows the word from text-criticism – a field devoted to reconstructing the most 'original' version of a text – where it denotes any accidental or intentional change to an original text. He readily admits the word can be understood to be pejorative, yet some scholars use the term in a neutral sense. Ultimately, he justifies and elucidates his usage of the term:

> I am therefore consciously employing irony in my denotation of the orthodox corruptions of Scripture. On the one hand, I am using the term in its technical text-critical sense of 'alterations of a text'; at the same time, I am using it to refer to the effect of rereading or rewriting of texts in the history of their transmission, claiming not that scribes misunderstood their texts and perverted them (as if corruption were necessarily pejorative), but that in their transmissions of the text they engaged in much the same process of interpretation and interaction that we all engage in, rereading and therefore rewriting our texts at every turn.[162]

---

158. Origen, *Origen: Contra Celsum*, trans. Henry Chadwick (Cambridge: Cambridge University Press, 1980).
159. Kelhoffer, *Miracle and Mission*, 480.
160. Lyons-Pardue, *Gospel Women*, 135.
161. Bart D. Ehrman, *The Orthodox Corruption of Scripture: The Effect of Early Christological Controversies on the Text of the New Testament* (Oxford: Oxford University Press, 1996), 29–31.
162. Ehrman, *The Orthodox Corruption of Scripture*, 31.

In other words, Ehrman chooses a deliberately controversial term, but does not necessarily use that term in the way that it might be understood. From one point of view, Ehrman's 'proto-orthodox corruptions', could just as easily been called 'proto-orthodox readings'. From another, the fact that they are deliberate and lasting alterations to a pre-existing text justifies a pejorative term. Ehrman sees this corruption as an almost natural process, which is not hostile to the text. Scribes did not act 'out of sheer malice or utter disregard for the constraints of the text', they 'knew exactly what the text said, or at least they thought they knew', and 'the changes they made functioned to make these certain meanings all the more certain'.[163] Allow me to engage with Kelhoffer, Lyons-Pardue and Ehrman's arguments, in the context of this chapter and Jenkins's contribution to the study of derivative texts.

It seems evident from the various endings to Mark that the text itself invited writers to finish it. Whether we wish to use the metaphor of archive, database, or simply text, Mark lay waiting to be expanded: Mark quickly became more than Mark originally was. Indeed, seeing how common the Longer Ending is in manuscripts, the most common Mark is a derivative Mark. And the Mark that was authoritative for most of Christian history was, to borrow Ehrman's term, a corrupted Mark. Taking the context of fan studies into consideration, 'corruption' may very well be an extremely useful term for derivative Mark. Though Ehrman is probably correct when he argues that ancient scribes were not hostile to the text and that, in a general sense, 'scribes altered their sacred texts to make them "say" what they were already known to "mean"',[164] this does not imply that the act of rewriting the ending to Mark was innocent nor is this true for many of the changes discussed in this chapter. If we see these scribes as Jenkins's poachers, their alteration of their sacred texts was an act of resistance. Scribes resisted current forms of the text and asserted their own authority over that of the evangelist. It would be extremely complicated to try to argue that *all* of the endings of Mark, with all their variety, were nothing more than scribes making texts 'say' what they already 'mean'.

We know that several scribes at different stages altered the ending to Mark, but what exactly do these alterations *imply*? On the one hand, they can be seen – as Kelhoffer or Ehman argue – as attempts by Christian scribes to make the text adhere better to a certain theological agenda. In this case the writers are seen as readers who recognize current debates in texts, and attempt to clarify passages that could be misunderstood. On the other, Lyons-Pardue shows that these 'clarifications' are hardly solely that, as they create new problems as well. Frustration with the text surely underlies many of the motivations of these ancient scribes. In some cases that may have been frustration that Mark was not clearly 'proto-Orthodox', as Ehrman and Kelhoffer argue, but this should not be taken too far. Theological frustration may underlie some fan production, but there are other forces at work

---

163. Ehrman, *The Orthodox Corruption of Scripture*, 280.
164. Ehrman, *The Orthodox Corruption of Scripture*, 276.

as well. The examples of refocalization, personalization, and recontextualization – three typical fan approaches – demonstrate that there is more to this process. When Lyons-Pardue argues that the Longer Ending is hardly a solution to theological criticism,[165] she hints to exactly this complication. Fan Studies has elucidated other, non-theological, motives that could have led to some significant additions to the gospel.

This leads us back to the categorization of these additions and changes: are they fakes, fictions, forgeries or, indeed as we just examined, corruptions? The discussion above highlights how complex the use of these terms is. These derivative texts have been created by careful readers and exist due to various forces. They are the outcome of affective production. Gaging the quality and value of texts based on their derivative nature, undervalues both them and their producers. When these texts are examined through fact/fiction, real/fake and authentic/forgery binaries, we limit the argument in ways that do not do justice to the texts or the forces that led to their creation. The use of the concepts immediately condemns derivative texts to the negative side of these binaries, with all the associated value judgements. Thus, ultimately, the terms themselves are not productive. In this chapter fan studies theory allowed a more nuanced discussion of the relationships between source and derivative texts, and a deeper understanding of the forces that led to the creation of these derivative texts. They are the products of fascinated writers, who have solved frustrations that they have with the source texts by creating new ones. They have not created forgeries to replace the authentic ones, nor fiction to replace fact. Rather, they borrowed these texts, creating a cultural and social identity for themselves. They struggled with them, articulating for themselves and others unrealized possibilities of these texts. The following chapter, where we will examine the concept of fan play, will further deconstruct these false dichotomies.

All in all, Jenkins's groundbreaking *Textual Poachers* has served as a fruitful theory to engage with the multiple endings to the Gospel of Mark. His conceptualization of fans as fascinated and frustrated producers allowed useful engagement with the forces that led to the creation of new, additional endings to pre-existing biblical texts.

---

165. Lyons-Pardue, *Gospel Women*, 135.

Chapter 2

NOSTALGIA, NOVELTY, AND TEXTUAL AUTHORITY IN THE TESTAMENTS OF THE TWELVE PATRIARCHS: WHAT POWER DOES A DERIVATIVE WORK HAVE?[1]

In this chapter we step away from texts that became canonical to one of the so-called Old Testament Pseudepigrapha. These parabiblical texts are 'attributed to (or ... primarily concerned with the history or activities of) an Old Testament character (or characters)',[2] making them derivative of the texts and traditions that came to be collected in the Hebrew Bible or Old Testament. Here we have, unlike in the previous chapter, full-blown derivative texts that are thousands of words long. These texts move beyond a simplistic 'fixing' of issues and require a more in-depth analysis of the forces that drive fan production.

When the paperback version of Anne Rice's *Christ the Lord: Out of Egypt* was published, she included a new introduction dated 12 July 2006.[3] As discussed earlier,[4] she uses this introduction to discuss the topic of fictionality, reinforcing that her account is both fictional and realistic. This double affirmation is important. On the one hand, she affirms her orthodox Catholic beliefs – she feels that everything she has written fits perfectly in her and the community's understanding of the key aspects of Jesus's life and ministry. Her rewriting of Jesus's life is nostalgic,

---

1. The research underlying this chapter inspired this entire project. Huge thanks go to Sonja Ammann, Mette Bundvad, and Frauke Uhlenbruch for putting together the Fan Fiction and Ancient Scribal Cultures unit at the European Association of Biblical Studies, and accepting my paper for its session in Berlin, 2017. A different version of this chapter was published in a special edition of *Transformative Works and Cultures*, edited by Frauke Uhlenbruch and Sonja Ammann. Tom de Bruin, 'Nostalgia, Novelty, and the Subversion of Authority in "The Testaments of the Twelve Patriarchs"', *Transformative Works and Cultures* 31 (2019), doi:10.3983/twc.2019.1553. The peer reviewers and copy editor at *Transformative Works and Cultures* helped me immensely, and I am extremely appreciative to them.

2. Hedley F. D. Sparks, ed., *The Apocryphal Old Testament* (Oxford: Clarendon Press, 1984), xv.

3. Anne Rice, *Christ the Lord: Out of Egypt: A Novel* (New York: Knopf, 2005), 457–66.

4. See pp. 2–4.

harkening back to earlier, personal engagements that she had with the gospels. Yet at the same time, she fully admits that she is fundamentally adding to the narrative of Jesus: 'history as well as the gospels is the source for this picture of a world in which Our Lord *might have lived*, as a little boy, in war and in peace, from day to day'.[5] She creates a world in which Jesus might have lived, a re-imagining of ancient Egypt and Palestine; and she attributes to the child Jesus 'emotions' and 'powers' that he might have had. Her derivative text is thus also novel: it creates something new for her and her readers to experience. These two forces, nostalgia and novelty, drive much of fan engagement, affect and production.

I will use the Testaments of the Twelve Patriarchs, one of the longer Pseudepigrapha, as a case study to further examine the forces that drive the writing of fan fiction and early Christian derivative works. Here I extend the discussion from the first chapter, by engaging with Paul Booth's emphasis on fan play and other recent fan studies theory on fan production. I will examine how both novel and nostalgic readings are constructed by fans and early Christian writers. Applying these two aspects to the Testaments, I demonstrate how a nostalgic interaction with the source narratives creates a new, yet traditional, reading of the 'Rape of Dinah' narrative that is preserved in Genesis 34. In the second part of the chapter, I show how the desire for novelty drives Christian readings of ancient, pre-Christian texts. These two aspects show a unified way of understanding the writer's engagement with their source traditions, and demonstrate how authority can be both reinforced and deconstructed in a single text.

The Testaments of the Twelve Patriarchs claim to be the final words of the twelve sons of Jacob (the progenitors of the ancient nation of Israel), given on their deathbeds to their children. The twelve testaments in this pseudepigraphal work all share the same form with minor variations. The patriarch knows he is dying, he calls his children, he reflects on his life, he exhorts his offspring, he talks about the future, and he dies. The Testaments contain many themes that have been explored, by including messianism, eschatology, ethics, anthropology, and demonology.[6] Though it is collected in the 'Old Testament Pseudepigrapha', the current version of the work makes explicit references to Jesus Christ. As most scholars agree,[7] the current form of the Testaments is written by a Christ follower, though some claim

---

5. Rice, *Christ the Lord*, i, emphasis mine.

6. See, for short discussions of these many topics: Vered Hillel, 'Patriarchs, Testaments of the Twelve', in *T&T Clark Encyclopedia of Second Temple Judaism*, ed. Loren T. Stuckenbruck and Daniel M. Gurtner (London: T&T Clark, 2019), 411–15; Tom de Bruin, 'Testaments of the Twelve Patriarchs', in *Critical Dictionary of Apocalyptic and Millenarian Movements*, ed. James G. Crossley and Alastair Lockhart, 14 October 2022, https://www.cdamm.org/articles/testaments-of-the-twelve-patriarchs.

7. David A. deSilva, 'The *Testaments of the Twelve Patriarchs* as Witnesses to Pre-Christian Judaism: A Re-Assessment', *Journal for the Study of the Pseudepigrapha* 23 (2013): 67, doi:10.1177/0951820713502411.

a hypothetical original form predates Christianity.⁸ Or to put this situation into fannish terms, the text is a remix of existing fan fictions about the Israelite forefathers created by a fan of Christ, somewhere in the second century CE.⁹

In this chapter, I will be looking at three parts of the Testaments that are indicative of the whole. These three parts are all related to the issue of authorship and authority, and the ways that the Testaments alternatively perpetuates and subverts the authority of the canonical material. First, I will examine the so-called paratext and the narrative frames of each testament. There the text and its writer engage in a dialectic on authority with the readers. Next, building on the nostalgia/novelty continuum expressed by Booth, I will examine Testament of Levi 5–6, a nostalgic reading in the Testaments, and Testament of Simeon 6.2–7, a novel reading. I will demonstrate how the Testaments' nostalgic reading 'fixes' perceived issues in the canonical material. I will then demonstrate how the novel reading subverts Scripture. In this reading the Israelite patriarchs, who predate Christ by a few millennia, are recast as Christ-followers.

Fan Play and Fan Economies

In the Introduction to this book, the most obvious reason why fan fiction is written was shortly examined: a desire to fill in the gaps of a narrative. Sheenagh Pugh gives us insight into that force at work in the creation of fan fiction:

> whenever a canon closes, someone somewhere will mourn it enough to reopen it. The wish to find out 'what happened next' – or invent it if it didn't – is familiar

---

8. Anders Hultgård, *L'eschatologie des Testaments des Douze Patriarches: I. Interprétation des textes*, Acta Universitatis Upsaliensis Historia Religionum 6 (Stockholm: Almqvist & Wiksell, 1977); Jürgen Becker, *Untersuchungen zur Entstehungsgeschichte der Testamente der zwölf Patriarchen*, Arbeiten zur Geschichte des antiken Judentums und des Urchristentums 8 (Leiden: Brill, 1970); Anders Hultgård, *L'eschatologie des Testaments des Douze Patriarches: II. Composition de l'ouvrage, textes et traductions*, Acta Universitatis Upsaliensis Historia Religionum 7 (Stockholm: Almqvist & Wiksell, 1981); Jarl H. Ulrichsen, *Die Grundschrift der Testamente der zwölf Patriarchen: Eine Untersuchung zu Umfang, Inhalt und Eigenart der ursprünglichen Schrift* (Uppsala: Almqvist & Wiksell, 1991); Stefan Opferkuch, 'Ein Rausch und seine Folgen. Parallelen zwischen der Erzählung von Noah als Weinbauer (Gen 9,20–27) und ihren Auslegungstraditionen und der Bilha-Episode in TestRub 3,11–15', *Zeitschrift für die neutestamentliche Wissenschaft* 108 (2017): 281–305, doi:10.1515/znw-2017-0011.

9. Origen's reference to this text in his *Homilies on Joshua* is often used to date the Testaments to the mid/late second century; Harm W. Hollander and Marinus de Jonge, *The Testaments of the Twelve Patriarchs: A Commentary*, Studia in Veteris Testamenti Pseudepigrapha 8 (Leiden: Brill, 1985), 82. Admittedly, we do not know if the text Origen cites is the same as the text that we have access to.

to most of us.... if we liked the story we may still not be ready for it to end, for the characters and milieu that have become real to us to be folded up and put back in the puppeteer's box.[10]

Putting aside, for the moment, the idea of the 'closing of the canon', the force at work here is that fans are not satisfied with a limited set of narratives. They need to react by expanding the text. In the previous chapter, I used Henry Jenkins's concepts of fascination and frustration to theorize the forces that underlie this fan interaction. Fans are fascinated with the world and, in Pugh's example, frustrated that the narrative is over. So, they put pen to paper and fill the gaps. In the context of early Christianity, this is surely the same force that drove the writers of the so-called infancy gospels.[11] The canonical gospels leave gaps in the narrative of Jesus, and ancient fans of Christ wanted to, to use Pugh's words, 'find out what happened or invent it'.

In the previous chapter, I framed fan interaction as a 'struggle', which is how Jenkins originally portrayed fans. And indeed, the reception of Jenkins's book led to fan fiction being increasingly read in political terms, as dissatisfied fans involved in a struggle with media producers.[12] Yet, for others, fan engagement is more akin to 'play'. To return to Anne Rice's *Christ the Lord*, she does not appear to be struggling with insufficiencies in the gospels, rather she is playing with them, exploring new possibilities. Or, as she claims, the novel was written 'with the hope of exploring and celebrating the mystery ... in a wholly fresh way'.[13] Paul Booth's *Playing Fans: Negotiating Fandom in the Digital Age* builds on the concept of play, and re-envisions that fascination/frustration paradigm as a continuum 'between nostalgia and novelty'.[14] On the one side there is 'a desire for fresh material, new takes on old genres, and changing paradigms of meaning', and on the other, 'an inherently nostalgic practice'.[15] This interplay between nostalgia and novelty undergirds the fannish production of texts. For Booth nostalgia is 'the sense of the text' and pops up in various ways.[16] Fans exist due to how a text originally affected them; they interact with moments in the text that they see as iconic.

---

10. Sheenagh Pugh, *The Democratic Genre: Fan Fiction in a Literary Context* (Bridgend: Seren, 2005), 47.

11. Tony Burke, 'Early Christian Apocrypha in Popular Culture', in *The Oxford Handbook of Early Christian Apocrypha*, ed. Andrew F. Gregory et al., Oxford Handbooks (Oxford: Oxford University Press, 2015), 433, doi:10.1093/oxfordhb/9780199644117.013.29.

12. See, e.g. Fathallah's analysis of fan fiction in the academy, Judith Fathallah, *Fanfiction and the Author: How Fanfic Changes Popular Cultural Texts*, Transmedia: Participatory Culture and Media Convergence (Amsterdam: Amsterdam University Press, 2017), 21–23.

13. Rice, *Christ the Lord* (2005, 2007), 466.

14. Paul Booth, *Playing Fans: Negotiating Fandom in the Digital Age* (Iowa City, IA: University of Iowa Press, 2015), 4.

15. Booth, *Playing Fans*, 6.

16. Booth, *Playing Fans*, 6.

These examples are defined by nostalgia. On the other side of the continuum is 'the sense of newness'.[17] Fans, though nostalgic for their original interaction with the text, are driven by a need for new, fresh narratives, takes, genres, and paradigms. On this side of the continuum fans are driven by change, fans explore different meanings, different perspectives, or different outcomes. These new texts are both original yet remind us of their precursors. Thus, fans are driven by two different forces. Nostalgia harkens back to the originally read texts; novelty, on the other hand, desires for something new.

The forces driving fans to create is only part of the economy that drives fan production. Fans, engaging through nostalgia and novelty with texts, feel a compulsion to create a fan work but, as discussed in the Introduction, fan work can only exist in a community. Fans create, and then they distribute them to other fans. Thus, while part of the drive to write fan fiction is a personal, affective engagement with a source material, at the same time there is an engagement with a community of consumers of that fan fiction. Thus, when we try to understand what a creator gets out of writing a text, we need to also think about labour and economy. A text comes into being by someone's labour and the creator would expect to receive something in return. Contemporary commercial authors receive some sort of capital in exchange for their labour, though as (for example) most academic authors know, the relationship between royalties and labour is terribly skewed. Nevertheless, academic authors do keep writing, for – one would assume – other reasons than royalties received. The same is true for conventional fan authors, who typically receive no monetary gains, yet keep writing.[18] The fan economy is not one of capital nor money, but of gifts. These gifts are reciprocal and end up creating and maintaining social solidarity.

Tisha Turk examined the gift economy of fandom.[19] She argues that each fan creation is considered a gift, sometimes for a single person, sometimes for the community as a whole. Each gift is reciprocated with more gifts. Turk describes that these gifts take on two specific forms: art objects, and creative work, that surround and undergird the pieces of art. The first are the easiest to imagine, these are works of art (texts, images, videos etc.) that a fan creates. These works require artistic skill to make and are highly valued. The second is much less obvious and less valued: this type of gift is all the work that keeps the fan engine running. Unseen, behind-the-scenes labour, that Turk lists as follows:

> commenting on stories, beta-ing vids, writing essays and recommendations, reviewing and screen-capping episodes, collecting links, tagging bookmarks,

---

17. Booth, *Playing Fans*, 6.
18. Hellekson calls them 'anticommercial'. Karen Hellekson, 'A Fannish Field of Value: Online Fan Gift Culture', *Cinema Journal* 48 (2009): 114, doi:10.1353/cj.0.0140.
19. Tisha Turk, 'Fan Work: Labor, Worth, and Participation in Fandom's Gift Economy', *Transformative Works and Cultures* 15 (13 August 2013), doi:10.3983/twc.2014.0518.

maintaining Dreamwidth and LiveJournal communities, organizing fests/
challenges/exchanges, compiling newsletters, . . . and the list could go on.[20]

Thus, the entire world of fannish production revolves around giving and receiving gifts, some more visible than others.

Karen Hellekson sees gifts functioning in a similar manner, but focusses on a specific outcome of the economy: social solidarity.[21] As gifts are created, received and reciprocated, ultimately each gift is exchanged for a 'gift of reaction'.[22] Each individual gift is lost in the sea of fan exchanges and reactions, and together they become something larger: they form a way for a community to create social cohesion. Returning to Turk, we can conclude that the gift of reaction is both a public and a private gift; and is arguably the largest force behind fan labour. Turk explains: 'Fans may write stories . . . because we feel an internal compulsion to do so, but we distribute them for other fans to read and watch. . . . Use is therefore the clearest sign of a gift accepted.'[23] In the fan community, fans receive more gifts than they give. While they might write a few texts, they will read many, many more. When they create a piece of art in reaction to someone's work, they will potentially receive thousands of 'gifts of reaction' to their art. This inequality is a part of the gift economy, where the reward for labour is distributed over a large community and thus becomes very valuable indeed.

Applying this context of labour and economy to ancient Christianity, we could argue for something similar. While, as discussed in the Introduction, it is not unthinkable that early Christian writers were in some way 'professionals',[24] there are different economies underlying, for example, the difference between the writings of Christian teacher Clement of Alexandria, and the Apocalypse of Peter written by an unknown person. The first is a more professional product, penned by a named author, and is authorized; the second is none of these. It seems rather obvious what a Christian teacher like Clement would have got out of writing a theological treatise like his *Stromata*, but what did the anonymous writer of the Apocalypse of Peter get? Could we imagine that they partook in an economy similar to the gift economy of contemporary fandom? Let me explore this briefly.

In contemporary fandom, a fan is driven to create fan art. This is circulated and reciprocated – either by gifts of art, of collection, of re-use, or simply of consumption. This gift economy is what drives the fan community. Ancient Christianity could be seen to have the same basic economy. Someone has an internal compulsion to write a text; they are fascinated by and frustrated with a Christian story. We know that these new texts were copied and translated extensively and read – liturgically,

---

20. Turk, 'Fan Work', para. 2.3.
21. Hellekson, 'A Fannish Field of Value'.
22. Hellekson, 'A Fannish Field of Value', 116.
23. Turk, 'Fan Work', para. 4.1.
24. See pp. 15–16.

publicly, and privately – for centuries. In this we have the same three types of gifts that the fan community has: art objects, behind-the-scenes labour, and reaction. The first is evident in the amount of texts that we have, and the way that these texts use and re-use other traditions. It is also evident in the very large amount of Christian art based on parabiblical narratives.[25] Behind-the-scenes labour exists in the codifying, copying and translating of these texts – people were doing extensive amounts of work so that these texts remain available and become available for new contexts. The gift of reaction is present in the copying, transmitting, and reading of these works, but is also undoubtedly evident in the way these texts were used in and become foundational for liturgical settings.[26]

Yet at the same time there are also differences between contemporary fan fiction and ancient parabiblical writings when it comes to the gift economy. As Candida Moss has recently pointed out, ancient texts were very often written (and read) by enslaved people, at the behest of their enslavers.[27] Though this has always been a well-known fact, scholars of early Christianity have hardly scratched at the surface of its implications. Case in point is Moss's 2023 appeal 'that, rather than continuing to rehearse Enlightenment models of solitary authorship or unwittingly reproducing ancient Roman slaveholder despotics, New Testament and early Christian scholarship should consider the role of enslaved or formerly enslaved secretaries in the production of Christian texts.'[28] Her forthcoming monograph *God's Ghostwriters* should contribute immensely to this discussion.[29] Recognizing the role of enslaved people in the production of Christian texts and other works, complicates concepts of writer- and authorship immensely, also for viewing ancient texts as fan objects. It is rather hard to imagine the forced labour of enslaved people as part of the gift economy of fan labour. At the same time, enslaved people did not factor into the elite's conceptualization of the literary landscape and the gift economy. These slaveholder despotics, 'present enslaved workers as prosthetic tools, as extensions of [the authors'] own bodies.'[30] It could

---

25. David Cartlidge and J. K. Elliott give hundreds of examples of this. David R. Cartlidge and J. K. Elliott, *Art and the Christian Apocrypha* (London: Routledge, 2001).

26. See, for example, Harald Buchinger, 'Liturgy and Early Christian Apocrypha', in *The Oxford Handbook of Early Christian Apocrypha*, ed. Andrew Gregory et al., Oxford Handbooks (Oxford: Oxford University Press, 2015), 361–77, doi:10.1093/oxfordhb/9780199644117.013.40.

27. Candida R. Moss, 'The Secretary: Enslaved Workers, Stenography, and the Production of Early Christian Literature', *The Journal of Theological Studies* 74, no. 1 (2023): 20–56, doi:10.1093/jts/flad001.

28. Moss, 'The Secretary', 24.

29. Candida R. Moss, *God's Ghostwriters: Enslaved Christians and the Making of the Bible* (Boston: Little, Brown and Company, 2024).

30. Candida R. Moss, 'Between the Lines', *Studies in Late Antiquity* 5, no. 3 (2021): 435, doi:10.1525/sla.2021.5.3.432.

well be argued that the elite felt they were partaking in a gift economy through their labour, not recognizing the labour and contributions of these highly educated scribes, who might have been Christ-followers themselves. Another important difference between ancient and contemporary fan communities when it comes to the gift economy, might be the anonymity of many ancient parabiblical texts. While most fan fiction is pseudonymous, this does not mean that it is anonymous: fan fiction authors create a persona around their *nom de plume*.[31] Thus they do receive status and honour for the artistic creations besides the gifts of codifying, transmission, use, and reaction. While we cannot say for certain, it stands to reason that the writers of ancient parabiblical writings would have social networks in which they read and shared their texts. Here ancient writers would receive status and honour similar to contemporary fan communities. The difference lies in the scale and extent of these gifts. Contemporary online fan communities are exceedingly large, and fan authors will receive thousands if not millions of gifts, networks for ancient writers would have been much smaller. Additionally, insofar as we know, these ancient texts were distributed as anonymous or pseudonymous works and thus writers would not receive honour and status outside of their direct network. This difference does not make the comparison of gift economy with the ancient parabiblical economy null, but shows a pious element that is also part of Christianity. Here we return to Anne Rice's motivations from the Introduction, which in her own words were not capitalistic, nor was she interested in the gifts that she would receive for writing the book. Her motivations were of the pious sort: she sees herself as gifting others the work itself for the glory of God. Certainly, there is an element of performative piety here, and her motivations must have included more than what she claims. At the same time her personal faith does play a role as well. Similarly, the ancient Christian fan artist – after receiving honour and status in their social networks – could see the gifts of reaction, use, codification and transmission, and conclude *Soli Deo gloria*.

Author's Notes and Paratextual Engagement in Authority

Fan fiction by necessity engages in a dialectic of authority. Fans, as they create derivative works, need to establish their agency, authorial voice and claim to authority.[32] Like all texts, fan texts are accompanied by paratext, defined by Gerard Genette as, 'a certain number of verbal or other productions, such as an author's name, a title, a preface, illustrations.... These accompanying productions, which

---

31. Maria Lindgren Leavenworth, 'The Paratext of Fan Fiction', *Narrative* 23 (2015): 44.
32. Alexandra Elisabeth Herzog, '"But This Is My Story and This Is How I Wanted to Write It": Author's Notes as a Fannish Claim to Power in Fan Fiction Writing', *Transformative Works and Cultures* 11 (2012): para. 1.3, doi:10.3983/twc.2012.0406, emphasis mine.

vary in extent and appearance, constitute ... the work's *paratext*'.³³ In this paratext, 'a discursive negotiation of the concepts of authorship and ownership' takes place.³⁴ Perhaps the most obvious paratext to accompany fan fiction is the 'Author's Notes' where there is a 'fannish negotiation of ownership and agency' which is ultimately about 'authority'.³⁵ A good example of this is given by Alexandra Herzog. She begins her article on Author Notes and authority with a quote from a fan named Caazie, who declares, 'this is *my* story and this is how *I* wanted to write it'.³⁶ Here the fan claims their own agency by using first person pronouns in relation to the narrative and their ownership of it. Author Notes are most important to my discussion as they provide a place for authors to enter a negotiation of meaning with their readers, where they take the authority found in the original text, reappropriate it, and repackage it for the readers.³⁷ In doing this, fan authors attempt to enforce authorial control on meaning, 'trying to dictate to the readers how "*the text is read properly*"'.³⁸

The Testaments of the Twelve Patriarchs, like all texts, is accompanied by paratext. Each individual testament has been given a title and a subtitle (which may or may not have been included in the most original texts); additionally, each testament begins with a narrative frame. The titles are all in the same vein: 'Testament of Reuben', 'Testament of Judah', 'Testament of Benjamin', and so on. As such they define the work as a testament, the (often very authoritative³⁹) last words of a famous patriarch of Israel. The subtitles also share a structure: they consist of the preposition 'concerning' followed by one or more substantives such as 'Envy', 'Compassion and Mercy', or 'Natural Goodness.'⁴⁰ In many cases the subtitle self-

---

33. Gerard Genette, *Paratexts: Thresholds of Interpretation* (Cambridge: Cambridge University Press, 1997), 1. Genette focussed only on the text as manifested in printed media. Georg Stanitzek extended the theory to other media, including film and television. Georg Stanitzek 'Texts and Paratexts in Media', *Critical Inquiry* 32, no. 1 (September 2005): 27–42, doi:10.1086/498002.

34. Judith May Fathallah, 'Statements and Silence: Fanfic Paratexts for *ASOIAF/Game of Thrones*', *Continuum* 30, no. 1 (2 January 2016): 86, doi:10.1080/10304312.2015.1099150.

35. Herzog, 'This Is My Story', para. 1.5.

36. Herzog, 'This Is My Story', para. 1.1, emphasis mine.

37. Herzog, 'This Is My Story', para. 3.1.

38. Herzog, 'This Is My Story', para. 2.4, original emphasis.

39. Kolenkow writes 'testaments were viewed as authoritative because no person would be expected to tell an untruth at the hour of death/judgment, nor would the dying person fail to give children both goods and truth (or warning)', Anitra B. Kolenkow, 'Testaments: The Literary Genre "Testament"', in *Early Judaism and Its Modern Interpreters*, ed. Robert A. Kraft and George W. E. Nickelsburg, The Bible and Its Modern Interpreters (Atlanta, GA: Scholars Press, 1986), 259.

40. The full list is: 'ideas', 'envy', 'priesthood and arrogance', 'courage, love of money and fornication', 'simplicity', 'compassion and mercy', 'anger and falsehood', 'natural goodness', 'hatred', 'the two aspects of vice and virtue', 'chastity', and 'a pure mind'.

evidently follows from the contents of the testament. In some cases, the link is harder to make.⁴¹ These subtitles guide readers in their reading of the text. They automatically see the titular theme as the dominant one. Thus, the subtitles function in a manner similar to the Author Notes, in that the readers are shown how to read the text 'properly'. Admittedly, the subtitles are most likely later additions to the Testaments.⁴² They therefore functioned as guides for the reader only at a later stage in their history. There is, however, a second part to the paratext which is not a later addition.

Each Testament begins with a narrative frame surrounding the last words of the patriarch. While the titles function to enforce authority over the interpretation of the text, the narrative frame functions to give the text itself authority. Without fail, each testament begins with the phrase 'a copy of the words of [a patriarch]'.⁴³ By portraying each of these works as the authentic last words of one of the twelve patriarchs, the texts are given great authority. Indeed, because the patriarchs themselves appear to be given agency over their own biographies, the narratives presented could be seen to supersede the third-person narratives of the canon itself. Fan fiction, using terminology borrowed from Christian tradition, similarly interacts with a canon, which is not an authoritative list of books but the interpretation of one or more texts that are core to the fandom.⁴⁴ In fan fiction the canon is decentred, and almost becomes 'a reference work that one *might* consult for character names and general ideas instead of being considered a bible that needs to be treated with reverence and awe and would conventionally represent the only valid text'.⁴⁵

An interesting dichotomy is thus created in fan studies. Fan fiction interacts with a canon, but this canon is not entirely authoritative, not definitive, and not sacred. However, while Herzog highlights the differences between how fan fiction depicts its canons and how contemporary culture views the relationship between

---

41. For example, T. Reuben receives the title 'about ideas/thoughts', which is not the most straightforward choice, as the theme is clearly fornication. See, Hollander and de Jonge, *Commentary*, 87. But the argument does concentrate 'on the relationship between fornication and the mind' and the testament 'shows how fornication begins in the mind itself', Tom de Bruin, *The Great Controversy: The Individual's Struggle between Good and Evil in the* Testaments of the Twelve Patriarchs *and in Their Jewish and Christian Contexts*, Novum Testamentum et Orbis Antiquus 106 (Göttingen: Vandenhoeck & Ruprecht, 2015), 140. T. Judah is entitled 'about courage, love of money and fornication'. Courage is the theme of the first nine chapters of T. Judah, fornication the theme of the last seventeen. The love of money is a minor topic, occurring only twice in the testament (T. Judah 18.2, 19.1).

42. Whether the titles are later additions is much less clear. See, on the titles and subtitles, de Bruin, *Great Controversy*, 80.

43. For more on the form of the Testaments, see the discussion and notes in de Bruin, *Great Controversy*, 42–47.

44. See pp. 24–25.

45. Herzog, 'This Is My Story', para. 3.2, emphasis mine.

religious groups and their canon(s), it does not appear that this contemporary difference is true for many first- and second-century Jews and Christians. Lee McDonald, using an example of how the first-century Jewish Qumran community 'did not hesitate to change the text', argues that, for Christians, only 'in later centuries, would [textual transformation] have been most unusual and almost unthinkable, given the perceived holiness of the text'.[46] Many Jews and Christians from the first centuries, then, had a very similar view of canon to contemporary fan authors. Canon is not a definitive text 'to be treated with reverence and awe', but as something with which one can take 'many liberties'; only much later did (some) Christians start to treat specific canons as sacrosanct.[47] Therefore, while the Testaments are part of a corpus of works derivative of Scripture and, in the eyes of contemporary readers, seen as less authoritative than canonical works, this is unlikely to have been the case for ancient readers.[48]

The Testaments thus assume a large amount of authority over the texts collected in the canon. Though the canon is viewed as authoritative, this does not mean that a parabiblical book *cannot* be authoritative as well. Building on Herzog's quote above, it seems that in this period Jews and Christians did not consider the Bible to be 'the bible' in the same way contemporary audiences might. Ancient and current sensibilities towards authorship do not fully overlap, specifically in the realm of ancient Jewish and Christian texts. One could argue that in the context of contemporary authorship, 'the purpose of literature is seen as being to express the self, and to that extent literature is seen to embody the self'.[49] Texts are strongly related to an author's self or persona. Consider, for example, G. R. R. Martin's famous claim that 'my characters are my children, I have been heard to say. I don't want people making off with them, thank you'.[50] By invoking the metaphor of genetic progeny, he shows the involvement of his self in his fictional characters, and thus his fiction.[51]

---

46. Lee Martin McDonald, *The Formation of the Biblical Canon: Volume II: The New Testament: Its Authority and Canonicity*, 4th ed. (London: Bloomsbury T&T Clark, 2017), 316. See also McDonald's Christian examples. McDonald, *Formation of the Biblical Canon II*, 331.

47. McDonald, *Formation of the Biblical Canon II*, 331.

48. Francis Borchardt, for example, recently examined canonicity and authority in ancient Judaism, concluding that 'these examples show that when considering the concept of authority in ancient Judean literature, we should be ever mindful of authorization as an act of reception. This leads to further conclusions: a text can be authorized for diverse reasons by different readers. Different texts can also be considered authoritative by separate reading communities'. Francis Borchardt, 'Influence and Power: The Types of Authority in the Process of Scripturalization', *Scandinavian Journal of the Old Testament* 29 (2015): 196.

49. Francesca Middleton, 'Abusing Text in the Roman and Contemporary Worlds', *Transformative Works and Cultures* 21 (2016): para. 2.9, doi:10.3983/twc.2016.0672.

50. G. R. R. Martin, 'Someone Is Angry On the Internet', *LiveJournal*, 7 May 2010, https://grrm.livejournal.com/151914.html.

51. See also Fathallah's discussion of the Romantic model of authorship as it relates to fan fiction and authority. Fathallah, 'Statements and Silence', 77.

For ancient religious texts, there is a different relationship. Annette Reed argues that the 'earliest Israelite/Jewish' texts attributed to famous figures 'appeal to them, not as authors with authority rooted in their own wisdom or virtue, but primarily as conduits for the transmission of divine knowledge to humankind ... [the] writer is not so much creator or author as tradent and guarantor'.[52] Indeed, discussing Jewish texts written between the fifth century BCE and first century CE, she argues that 'the practice of penning books in one's own name remains surprisingly rare among Second Temple Jews.'[53] Thus, in ancient Judaism of that period authorship and authority are less related to the writer's self, and are instead more related to the writer's access to divine revelation. Yet, noting a shift in the literary landscape, including a steady growth of attributing previously anonymous texts to 'famous figures', Reed suggests that this shows a renewed interest in the writers themselves and thus a 'reinterpretation of biblical history as a series of ancient heroes'.[54] She argues that this reinterpretation 'may reflect—at least in part—a response to Hellenistic views of the authority of a text as tied [to] its author'.[55]

The Testaments show both sides of this sensibility, emphasizing both the heroic nature of the twelve sons of Jacob,[56] and their unfettered access to additional divine revelation.[57] Considering these differences in the understanding of authorship and authority, there is a large difference between how authority and derivative works are understood and interpreted in ancient Jewish and Christian circles and contemporary fan communities. Because for ancient readers, the canon was seen as less 'sacred' and the actual writer of the text was less important than the implied author/narrator, the authority of the Testaments could readily supersede that of the canonical narratives.[58]

---

52. Annette Yoshiko Reed, 'Pseudepigraphy, Authorship, and the Reception of "the Bible" in Late Antiquity', in *The Reception and Interpretation of the Bible in Late Antiquity*, ed. Lucian Turcescu and Lorenzo DiTommaso, The Bible in Ancient Christianity 6 (Leiden: Brill, 2008), 476–77, doi:10.1163/ej.9789004167155.i-608.116.

53. Reed, 'Pseudepigraphy, Authorship, Reception', 478.

54. Reed, 'Pseudepigraphy, Authorship, Reception', 478.

55. Reed, 'Pseudepigraphy, Authorship, Reception', 478.

56. For example, consider Philonenko's comparison of how Judah is portrayed in a way similar to Hercules/Herakles. Marc Philonenko, 'Juda et Hérakles', *Revue d'histoire et de philosophie religieuses* 50 (1970): 61–62.

57. See the discussion below, or the discussions in Robert A. Kugler, *The Testaments of the Twelve Patriarchs*, Guides to Apocrypha and Pseudepigrapha (Sheffield: Sheffield Academic Press, 2001), 14; Hollander and de Jonge, *Commentary*, 39–41.

58. Robert Kugler argues a similar point, from a slightly different point of view, he writes that *The Testaments* (together with many other Jewish and Christian works) capitalize 'on the emerging authority of the Hebrew Scriptures by invoking key figures in them to make fresh claims regarding the nature of being human in relationship with Israel's God'. Robert A. Kugler, 'The *Testaments of the Twelve Patriarchs*: A Not-So-Ambiguous Witness to Early Interpretive Practices', in *A Companion to Biblical Interpretation in Early Judaism*, ed. Matthias Henze (Grand Rapids, MI: Eerdmans, 2012), 355.

In their paratext, then, the Testaments attempt to assume authority over the canon. As we consider the text itself, we see marked differences between canon and the Testaments. The biographical sections repeat and consolidate common canonical material, but they also adapt, extend and change this material.[59] In this way, they replace ancient, third-person, canonical readings with new, authoritative, first-person ones. In the next section I will analyse an example of how the canonical details of biblical characters' lives are altered in the Testaments. In creating a fannish reading of the canonical framework and other associated traditions, the character, ethics, and beliefs of the patriarchs are adapted to meet the needs of the religious community as perceived by the writer. However, this reading remains on the nostalgic side of Booth's continuum. There is little impulse to create completely novel readings.

Nostalgic Fan Fiction

Ancient non-canonical Jewish and Christian writings currently tend to be examined as witnesses to thought that is not represented in the canon. This is, from the outset, a somewhat anachronistic endeavour, as there is little reason to assume that Jewish and Christian communities at the time were concerned with the idea of a canon; they were 'not canon conscious'.[60] Yet at the same time, most communities would have seen some books as 'core' and others as 'fringe'.[61] Allow me to introduce a couple of examples, before giving some more critical notes.

In his introduction to non-canonical writings, David deSilva explains that these texts 'are of immense value as windows into the development of *biblical interpretation*, theology, ethics, and liturgy in Early Judaism and Christianity, as well as into the sociocultural and historical contexts within which these developments occurred'.[62] Most applicable to this discussion is specifically how these writings function as witnesses to ancient interpretative practices. As such, deSilva points out that they give us insight into how ancient people, or ancient fans, engaged with their canonical narratives and figures. A major theme we can note in ancient interpretation is the solving of perceived flaws in the narrative. As James Kugel explains:

> ancient interpreters ... set out to give the text the most favorable reading they could and, in some cases, to try to get it to say what they thought it really meant to say, or at least ought to say. They did this by combining an extremely meticulous

---

59. de Bruin, *Great Controversy*, 63–71.

60. Lee Martin McDonald, *The Biblical Canon: Its Origin, Transmission, and Authority* (Grand Rapids, MI: Baker Books, 2006), 191.

61. McDonald, *Biblical Canon*, 190–92.

62. David A. deSilva, 'Apocrypha and Pseudepigrapha', in *Oxford Bibliographies in Biblical Studies* (Oxford: Oxford University Press, 2020), doi:10.1093/OBO/9780195393361-0007, emphasis mine.

examination of its words with an interpretative freedom that sometimes bordered on the wildly inventive.[63]

This inventive freedom led to the creation of derivative works with widely diverging narratives. Kugel's and deSilva's work are indicative of a major theme in the way that 'canonical' and 'non-canonical' texts are often studied.[64] As shortly discussed in Chapter 1,[65] terming these texts 'rewritten Bible', implicitly places them as secondary to a canon, although that canon most likely did not exist at the time these texts were written. Eva Mroczek has recently critiqued these assumptions because a canonical focus obscures important facets of ancient literary practices.[66] She argues for fostering an appreciation of the way writers react to already existing traditions and texts without invoking a hierarchy of texts. Mroczek is surely correct in emphasizing the need to decentre the canon, and her conclusions support this project.[67] By their very natures, these texts react to and interact with (earlier) versions of the same narratives that have come to be preserved in the canon. At the same time, it is important to note that by the second century CE, the text of Genesis – the primary text the Testaments react to – was more or less fixed.[68] The Testaments is certainly in discussion with the parabiblical texts as well, but in an attempt to keep the discussion in this chapter somewhat manageable, I will only focus on how the Testaments engages with Genesis, leaving the analysis of how hundreds of texts and traditions interact in fan cultures for the following chapters. The section of the Testaments that I will discuss appears to be novel to the Testaments. Mary Anna Bader has examined all known parabiblical texts containing the narrative, and

63. James L. Kugel, *How to Read the Bible: A Guide to Scripture, Then and Now* (New York: Free Press, 2007), 12.

64. The best examples of this can be found in James L. Kugel, *Traditions of the Bible: A Guide to the Bible As It Was at the Start of the Common Era* (Cambridge, MA: Harvard University Press, 1998); Kugel, *How to Read the Bible*; deSilva, 'Witnesses'; deSilva, 'Apocrypha and Pseudepigrapha'.

65. See pp. 52–53.

66. Eva Mroczek, *The Literary Imagination in Jewish Antiquity* (New York: Oxford University Press, 2016).

67. Though admittedly, in the second century CE context we examine here, the status and contents of the canon would have been more generally fixed than in the 'precanonical' world Mroczek examines.

68. See the discussions in Alexander Fantalkin and Oren Tal, 'The Canonization of the Pentateuch: When and Why? (Part I)', *Zeitschrift für die alttestamentliche Wissenschaft* 124, no. 1 (2012): 1–18, doi:10.1515/zaw-2012-0001; Alexander Fantalkin and Oren Tal, 'The Canonization of the Pentateuch: When and Why? (Continued, Part II)', *Zeitschrift für die alttestamentliche Wissenschaft* 124, no. 2 (2012): 201–12, doi:10.1515/zaw-2012-0015; Thomas Römer, 'Moses Outside the Torah and the Construction of a Diaspora Identity', *Journal of Hebrew Scriptures* 8 (2008), doi:10.5508/jhs.2008.v8.a15.

concludes that 'the information ... [in the Testaments is] new to the reader, when compared to other texts examined'.[69]

In my analysis of the Testaments, I build on the details of Chapter 1. In a sense what we see here is similar to the fix-it fic genre discussed in detail there. Fans relate to texts with a mixture of fascination and frustration. They are attracted to these texts as they offer the best vehicle for exploring certain topics, but are disenchanted as the texts do not fully meet their desires.[70] Frustrated yet fascinated authors set out to solve this divide between their expectations and the text of the canon by creating narratives that solve or address these tensions. Fans are nostalgic for how the text originally affected them, and attempt to keep the whole of the text(s) in line with that 'imagined ideal text'.[71] Novelty does not play a large role here.

A prime example of this practice can be seen in the Testament of Levi 5-6. In this passage the author retells a canonical narrative often called the 'rape of Dinah' (Genesis 34:1-31). In the second century context of the Testaments, it is more than likely that the account of this narrative in Genesis would have been considered 'canonical' or at least authoritative. The story goes: Dinah, the sister of the twelve patriarchs, is assaulted and raped by a prince named Shechem. He then falls in love with her and wishes to marry her. Her twelve brothers (the patriarchs), hearing of this assault, are outraged. But Shechem's father intercedes and begs for marriage. He promises anything they desire. The brothers deceive him and ask that he, his son, and all the men in his city be circumcised. While the men are recovering from this surgery, Simeon and Levi, two of the twelve brothers, enter the city and kill them. The other ten brothers plunder everything: flocks, wealth, children, women. Their father is upset by this as he fears retaliation.

For many ancient and contemporary readers the ethics of the patriarchs in this narrative are highly ambiguous:[72] Simeon and Levi deceive and kill all the men, their brothers take all the women, children and livestock as their own, and their father Jacob, upon hearing this, is worried about his 'reputation and security', not about the terrible deeds of this sons.[73] Accordingly, the Testament of Levi tells a

69. Mary Anna Bader, *Tracing the Evidence: Dinah in Post-Hebrew Bible Literature*, Studies in Biblical Literature 102 (New York: Lang, 2008), 93.

70. Henry Jenkins, 'Reception Theory and Audience Research: The Mystery of the Vampire's Kiss', in *Reinventing Film Studies*, ed. Christine Gledhill and Linda Williams (London: Arnold, 2000), 175.

71. Booth, *Playing Fans*, 19.

72. See, for example, Bader's introduction to her analysis of rewritings of the Dinah narrative. Bader, *Tracing the Evidence*, xiii–xvi.

73. Bruce N. Fisk, 'One Good Story Deserves Another: The Hermeneutics of Invoking Secondary Biblical Episodes in the Narratives of Pseudo-Philo and the Testaments of the Twelve Patriarchs', in *The Interpretation of Scripture in Early Judaism and Christianity: Studies in Language and Tradition*, ed. Craig A. Evans, Journal for the Study of the Pseudepigrapha Supplement Series 33 (Sheffield: Sheffield Academic Press, 2000), 233.

different story, one unique to this text. Levi receives a vision from God in which he is ordained as a priest (T. Levi 5.1–3). An angel gives him a sword and a shield, saying 'retaliate against Shechem on account of Dinah, I will be with you because the Lord has sent me' (T. Levi 5.3).[74] Levi is furious about the rape of his sister and urges his father and elder brother to tell the Shechemites to become circumcised (T. Levi 6.3). Levi kills Shechem, and Simeon kills Shechem's father (T. Levi 6.4). The other brothers then kill the rest of the town (T. Levi 6.5). Upon hearing this Levi's father, Jacob, is angry and irritated, but not because of his reputation and security. He is upset because 'they had been circumcised and after this had been killed. ... We [the brothers] had sinned by doing this against his judgement' (T. Levi 6.6–7). But Levi is of another mind, he understood that this sexual assault was simply the latest of a long series of violent acts against Israelite women (T. Levi 6.8).[75] This fictional narrative saves Levi and Jacob from many ethical accusations. Levi is no longer an angry brother out for revenge; he is a warrior of the Lord sent to bring righteous judgement, and he is even accompanied by an angel.[76] In the same vein, Jacob's worries are now about having killed these fresh converts rather than the 'selfish' exclamations of Genesis account.

As introduced in Chapter 1, in the context of contemporary fan fiction such 'fixing' of canon is a common occurrence. Lesley Goodman quotes a fan who writes: 'Fan fiction is 60% fun, 30% porn and 120,000,000% fixing canon because canon is WRONG and needs to go sit in the corner and think about what it's done'.[77] The fiction in the Testament of Levi may not contain the 30% porn (for that we should probably turn to the Testaments of Reuben or Judah), but it does fix

---

74. All translations of the Testaments are my own, based on the Greek text of Marinus de Jonge et al., *The Testaments of the Twelve Patriarchs: A Critical Edition of the Greek Text*, Pseudepigrapha Veteris Testamenti Graece 1 (Leiden: Brill, 1978). English translations can be found in Hollander and de Jonge, *Commentary*; Marinus de Jonge, 'The Testaments of the Twelve Patriarchs', in *The Apocryphal Old Testament*, ed. Hedley F. D. Sparks (Oxford: Clarendon Press, 1984), 505–601.

75. This reading is not immediately obvious from the text, which seems to imply the sexual assault of the long-dead Sarah, great-grandmother of the twelve brothers. Fisk has argued how the author links this narrative from Genesis 34 with and earlier narrative in Genesis 20. There, the married Sarah, the 'mother' of Judaism, is inducted into the foreign king Abimelech's harem. This sexual assault, thus, becomes indicative of the way people treat Jewish women. Fisk, 'One Good Story', 234–35.

76. Cf. Bader's analysis of Levi in this narrative. She concludes: 'God acted on behalf of Israel, ridding the Israelites/Hebrews of the sons of Hamor. In close partnership with the Divine, Levi acted on behalf of God, cleansing Israel. Levi's actions, according to T. Levi, were sanctioned and empowered by the Divine', Bader, *Tracing the Evidence*, 92.

77. Lesley Goodman, 'Disappointing Fans: Fandom, Fictional Theory, and the Death of the Author', *The Journal of Popular Culture* 48, no. 4 (August 2015): 664, doi:10.1111/jpcu.12223.

canon.[78] A useful way to understand the tensions between the author, canon, and the collection of fan writings is to make distinctions between three authoritative objects or discourses, as outlined in Chapter 1.[79] There we noted that Goodman defines these as (1) the universe, (2) the canon, and (3) fandom.[80] In their original work the author creates a universe, which we could call fictional or constructed.[81] At this point that single work is both the entire canon *and* the fictional universe. Subsequent works by the author add to the canon, and are situated in that same universe and expand it. With the introduction of a second canonical text, 'there is now room for contradiction and inaccuracy, room for other differences between one of the texts and the fictional universe'.[82] In fact, even inside of one text there is room for these inaccuracies and differences. Thus, fans see the need and their right to fix canon to match their perception of the universe.

---

78. T. Reuben discusses the topic of fornication, and deals with both the narrative of Reuben's fornication with Bilhah and the fornication between the daughters of men and the angelic Watchers. See, for a discussion of these passages, Tom de Bruin, 'A Bad Taste in My Mouth: Spirits as Embodied Senses in the Testaments of the Twelve Patriarchs', *Journal for Interdisciplinary Biblical Studies* 4, no. 1 (2022): 22–26, doi:10.17613/tv6x-xw92; de Bruin, *Great Controversy*, 139–49; William Loader, *Philo, Josephus, and the Testaments on Sexuality: Attitudes towards Sexuality in the Writings of Philo and Josephus and in the Testaments of the Twelve Patriarchs* (Grand Rapids, MI: Eerdmans, 2011), 371–90; Ishay Rosen-Zvi, 'Bilhah the Temptress: The *Testament of Reuben* and "The Birth of Sexuality"', *Jewish Quarterly Review* 96 (2006): 65–94, doi:10.1353/jqr.2005.0098. T. Judah discusses Judah's marriage with a Canaanite Bathshua and his fornication with his daughter in law, see de Bruin, 'Bad Taste', 26–28; Tom de Bruin, 'Joseph the Good and Delicate Man: Masculinity in the Testaments of the Twelve Patriarchs', *Lectio Difficilior* (2020); Felix Opoku-Gyamfi, 'Retelling the Story of Judah and Tamar in the Testament of Judah', *Ilorin Journal of Religious Studies* 4, no. 2 (2014): 41–52; Esther Marie Menn, *Judah and Tamar (Genesis 38) in Ancient Jewish Exegesis: Studies in Literary Form and Hermeneutics*, Supplements to the Journal for the Study of Judaism 51 (Leiden: Brill, 1997), 107–213, doi:10.1163/9789004497764; Cecelia Wassén, 'The Story of Judah and Tamar in the Eyes of the Earliest Interpreters', *Literature and Theology* 8 (1994): 355–59, doi:10.1093/litthe/8.4.354; Lewis John Eron, '"That Women Have Mastery Over Both King and Beggar" (TJud. 15.5) – The Relationship of the Fear of Sexuality to the Status of Women in Apocrypha and Pseudepigrapha: 1 Esdras (3 Ezra) 3–4, Ben Sira and the Testament of Judah', *Journal for the Study of the Pseudepigrapha* 9 (1991): 43–66, doi:10.1177/095182079100000904.

79. See pp. 41–42.

80. Goodman, 'Disappointing Fans', 665–66.

81. See Chapter 5 for a more in-depth discussion on the creation of storyworlds and fictional universes.

82. Goodman, 'Disappointing Fans', 665.

In the case of the Testament of Levi the process is comparable. Ancient readers would have imagined that the canonical narrative portrayed the actual world, not a fictional universe.[83] Yet they could easily have seen a contradiction between the way these actual people would have or should have acted, and the way canon portrays them. Here is the same 'contradiction and inaccuracy', the same 'differences' between the expectation of the patriarchs' behaviour and the canon that Goodman discusses. This entails the same perceived need and right to fix canon, based on nostalgia for a certain perception of the universe. Booth writes that 'fan nostalgia, however, is not just about a historic memory but also about the affective connection between an imagined ideal fan text and the initial experiences of the fan'.[84] In other words, the fan becomes nostalgic for a non-existent ideal text and frustrated with the actual canonical text. There is a tension between the narrative and the reader's (ethical) expectations: the patriarchs, who should be the epitome of ethical perfection, act dishonourably, selfishly and violently. This combination of nostalgia for the patriarchs' (idealized) noble characters and frustration at the canon's portrayal of them serves as the impetus for creating these derivative works.

There are also marked differences between contemporary fix-it fiction and ancient derivative works when it comes to nostalgia. Fan fiction in general, and fix-it fic especially, is apologetic, and accepts its secondary status. Judith Fathallah, examining *Game of Thrones*[85] fan fiction, notes the verb choices of the authors. They use 'wish, wishing, would've', verbs that portray non-authoritative readings. Fathallah concludes that 'though fix-it fic is appreciated, it is not author-ized at the level of canon'.[86] At the same time, the authority of the canon 'is obviously deconstructed via fanfic', and Fathallah points to other fandoms that are decidedly less apologetic.[87]

The Testament of Levi, on the other hand, does all that it can to raise its authority to that of the level of canon. Besides the steps taken in the paratext, the work

---

83. The distinction between the Actual World and fictional universes is hard to define in religious studies, where fiction and reality easily mix. See, for example, Markus Altena Davidsen, 'Fiction-Based Religion: Conceptualising a New Category against History-Based Religion and Fandom', *Culture and Religion* 14 (2013): 378–95. The difficulty does not complicate this discussion as the tendency is to believe that fiction *is* reality, and not vice versa.

84. Booth, *Playing Fans*, 19.

85. *Game of Thrones* was the first book in a series of books by George R. R. Martin, commonly called the *A Song of Ice and Fire* novels. It became a hugely popular fantasy TV series on HBO, which ran for 8 seasons, from 2011 to 2019. Fanfiction of *A Song of Ice and Fire* was rare before the TV series. The transmedia enterprise now includes comic books, cooking books, video games, board games, spin off TV shows, and a large collection of merchandise, including replica weapons, toys, and even whiskeys.

86. Fathallah, *Fanfiction and the Author*, 148.

87. Fathallah, *Fanfiction and the Author*, 155.

attributes its unique knowledge to many authoritative, revelatory sources: 'a spirit of knowledge from the Lord' (T. Levi 2.3), a meeting with the Lord (T. Levi 5.1), the writings of Enoch, a person famous for their exceptionally close relationship to God (T. Levi 14.1), heavenly tablets (T. Levi 5.4), and Levi's forefathers (T. Levi 10). The narrator is presented as a conduit of divine knowledge, the basis of ancient Christian and Jewish authority.[88] Additionally, by putting historical events into the mouth of an ancient person in the form of prophecies, that is, by letting Levi prophesy about events that are sure to happen, because they have already happened and the author is writing retrospectively, the trustworthiness of the revelations of Levi is further strengthened.[89] The writer does everything possible to make this text authoritative. The Testaments are not meant to be seen as secondary at all – in fact, the author attempts to portray this writing as superior to canon itself. This authoritative step is easier to make in the ancient world, where canon is not so strictly and unequivocally defined, nor seen as the sole authoritative text.

In this section, I focussed on how the writer of the Testaments could be seen to be writing fix-it fan fiction. There are many similarities between fix-it fic and the way the Testament of Levi retells the narrative of the rape of Dinah. Both fix-it fic and the Testament of Levi function as though they are attempting to reconcile differences between the universe and the texts of the canon. As the Testament of Levi reconciles these differences and attempts to make its reading of Scripture authoritative, it both perpetuates and subverts the canonical material. On the one hand, in retelling the narrative in a way that removes certain difficulties, it reinforces the normativity of the canon. Any critique of or questions about the canon that a reader might have had are resolved. While the fan's nostalgia for the canonical narratives leads to the production of fiction, it is the authority claimed by the derivative work (through e.g. the genre, the spirit of the Lord, a meeting with a Lord, the writings of Enoch) that perpetuates the canonical material. The text presumes the inherent authority of the narrator as a recipient of divine revelation, and thus the canonical material is perpetuated by the derivative work. On the other hand, as the text adjusts fundamental parts of the canonical narrative, it subverts the canon as well. The act of fixing the narrative to fit the writer's conceptions of the patriarchs shows that there is a cognitive dissonance between those conceptions and the text of the canon. The canonical narrative simply must be wrong. The author subverts canonical authority, creating a new authoritative reading that replaces the authority of the canon.

In the case of the narrative of the rape of Dinah, the nostalgic motivation of the author seems straightforward. It is not necessarily hostile to the text. In the next section I will examine a novel reading. In the Testament of Simeon, going against the grain of the canonical narratives, the author claims the Israelite patriarchs to be ancient followers of Christ.

---

88. Reed, 'Pseudepigraphy, Authorship, Reception', 477.

89. For an analysis of how the writer of the Testaments attempts to establish authority, see de Bruin, *Great Controversy*, 70–72, 75–78.

Novel Fan Fiction

The example from the Testament of Levi leans towards the nostalgic side of Booth's nostalgia–novelty continuum.[90] It attempts to adapt, solve, and fix difficulties that the author sees in the canonical narrative. Little about the canonical narrative is revised in the above example, but elsewhere in the Testaments we find much more novel revisions.[91] Allow me to explore the fannish 'desire for fresh material'[92] through one of the passages about the future from the Testaments. These passages are generally either prophecies about Israelite history and the life of Jesus Christ or predictions about the end of days.[93] The predictions of the future have several roles in the text. Most significantly, they demonstrate the future consequences of the descendants' behaviour and they function to establish authority of the patriarch in question.[94] I have discussed authority above, however two methods the Testaments employs to enlarge the authority through prophecy need further exploration. First, the patriarchs claim access to hidden knowledge. The patriarchs show knowledge of events occurring after their death from sources that 'provide them with the information'.[95] Often they refer to esoteric teachings received from their forefathers or even heavenly documents. The patriarchs therefore have access to secret sources of authoritative information, which are not available to the audience. This strengthens the words of the patriarchs in the minds of the audience. Second, 'the author could ... put events that he knew would occur into the mouths of the patriarchs as predictions. These ... function to establish prophetic authority'.[96] The patriarchs 'predict' future events, showing that they must have supernatural knowledge.

As one might expect, in these sections that are more novel than nostalgic, the more subversive aspects of the Testaments come into focus. The Testament of Simeon contains an excellent example, when it gives a prophecy in 'hymnic form':[97]

> If you remove all jealousy and stubbornness from yourselves,
> my bones will blossom like a rose in Israel,
> and my flesh will blossom like a lily,
> and my fragrance will be like the fragrance of frankincense,
> and holy people will be multiplied from me like cedars forever,

---

90. Booth, *Playing Fans*, 6.
91. Some novelty is present in T. Levi as well. Levi's journey into the heavens where he is invested as a priest cannot be found in the canon (T. Levi 2.1–9.14).
92. Booth, *Playing Fans*, 6.
93. de Bruin, *Great Controversy*, 44.
94. de Bruin, *Great Controversy*, 74–80.
95. Kugler, *Testaments*, 14.
96. de Bruin, *Great Controversy*, 75.
97. Hollander and de Jonge, *Commentary*, 121; cf. Kugler, *Testaments*, 46.

and their branches will stretch far.
Then, the seed of Canaan will perish,
and nothing will remain for Amalek,
and all the Cappadocians will pass away,
and all the Hittites will utterly destroyed.
Then, the land of Ham will fail,
and all the people will perish.
Then, all the earth will take a break from upheaval,
and everything under the sky will rest from war.
Then, Shem will be glorified,
because the great God of Israel is Lord,
he will appear on earth like a person,
and will save Adam through him.
Then, all the spirits of deceit will be trampled,
and humans will rule over the evil spirits.
Then, in joy I will arise,
and I will praise the Most High on account of his marvellous deeds:
because God has saved humanity,
by taking on a body and eating with humans.

(T. Simeon 6.2–7)

This hymn contains a prediction that spans many centuries (though not necessarily in chronological order). The prediction references both the history of the Israelite people and the life of Christ. A poetic description of the 'glory of all Simeonites' is quickly followed with a description of the fall of Israel's enemies (T. Simeon 6.2–3).[98] Then we get predictions that occur chronologically after the events contained in the Hebrew Bible: God will appear on earth as a human saving all humankind and there will be peace on earth (T. Simeon 6.5). The forces of evil will be conquered, and then Simeon will rise from the dead (T. Simeon 6.6–7). Simeon will praise God, because God became a human, ate with humans and saved humanity (T. Simeon 6.8). Expectations of a messiah were fairly common among religions in Afro-Asia, including the varieties of Judaism,[99] and the messianic predictions here fit in that broader religious context. Yet the specificities of the predictions (God becoming human and eating with humans) appear to indicate that the writer is thinking of Jesus Christ as the messiah. They are doing what many Christ-followers did, reading Jesus back into ancient, pre-Christian texts.

---

98. Kugler, *Testaments*, 46.

99. See, for example, Serge Ruzer, *Early Jewish Messianism in the New Testament: Reflections in the Dim Mirror*, Jewish and Christian Perspectives Series 36 (Leiden: Brill, 2020), doi:10.1163/9789004432932; Magnus Zetterholm, 'Introduction', in *The Messiah: In Early Judaism and Christianity*, ed. Magnus Zetterholm (Minneapolis, MN: Fortress Press, 2007), xxi–xxvii.

According to the Testament of Simeon, Simeon – one of the foundational figures of the Israelite nation – was actually a Christ-follower all along. He believed in Jesus Christ and praised God for Christ's sacrifice to save humanity. While the canonical accounts of Simeon give no indication that he expected God to one day become a human and save humanity, the Christ-following fan author added these details into Simeon's biography in the Testaments. This text implies that Simeon was already aware of the salvific nature of Jesus Christ and appreciated his ministry and sacrifice. It also suggests he was aware of the Christian theology that God has a plan to save humanity through Jesus Christ and his incarnation. Christian beliefs are thus recast back into the time of the patriarchs. The Testament of Simeon argues that Christianity is the true faith, and the true understanding of the relationship between God and humanity, even according to the founding fathers of the Israelite nation.[100] In this way, the text subverts these Israelite characters and narratives. Though the canonical text makes no mention of their expectations of and belief in Jesus, they are now christened millennia after the fact.[101]

The Testament of Simeon is not the only testament to adjust history like this. In the Testament of Reuben, amongst others, Jesus Christ is called the fulfilment of time, and said to invalidate the Jewish priesthood (T. Reuben 6.8).[102] This is

---

100. This is similar, though not necessarily the same, to how early Christian writers (including writers of the New Testament) interpret ancient prophecies as speaking of Jesus. Examples abound, a few that immediately spring to mind are Matthew 1:18–25 citing Isaiah 7:14; Matthew 2:1–6 citing Micah 5:1–3; Luke 4:17–21 citing Isaiah 61:1–2, and Acts 8:32–35 citing Isaiah 53:7.

101. This is not an uncommon strategy in early Christian texts. See the similar way that Christian writers have treated the Jewish philosopher Philo of Alexandria. Otto writes: 'with the passing of time, Philo's status as a Jew became increasingly troublesome for his Christian readers. As the boundary lines between Christian and Jew became enshrined in law, some Christians sought to make a convert out of Philo centuries after his death, crafting the legend of "Philo Christianus." In this vein, Jerome expands on Eusebius's claim that Philo met Peter during his embassy to Gaius in Rome, suggesting that the Alexandrian envoy and the Palestinian apostle struck up a friendship. The fifth-century Acta Johannis includes a curious – and spurious – account of Philo's baptism by the apostle John. According to one fifth-century Byzantine catena, Philo was even ordained a Christian bishop'. Jennifer Otto, *Philo of Alexandria and the Construction of Jewishness in Early Christian Writings* (Oxford: Oxford University Press, 2018), 199–200. Anne Rice's *Christ the Lord* doesn't go so far as to make Philo Christian, but does make him very impressed by Jesus, wishing to keep Jesus on as a pupil. Rice, *Christ the Lord*, (2005), 19–20.

102. See also T. Levi 10.2, 14–18, T. Zebulon 9.8–10.3, T. Benjamin 9–10, and Harm W. Hollander, 'Israel and God's Eschatological Agent in the Testaments of the Twelve Patriarchs', in *Aspects of Religious Contact and Conflict in the Ancient World*, ed. Pieter W. van der Horst, Utrechtse Theologische Reeks 31 (Utrecht: Faculteit der Godgeleerdheid, Universiteit Utrecht, 1995), 96–104.

probably in reaction to the Roman destruction of the Jerusalem temple in 70 CE, about a generation after Jesus's death. This destruction naturally caused major rethinking – though not necessarily the annulment[103] – of the Jewish priesthood, and contributed to the early Christian view that Jesus represented an improved priesthood.[104] Yet, when the Testaments, written about a century after the destruction, claim that the Jewish priesthood is invalidated, a foundational aspect the canonical texts has been disowned or removed. The Testaments therefore perform a Christian fannish reading of the canon similar to what Jenkins describes as 'resistive reading':

> The reader is drawn not into the preconstituted world of the fiction but rather into a world she has created from the textual materials. Here, the reader's pre-established values are at least as important as those preferred by the narrative system.... The raw materials of the original story play a crucial role in this process, providing instructions for a preferred reading, but they do not necessarily overpower and subdue the reader.... Some groups' pleasure comes not in celebrating the values of their chosen works but rather in 'reading them against the grain', in expressing their opposition to rather than acceptance of textual ideology.[105]

Analogically, the writer of the Testaments is interested in the textual world of the canon, but is more readily drawn to their own contextual Christian worldview, established based on the canonical narratives. The patriarchs and their lives suggest a preferred reading, but the writer expresses opposition to that reading. Though the text gives no indication that Simeon was aware of Jesus, the fan author prefers to see Simeon as a Christ-follower. They read 'against the grain', subverting the inherent ideology of the narratives. Therefore, this work also falls neatly into Nickolas Pappas's definition of subversive readings: 'a subversive reading will release the reader from the power of the author ... [which is experienced] as limitations upon the creation of meanings'.[106] Though Pappas speaks of an author, contextualizing this for the ancient world, we may want to replace the word 'author'

---

103. Philip S. Alexander, 'What Happened to the Jewish Priesthood after 70?', in *A Wandering Galilean: Essays in Honour of Seán Freyne*, ed. Zuleika Rodgers, Margaret Daly-Denton, and Anne Fitzpatrick-McKinley, Supplements to the Journal for the Study of Judaism 132 (Leiden: Brill, 2009), 5–33, doi:10.1163/ej.9789004173552.i-622.9.

104. See, for example, Hebrews 7–9. See also Eric Mason, *'You Are a Priest Forever': Second Temple Jewish Messianism and the Priestly Christology of the Epistle to the Hebrews* (Leiden: Brill, 2008), doi:10.1163/ej.9789004149878.i-228.

105. Henry Jenkins, *Textual Poachers: Television Fans & Participatory Culture* (London: Routledge, 1992), 64.

106. Nickolas Pappas, 'Authorship and Authority', *Journal of Aesthetics & Art Criticism* 47 (1989): 328.

with 'text' or 'context'. The original context of the canonical narratives, and indeed the text itself, is not permitted to limit their meanings. Instead, that authority is unseated by 'carrying on some activity the author has instigated, to a point at which it is no longer relevant to ask about the author's own desires.'[107] 'The authors' desires drop out of the picture – not because they cannot be known, but because the authors' desires or intentions do not determine the outcome of this sort of reading. These readers have gone over the authors' heads'.[108] The context of the canonical narratives loses its authority over the readings. The new composer takes over what authority the texts had and creates a new, authoritative reading, with a decidedly Christian focus.

Subversive readings, or readings against the grain, seem to be a topic of debate in fan fiction. Slash fiction is a good example of a type of fan fiction that is most commonly seen as subversive.[109] Slash (generally) describes 'erotic encounters between television characters . . . of the same sex'.[110] It is seen as subversive because it deliberately goes against the characters' heterosexuality as implied, stated, or shown in the canon. Sara Gwenllian Jones argues that this 'paradigm rests upon an understanding of the text as an inviolable and discrete semiotic surface'.[111] She explores whether slash fiction based on a cult tv series can be seen *not* as a resistant reading, but as an 'actualization of latent textual elements'.[112] Arguing that maintaining the exotic and adventurous nature of the characters requires 'exotic erotics', she concludes that it 'is the cult television series itself which implicitly "resists" the conventions of heterosexuality'.[113] What the fans love about these texts requires the adventurous, anti-realist eroticism of slash fiction. These texts are inherently queer, though not explicitly so. Jeremy Swist has demonstrated a similar fannish engagement, though with a decidedly different outcome, among right-wing fans of metal music. These fans subvert Greco-Roman sources to create wolf-like, pagan, and far-right readings, activating the latent hypermasculine, elitist, patriarchal and racist elements of Roman and Spartan culture.[114] The Testaments

---

107. Pappas, 'Authorship and Authority', 328, 325.

108. Pappas, 'Authorship and Authority', 328, 325.

109. Cf. Jenkins's important discussion on slash fiction in Chapter 6 of *Textual Poachers*, and his quote of Joan Martin's 'informally circulated introduction to slash fiction': 'Slash is a wonderfully subversive voice whispering or shouting around the edges and into the cracks of mainstream culture', Jenkins, *Textual Poachers*, 207.

110. Sara Gwenllian Jones, 'The Sex Lives of Cult Television Characters', in *The Fan Fiction Studies Reader*, ed. Karen Hellekson and Kristina Busse (Iowa City, IA: University of Iowa Press, 2014), 116–17.

111. Jones, 'Introduction', 118.

112. Jones, 'Introduction', 119.

113. Jones, 'Introduction', 127–28.

114. Jeremy Swist, '"Wolves of the Krypteia": Lycanthropy and Right-Wing Extremism in Metal's Reception of Ancient Greece and Rome', *Metal Music Studies* 8, no. 3 (2022): 309–25, doi:10.1386/mms_00083_1.

engage with Scripture in a similar way to these examples. Fans of Jesus Christ appreciate these ancient texts, specifically because they speak to them about *Christian* interests. Their expectations implicitly resist a solely pre-Christ reading, and thus they need to actualize what, following Jones, we might call 'latent' Christian elements, that is, elements that are particularly suited for a Christ-focussed reading or tie in with concerns Christ-followers specifically might have. Thus, following Hellekson and Busse's argument that 'slash fan fiction may indeed be more textual and bound to the possibilities presented in the canonical source, and far less subversive than slash theorists have wanted to claim',[115] we could conclude that this reading of the Scripture is bound to the interstices available in the canon. In doing so, we would have to keep acknowledging the way the original contexts and characters are usurped and recast.

All in all, using the authority of the genre, the first-person narration, 'prophecies', and the access to hidden writings, the Testaments create an authoritative, Christ-focussed reading of the patriarchs, displacing other, canonical traditions. The writer of the Testaments seems to be creating a subversive reading in which their fandom of Christ is placed in these existing narratives. This reimagining of the patriarchs is no longer a simple fix-it fic necessitated by the unfavourable portrayal of beloved characters; it is a novel recasting of canon.

Conclusions

The writer of the Testaments creates a collection of twelve first-person biographies of the ancient Israelite patriarchs. In this collection of what we may anachronistically call fan fiction, they adapt the canonical material (and associated traditions) from a position of authority. Displacing the authors of the Scripture by appealing to hidden knowledge and authentic first-person narratives, the author subverts the authority of the canon by presenting their own readings as authoritative.

In some cases, the Testaments retell narratives, fixing or correcting how the patriarchs are portrayed in the canon. Deriving from a nostalgia for the characters, the writer reinterprets events to 'fix' perceived problems with the patriarchs' ethics. This makes clear the writer's frustration with the dissonance between the canon's portrayals and how the writer of the Testaments feels the universe and characters should be depicted. New narratives are created that fix these 'errors' in canon. In other cases, the Testaments create novel readings that are more subversive of the text. The original – textual and historical – contexts are displaced by resistant readings, where the writer introduces Christian material into these narratives. In this way, the writer activates latent possibilities of these narratives to create new readings that resonate with their fandom of Christ.

---

115. Karen Hellekson and Kristina Busse, 'Fan Identity and Feminism', in *The Fan Fiction Studies Reader*, ed. Karen Hellekson and Kristina Busse (Iowa City, IA: University of Iowa Press, 2014), 79.

Fan studies gives us a unified theoretical framework in which to discuss these hermeneutical strategies of both nostalgia and novelty. Fan play gives us a single model that allows the analysis of these – in the eyes of many – contradictory textual strategies, which traditionally have often been examined separately.[116] This allows the introduction of a more nuanced reading of how the Testaments engage with their source material(s), than traditionally done. For example, Robert Kugler[117] and James Kugel[118] have both significantly interacted with the Testaments as a derivative work. Kugler has focussed on the way that derivative works use these

---

116. There are numerous works that discuss the nostalgic elements in the Testaments, for example the retelling of the Dinah episode: Fisk, 'One Good Story'; H. Dixon Slingerland, 'The Nature of Nomos (Law) Within the *Testaments of the Twelve Patriarchs*', *Journal of Biblical Literature* 105 (1986): 39–48; Tjitze Baarda, 'The Shechem Episode in the Testament of Levi: A Comparison with Other Traditions', in *Sacred History and Sacred Texts in Early Judaism: A Symposium in Honour of A. S. van der Woude*, ed. J. N. Bremmer and F. García Martínez (Kampen: Kok Pharos, 1992), 11–74; Kugel, *Traditions*; Howard C. Kee, 'The Ethical Dimensions of the Testaments of the XII as a Clue to Provenance', *New Testament Studies* 24 (1978): 259–70, doi:10.1017/S002868850000789X; Bader, *Tracing the Evidence*; James L. Kugel, 'The Story of Dinah in the Testament of Levi', *Harvard Theological Review* 85 (1992): 1–34. Though these generally focus on how these readings are *novel* not nostalgic. There are, similarly, several analyses of the re-readings of Jewish history: Marinus de Jonge, 'The Future of Israel in the Testaments of the Twelve Patriarchs', *Journal for the Study of Judaism in the Persian, Hellenistic and Roman Period* 17 (1986): 196–211; Hollander, 'Eschatological Agent'; Michael E. Stone, 'Ideal Figures and Social Context: Priest and Sage in the Early Second Temple Age', in *Ancient Israelite Religion: Essays in Honor of Frank Moore Cross*, ed. P. D. Miller, Paul. D. Hanson, and D. McBride (Philadelphia, PA: Fortress Press, 1987), 575–86; Marinus de Jonge, 'The Pre-Mosaic Servants of God in the Testaments of the Twelve Patriarchs and in the Writings of Justin and Irenaeus', *Vigiliae Christianae* 39 (1985): 157–70. Very little can be found that incorporates both sides of that coin in a single framework.

117. For example, Kugler, 'Not-So-Ambiguous Witness'; Kugler, *Testaments*.

118. Examples include James L. Kugel, 'Some Translation and Copying Mistakes from the Original Hebrew of the Testaments of the Twelve Patriarchs', in *The Dead Sea Scrolls: Transmission of Traditions and Production of Texts*, ed. Sarianna Metso, Hindy Najman, and Eileen Schuller, Studies on the Texts of the Desert of Judah 92 (Leiden: Brill, 2010), 45–56; Kugel, *How to Read the Bible*; Kugel, *Traditions*; James L. Kugel, 'Reuben's Sin with Bilhah in the Testament of Reuben', in *Pomegranates and Golden Bells: Studies in Biblical, Jewish, and Near Eastern Ritual, Law, and Literature in Honor of Jacob Milgrom*, ed. David P. Wright, David N. Freedman, and Avi Hurvitz (Winona Lake, IN: Eisenbrauns, 1995), 525–54; James L. Kugel, 'Levi's Elevation to the Priesthood in Second Temple Writings', *Harvard Theological Review* 86 (1993): 1–64; Kugel, 'The Story of Dinah in the Testament of Levi'; James L. Kugel, *In Potiphar's House: The Interpretive Life of Biblical Texts* (New York: HarperCollins, 1990).

new narratives of canonical characters to make 'fresh theological arguments',[119] that is, novel readings. He claims that the Testaments – together with many Jewish and Christian texts – exploit the authority of Jewish Scriptures. Kugel, on the other hand, sees these narratives more in the context of solving major problems in the text,[120] that is, nostalgic readings. He sees ancient writers as highly inventive readers struggling to find favourable readings. In some ways these two readings overlap,[121] yet they are based on wholly contradictory assumptions: Do the Testaments provide fresh theological arguments that add to canon or do they solve contradictions that are inherent to canon? The writer is either exploitative (Kugler)[122] or a clever explainer (Kugel).[123]

Clearly, both nostalgia and novelty are present in the Testaments, and Booth's continuum of fan play allows for both to exist side-by-side and build on one another. The writer now has a unified strategy for their derivative works. They are a fan; and 'to engage a fan, a text needs to be both familiar and novel at once; it must both surprise and appease'.[124] We can expect nothing else from a text copied for thousands of years by fans. In this fan-based model, the writer's hermeneutics in both reading and rewriting canon is no longer divided between two poles, but unified on a single continuum of negotiation and dialogue with canon(s) and community.[125] Thus we can conclude that the fan author, as a creator of a derivative work, is driven by the desire for new material within the context of the canon.

All in all, the Testaments (and other derivative texts) play a nuanced fannish game of perpetuating and subverting canonical authority. Picking and choosing topics, themes and narratives the authors, editors, readers and transmitters enter into a negotiation of power: changing, adapting, and enforcing readings that suit the personal and communal needs of their religious and sociocultural context.

---

119. Kugler, 'Not-So-Ambiguous Witness', 356.
120. Kugel, *How to Read the Bible*, 10–14.
121. Kugler, for example, suggests some more 'motifs' to add to those of Kugel. Kugler, 'Not-So-Ambiguous Witness', 356–58. Kugel admits that ancient interpreters might be 'playing fast and loose with the text's real meaning', Kugel, *How to Read the Bible*, 13.
122. Kugler, 'Not-So-Ambiguous Witness', 355.
123. Kugel, *How to Read the Bible*, 14.
124. Booth, *Playing Fans*, 6.
125. Booth relates this negotiation and dialogue between fans and the media industry, that is the sanctioned producers of new canonical narratives. In the context of second century Christianity, where the media industry would not be formalized, this would most likely be represented by the fan authors themselves, the diverse communities, the existing canon, and other derivative works. Booth, *Playing Fans*, 1.

Chapter 3

CANONICITY AND THE POLITICS OF CANON: HOW DO PEOPLE (DE-)AUTHORIZE DERIVATIVE WORKS?[1]

Early Christians lived in a vast Christian literary universe. Thousands of texts – writings, art, liturgies, and hymns – work together to create a storyworld that surpasses each individual work. Yet, there is a hierarchy in these texts. Many people nowadays, for example, consider the writings collected in the canon to be more historically accurate than those outside. Others assert that written texts are more accurate than art or hymns. In this chapter I will examine how such hierarchies arise, are reinforced and are maintained – I will explore the creation and policing of lists of canonical texts.

In the Introduction I discussed how Anne Rice portrays non-canonical texts as fanciful legends, yet includes them in her book on the Jesus of the gospels.[2] As discussed in the Introduction, she devotes a number of pages of her Author's Note to defending this inclusion.[3] Nevertheless, her decision did lead to many questions by readers and reviewers. Rice has always been famous for doing large amounts of historical research for her books on vampires. And Jenny Diski, reviewing for British newspaper *The Guardian*, notes Rice's claim to have 'lost none of the

---

1. My thanks go to Allen Wilson, for co-authoring an article for the *Ancient Jew Review* on policing New Testament variants with me. The discussions we had helped up me frame some of the discussion in this chapter (and other parts of this book). Allen Wilson and Tom de Bruin, 'Teaching the New Testament as an Expanded Universe', *Ancient Jew Review*, 16 August 2021, https://www.ancientjewreview.com/read/2021/8/16/teaching-the-new-testament-as-an-expanded-universe. Thanks also go to Kees Meiling for double-checking and improving my Latin translations in this chapter. As for many chapters in this book, I'm also highly indebted to Kelsie Rodenbiker for her extensive feedback on a draft of this chapter.

2. Anne Rice, *Christ the Lord: Out of Egypt* (London: Arrow, 2007).

3. See pp. 3–5.

historical accuracy' for which she is known.[4] Diski seems to disagree with Rice's self-evaluation:

> The life of Christ comes to us largely from the Gospels, the historicity of which has been the subject of disagreement between scholars, theologians and historians from then to now. The childhood of Jesus is virtually invisible in the historical record and mentioned only once, after the nativity, in the Gospels. The rest is speculation, folk stories collected into apocryphal books and, well, fiction. Rice uses a good deal of material from the apocryphal Infancy Gospel of Thomas. Hardly the historical accuracy which she insists is so important.[5]

Diski levels common allegations also heard elsewhere – the same allegations Rice seems to have foreseen: the Apocrypha are folk stories, speculation. The 'historical record' includes the gospels of the canon, but not the Infancy Gospel of Thomas.[6] Other reviewers of Rice's book focus on an aspect Rice did not address in her Author's Note. Lee Harmon, for example, writes that 'scholars will recognize the story from the Infancy Gospel of Thomas, which Rice latches onto and includes in her book, caring not that no historian of this gnostic gospel considers it to be true. The story is pure mythology, and not even Biblical myth'.[7] Leaving aside Harmon's differentiation of mythology and biblical myth, the indictment is clear: Rice uses 'gnostic' texts. By using this term, Harmon invokes a long history of Christian stigmatization of certain thinking and certain texts as heretical. He also includes Rice's work as part of the much more controversial world of Dan Brown's biblical fiction.[8]

---

4. Jenny Diski, 'God Almighty', *The Guardian*, 12 March 2005, https://www.theguardian.com/books/2005/dec/03/fiction.annerice.

5. Diski, 'God Almighty'.

6. While the general scholarly consensus is that these gospels are not the most reliable historical sources, there are two caveats. First, this consensus may also be due to the criteria that scholarship uses to define historical reliability, see Simon J. Gathercole, 'Other Apocryphal Gospels and the Historical Jesus', in *The Oxford Handbook of Early Christian Apocrypha*, ed. Andrew Gregory et al., Oxford Handbooks (Oxford: Oxford University Press, 2015), 264–65, doi:10.1093/oxfordhb/9780199644117.013.37. Second, some scholars do argue for reliability for some aspects, see Richard Bauckham, 'The Brothers and Sisters of Jesus: An Epiphanian Response to John P. Meier', *Catholic Biblical Quarterly* 56, no. 4 (1994): 695–96.

7. Lee Harmon, 'Book Review: Christ the Lord: Out of Egypt', *Dubious Disciple*, 20 December 2010, https://www.dubiousdisciple.com/2010/12/book-review-christ-the-lord-out-of-egypt.html.

8. For an examination of 'heresy hunting' in Dan Brown's work, see Tony Burke, 'Heresy Hunting in the New Millennium', *Studies in Religion/Sciences Religieuses* 39, no. 3 (2010): 405–20, doi:10.1177/0008429810373319.

Harmon was clearly not alone in his reactions, for Rice expressly reflects on these allegations in her note for the later paperback edition:

> Since the book was published there has been talk in some circles about my use of 'the apocrypha.' I now feel that 'apocrypha' is a very poor word for the material I used. Apocrypha means too many things to too many people. And the word has been connected in the public mind with late date Gnostic 'gospels' for which recent scholars have made rather spectacular and controversial claims. I would like to make clear here: the material I used in this novel, pertaining to Our Lord's childhood and the life of His Mother, has nothing, absolutely nothing, to do with these late date Gnostic gospels. Nothing at all. What I used was material that is best referred to as 'early legends' pertaining to the life of Christ – and these legends have indeed been used by Christian artists for two thousand years. These stories have been the source for Christians of devotion to St. Anne and St. Joachim, the parents of Mary, and the source of devotion to St. Joseph, the foster father of the Lord. Some of the earliest traditions connected with the Virgin Mary are in these stories.[9]

Rice, naturally, defends her usage of these parabiblical sources. She argues that the narratives she included have 'nothing at all' to do with 'gnostic' gospels. What she included were 'early legends', these are the sources that Christian artists used, and the foundation for Christian devotion of saints. And she argues that there is an issue of dating: *her* legends are early, *those* gospels are 'late date'. The distinctions she makes are highly problematic from a historical point of view,[10] but I am more interested in the way these points are argued. Diski argues that the historical record contains nothing of Jesus's childhood, despite knowing of the infancy gospels – they must therefore not be historic. Harmon stigmatizes the parabiblical narratives as gnostic, a common scapegoat – they must therefore not be orthodox.[11] He also calls them mythology – they must be untrue. Anne Rice defends by claiming the texts she used are early – they must be reliable. They are also often used by Christian artists – they must be true.

Anne Rice and her reviewers here are engaged in a discussion of authority. They have different ideas of which texts should be authorized and which de-authorized. They defend their decisions with various arguments, from the wholesale stigmatization of sources as gnostic (therefore heretical) or speculation (therefore

---

9. Rice, *Christ the Lord*, 462–63.

10. See, for example, Annette Yoshiko Reed, 'The Afterlives of New Testament Apocrypha', *Journal of Biblical Literature* 134, no. 2 (2015): 405, doi:10.15699/jbl.1342.2015.2916.

11. See, Burke, 'Heresy Hunting in the New Millennium'; Tony Burke, 'Early Christian Apocrypha in Contemporary Theological Discourse', in *The Oxford Handbook of Early Christian Apocrypha*, ed. Andrew F. Gregory et al., Oxford Handbooks (Oxford: Oxford University Press, 2015), 441–58, doi:10.1093/oxfordhb/9780199644117.013.30.

a-historic) to uncritical assumptions of early date (therefore reliable) and ubiquity (therefore reliability). In the rest of this chapter, I will trace similar discussions about derivative texts in early Christianity and fan communities.

Christian Apocrypha

Most publications on the Apocrypha deal in some way with their obvious derivative status. 'Since their origins' they have been, to borrow Tony Burke's words, 'maligned by critics'.[12] Allow me to shortly explore this through the examples of the editors of the two most well-known English collections of Apocrypha: M. R. James and J. K. Elliott. James, who wrote scholarly works and fictional ghost stories, published his influential *The Apocryphal New Testament* 1924. There he writes:

> Interesting as they are ... [the Apocrypha] do not achieve either of the two principal purposes for which they were written, the instilling of true religion and the conveyance of true history. As religious books they were meant to reinforce the existing stock of Christian beliefs.... As books of history they aim at supplementing the scanty data (as they seemed) of the Gospels and Acts.[13]

James, at first glance, does not dismiss these books purely because of their secondary status, rather it is their contents with which he claims to take issue. He postulates that these secondary writings had two goals: reinforcing or, as becomes clear in his discussion, creating new theology and filling historical gaps in better-known narratives. James feels that it is obvious that these books fail in this regard. They attempt to imitate the style of canonical authors, but end up either too theatrical or 'jejune' (i.e. unsophisticated). Furthermore, they are, he claims, clearly historically inaccurate.[14]

James goes on to argue that despite their dubious historical, religious and literary value, they are still worth reading, an unsurprising statement for the preface to a collection of Apocrypha. He gives several reasons why they should be read, ironically further stigmatizing them in the process. He sees the texts as a way into the mind of the 'unlearned Christians of the past ages',[15] showing their interests, ethical ideals, and expectations for the afterlife. Though they are not high literature, they are 'precious' as 'folk-lore and romance'.[16] As an author of fictional

---

12. Tony Burke, 'Introduction', in *Fakes, Forgeries, and Fictions: Writing Ancient and Modern Christian Apocrypha: Proceedings from the 2015 York University Christian Apocrypha Symposium*, ed. Tony Burke (Eugene, OR: Cascade Books, 2017), 1.

13. Montague R. James, *The Apocryphal New Testament Being the Apocryphal Gospels, Acts, Epistles and Apocalypses* (Oxford: Clarendon, 1924), xii.

14. James, *Apocryphal New Testament*, xii.

15. James, *Apocryphal New Testament*, xiii.

16. James, *Apocryphal New Testament*, xiii.

tales himself, James naturally has some skin in this game. His own fiction, on the other hand, was known to be 'scholarly [and] formalised', the exact opposite of what he calls these narratives.[17]

Most importantly for James – though he uses different terminology – the parabiblical texts are an insight into the vast media landscape of Christianity:

> They reveal the source of no inconsiderable part of his material and the solution to many a puzzle. They have, indeed, exercised an influence (wholly disproportionate to their intrinsic merits) so great and so widespread, that no one who cares about the history of Christian thought and Christian art can possibly afford to neglect them.[18]

Having clearly mastered the art of the backhanded compliment, James argues that they are indispensable for understanding Christian history. All of James's arguments for reading the books seem to function to malign them further. He concludes his discussion with his regrets that many more apocrypha were lost, 'but with the verdict that consigned them to obscurity and then to destruction I cannot quarrel'.[19] Just to be clear, most contemporary scholars would argue that James's opinion on the literary and historical value of these books is by no means based on the inherent qualities of the works but rather on his preconceived opinions of their aesthetics and worth.

J. K. Elliott's 1993 'thorough rewriting' of James's publication, does little to remove the unwarranted stigma against these books.[20] When he tries to 'justify the publication of a volume of such literature', he decides that he 'can most fittingly cite a few paragraphs written by M.R. James'.[21] He then proceeds to cite the exact passage I referred to and summarized above, including the judgements that they are theatrical, jejune and that they 'are neither good books of history, nor of religion, nor even as literature'.[22] Elsewhere in his collection, Elliott refers to these texts as 'crudely sensational', 'imaginative reconstructions', 'fanciful', 'legendary', and 'a large collection of fantasies'.[23] This is peculiar, as in other publications Elliott

---

17. Gina Wisker, *Horror Fiction: An Introduction*, Continuum Studies in Literary Genre (New York: Continuum, 2005), 79.

18. James, *Apocryphal New Testament*, xiii.

19. James, *Apocryphal New Testament*, xiii.

20. J. K. Elliott, *The Apocryphal New Testament: A Collection of Apocryphal Christian Literature in an English Translation* (Oxford: Clarendon Press, 1993), ix.

21. Elliott, *Apocryphal New Testament*, xiv.

22. Elliott, *Apocryphal New Testament*, xiv.

23. Elliott, *Apocryphal New Testament*, 69, 165, 100. See, for more examples, Janet Spittler, 'The Development of Miracle Traditions in the Apocryphal Acts of the Apostles', in *Between Canonical and Apocryphal Texts: Processes of Reception, Rewriting and Interpretation in Early Judaism and Early Christianity*, ed. Jörg Frey, Tobias Nicklas, and Claire Clivaz (Mohr Siebeck, 2019), 357–59, doi:10.1628/978-3-16-155232-8.

defends the enduring influence and value of the Apocrypha. In a 2008 introduction to a book on the non-canonical gospels, he concludes:

> The non-canonical writings have played their part in moulding Christian thought; they reflected and influenced popular piety and devotion; their influence can be seen in art and the arts. They seldom aspire to great literature, although the occasional purple passage stands out; but in many cases they tell a racy tale, encapsulate a well-turned phrase, even recall a *bon mot* of Jesus – one which may even be among his *ipsissima verba* [actual words] – and certainly they provide the researcher plotting the history of Christianity with a rich seam that only nowadays is being recognized as the origin of much that is firmly fixed in its traditions.[24]

Here Elliott points to many reasons why the Apocrypha are valuable for the study of Christianity – including the potential that they may include historically accurate details. Though, whatever their historical value, the unmerited aesthetic judgement of James echoes through in Elliott's words: 'They seldom aspire to great literature.'

In contemporary scholarship there seems to be general agreement that the Apocrypha have historical value. Philip Tite, writing in 2019, speaks of a 'renaissance in [Christian Apocrypha] scholarship over the past few decades'.[25] When it comes to historical value, there remains some debate whether these texts simply reflect the 'continued reflection about Jesus, his family, and his first followers, ... in late antique and medieval cultural memory', or whether they 'shed light on the beliefs of Jesus and his earliest followers'.[26] Nevertheless, both sides agree on their historical importance. However, throughout contemporary scholarship snippets of unjustified denigration of their aesthetic and historical value remain: from 'no one would mistake the *Infancy Gospel* for great literature',[27] to the recently republished opinion that 'the New Testament apocryphal writings exerted an influence out of all proportion to their fundamental worth'.[28]

---

24. J. K. Elliott, 'The Non-Canonical Gospels and the New Testament Apocrypha: Currents in Early Christian Thought and Beyond', in *The Non-Canonical Gospels*, ed. Paul Foster (London: T & T Clark, 2008), 11.

25. Philip L. Tite, 'It's Not So Secret Anymore: Shifts in the Study of Christian Apocrypha', *Bulletin for the Study of Religion* 48, no. 3–4 (2020): 1, doi:10.1558/bsor.41168.

26. Reed, 'The Afterlives of New Testament Apocrypha', 403.

27. Christopher A. Frilingos, 'Parents Just Don't Understand: Ambiguity in Stories about the Childhood of Jesus', *Harvard Theological Review* 109, no. 1 (2016): 37, doi:10.1017/S0017816015000474.

28. R. K. Harrison, 'Old Testament and New Testament Apocrypha', in *The Origin of the Bible*, ed. Philip Wesley Comfort (Wheaton, IL: Tyndale House, 2020), 94.

Canon, Canonicity and Tiers of Canon

The consistent maligning of the Apocrypha as poorly written, non-historical popular literature, as evidenced in engagement with Rice's book and my summary of scholarship on these texts, lead me to the specific concerns of this chapter. Here I am interested in the reasons why and ways that ancient Christians policed canon. To allow critical reflection on these topics, let me introduce some critical fan studies theory. Henry Jenkins argues that:

> More and more, storytelling has become the art of world building, as artists create compelling environments that cannot be fully explored or exhausted within a single work or even a single medium. The world is bigger than the film, bigger even than the franchise – since fan speculations and elaborations also expand the worlds in a variety of directions.[29]

Early Christians are engaged in a similar process, exploring the world of Jesus and the disciples in a variety of directions. Important for my discussion is to consider the politics inherent to world building, as constant choices must be made to authorize some aspects and de-authorize others. Dan Hassler-Forest reflects on 'transmedia world building as a practice that is defined by this very tension between the authoritative desire to unify on the one hand and the hybrid, constructed nature of "heteroglot" utterances on the other'.[30] This tension will underlie much of the discussion of this chapter: the tension between unity of meaning and diversity of voices. Hassler-Forest notes that 'writers, producers, and critics' spend most of their time and energy addressing this tension. They attempt to unify their storyworld, to ensure that its 'chronology, characters and events' remain coherent over texts and media. This is a discourse of authority, and the various authorities produce authoritative rulings on what is, and what is not part of the storyworld: 'transmedia adaptations like Tolkien's world of Middle-earth or the *Star Wars* franchise have established elaborate narrative canons that identify clearly which texts are considered part of the "real" imaginary world and that are discarded by the storyworlds' "authoritative" center'.[31]

In this discourse of a storyworld's centre and periphery there are two main places of authority: the producers and the consumers. The producers are the more obvious authority: the author of the text or, more often now, the media conglomerate

---

29. Henry Jenkins, *Convergence Culture: Where Old and New Media Collide* (New York: New York University Press, 2006), 114.

30. Dan Hassler-Forest, 'The Politics of World Building: Heteroglossia in Janelle Monáe's Afrofuturist WondaLand', in *World Building. Transmedia, Fans, Industries*, ed. Marta Boni, Transmedia: Participatory Culture and Media Convergence (Amsterdam University Press, 2017), 381, doi:10.5117/9789089647566/ch21.

31. Hassler-Forest, 'Politics of World Building', 381.

has the power to create texts and make authoritative declarations about their interpretation. The consumers or, in the context of this book, the fans poach these authorized texts and statements, creating different hierarchies and even alternative storyworlds. In contemporary fan circles this negotiation of authority and meaning is strongly related to the canon of a fandom. The canon is a source of meaning and authority. Yet, the interpretation of canon, and even the contents themselves, are at the same time negotiable. The canon – both meaning and contents – are created and policed through the authority of fan hierarchies. Before exploring these fan hierarchies in more detail, let me comment on how canon is negotiated.

In fandom canon can mean both the list of texts considered canonical *and* 'the complete fictional universe deemed ... an accurate history of that story world'.[32] Neither of these are self-evident, especially when storyworlds become transmedial, that is, when they spread over different media. To take the *Star Wars* franchise as an example, there is a large collection of films, TV shows, video games, comics, toys, board games, novels, and the like.[33] Canonicity spread over thousands of transmedial narratives became so extremely complex that for many years Lucasfilm, the copyright holder, had six levels of canon (G, T, C, S, N and D) in descending authority.[34] Contradictions between texts would be solved by this hierarchy of canonicity, and a new text of say G-canon could override the authority of existing N-canon texts.[35] 'However, this was not always absolute, and the resolution of all contradictions was handled on a case-by-case basis'.[36] Here we see the authoritative attempt to create a univocal storyworld. But, many of these texts, no matter which level, were canonical to some people at some time – this is the heteroglossic reality.[37] The situation became increasingly complex when Disney

---

32. Paul Booth, *Digital Fandom 2.0: New Media Studies*, 2nd ed., Digital Formations 114 (New York: Peter Lang, 2017), 28.

33. *Star Wars* is a multi-billion dollar multimedia franchise, currently owned by Disney. It finds its origins in the 1977 film *Star Wars* (retroactively renamed *Star Wars: Episode IV – A New Hope*) created by George Lucas. Lucas's Lucasfilm was the copyright holder for decades, maintaining an ever-increasing transmedia world. The transmedia enterprise includes films, books, videogames, board games, toys, TV shows, and theme park attractions.

34. *Star Wars* is by no means the only transmedia enterprise that has tiers of canon, see Meredith Warren's discussion of the tiers of fandom canon as they relate to biblical studies. Meredith Warren, 'My OTP: Harry Potter Fanfiction and the Old Testament Pseudepigrapha', *Scriptura* 8 (2006): 59–61.

35. Mark J. P. Wolf, *Building Imaginary Worlds: The Theory and History of Subcreation* (New York: Routledge, 2013), 271, doi:10.4324/9780203096994.

36. 'Canon', *Wookieepedia*, 24 October 2021, https://starwars.fandom.com/wiki/Canon#Canon_in_the_Holocron_continuity_database.

37. See, for example, Apocrypha scholar Brandon Hawk's personal reflections on the canonicity of the now non-canonical Star Wars Customizable Card Game. Brandon W. Hawk, 'Canonizing Star Wars', *Brandon W. Hawk* (blog), 1 May 2022, https://brandonwhawk.net/2022/01/05/canonizing-star-wars/.

acquired *Star Wars*, and decanonized most *Star Wars* transmedia. While seven *Star Wars* films and a TV series remained canon, the producers determined that the rest would no longer limit the 'freedom' of creators.[38] In language that mirrors Anne Rice's terminology for the Apocrypha she included in her book on Jesus, Disney declared all other *Star Wars* media 'legends'.[39] Of course, this reflects the producer's point of view. As I will discuss below, the reality for fans is a different story altogether.[40]

The *Star Wars* canon is an example of an attempt by the copyright holder to strongly police a single, univocal storyworld. Even in such a situation, as will be discussed below, the reality of what is considered canonical by the fans is complex and contested. In other fandoms it is much less clear what the producer intends canon to consist of, and sometimes the producer does not seem to want to regulate this at all. For *The Hitch Hiker's Guide to the Galaxy*,[41] for example, no attempts have been made to standardize the large narrative differences between the radio plays, novels, and TV show – all written and authorized by Douglas Adams. Similarly, 'what should be included in the "official" narrative of extensive franchises like *Lord of the Rings* or the Marvel comics is subject of fierce debate'.[42] Meredith Warren gives an in-depth example of the canonical debate within one specific fandom and how similar it is to canon debates about the Bible.[43] In contemporary fandom, like in ancient ones, what is considered canon often differs from community to community.

The differences in what are considered to be canon in fandom is further complicated by issues of access. Many contemporary fandoms are extremely large transmedia enterprises where most fans will not have consumed the entirety of the products of the fandom. Roy Cook gives the example of *Batman*, which is but a small part of the DC Comics fandom, 'if one reads one comic page per minute, two hours per day, seven days per week, three hundred sixty-five days per year, it would take (approximately) five years of sustained effort to read every comic book in which Batman is the main character or a regular member of the headlining team'.[44]

---

38. 'The Legendary Star Wars Expanded Universe Turns a New Page', *Star Wars*, 25 April 2014, https://www.starwars.com/news/the-legendary-star-wars-expanded-universe-turns-a-new-page.

39. 'Legendary Star Wars Expanded Universe'.

40. Hawk, 'Canonizing Star Wars'.

41. The *Hitch Hiker's Guide to the Galaxy* started as a BBC Radio 4 play in 1978, authored by Douglas Adams. The storyworld currently includes several books, a TV show, a film, 2 video games, illustrated novels, and comic books.

42. Stijn Reijnders et al., 'Fandom and Fan Fiction', in *The International Encyclopedia of Media Effects*, ed. Patrick Rössler, Cynthia A. Hoffner, and Liesbet Zoonen (Hoboken, NJ: Wiley, 2017), 1–12, doi:10.1002/9781118783764.wbieme0176.

43. Warren, 'My OTP', 59–62.

44. Roy T. Cook, 'Canonicity and Normativity in Massive, Serialized, Collaborative Fiction', *The Journal of Aesthetics and Art Criticism* 71, no. 3 (2013): 271, doi:10.1111/jaac.12021.

If we add to this the hundreds of Batman TV episodes, the scores of films, the fifty plus video games, the several theme park rides, and thousands of toys, it quickly becomes clear that it is extremely unlikely that 'a single person can, or will, experience all parts of the fiction'.[45] This means that, for many fandoms, different fans will have consumed different parts of the canon. And that for an individual fan, canon is highly associated with embodiment, influenced by topics such as access, interest, and ability. Furthermore, for such vast canons, various fans will enter the canon via different works and thus prioritize different and peculiar parts of canon. This, naturally, resembles early Christianity, where access to certain texts would have varied from community to community.

At this juncture it is vital to re-emphasize how fan studies and fandom uses the term canon in a different sense than scholars of early Christianity. In fandom, as mentioned above, canon can mean both a collection of texts – which is similar to the way canon is used in biblical studies – and the events described in those texts. In other words, an event or a factoid is 'canon' if it can be found the generally accepted texts. This second meaning is completely foreign to the field of early Christianity, yet is the more common meaning in fandom. But even the first meaning is different in fandom than in how many people use the term in studying Christianity. Biblical scholars will often make a distinction between authoritative texts and canonical texts, and between 'a collection of authoritative books' and 'an authoritative collection of books'.[46] In both of these dichotomies, the first usage reflects the common usage in fan studies and fandom (and, I would argue, also reflects the reality of early Christianity). In fandom, canon is a collection of texts that a group of fans consider authoritative. In what follows, I will follow the usage more common in fan studies, and I will continue to use terms like 'canon' and 'canonize' in this loose sense that mirrors the sense in fan studies.

The complexity of *Star Wars* canon makes for rich ground for analysis of how canon is formed, agreed upon, reinforced, and dismantled. In the case of *Star Wars*, the producer has made clear and definitive statements on canon. Suzanne Scott reflects on the implications of levels of canon for fans and consumers, 'the transmedia author's power to demarcate primary and secondary texts, inducting some extensions of the transmedia story into the canon and excluding others, creates "tiers" of canon [that] leads directly to tiers of perceived narrative

---

45. Cook, 'Canonicity and Normativity', 271.

46. Bruce M. Metzger, *The Canon of the New Testament: Its Origin, Development, and Significance* (Oxford: Clarendon Press, 1987), 283. For a useful discussion of the definition of canon in the field of biblical studies, see Eugene Ulrich, 'The Notion and Definition of Canon', in *The Canon Debate : On the Origins and Formation of the Bible*, ed. Lee Martin McDonald and James A. Sanders (Peabody, MA: Hendrickson, 2002), 21–35.

value for fans'.⁴⁷ In other words, the levels of canon reflect more than just canonicity, they also share an inherent aesthetic and narrative value. A *Star Wars* text of 'G canon' status, that is something authored by George Lucas himself, is highly authoritative and can overrule other texts, but it is also seen as inherently better, aesthetically more pleasing. The top-level texts are seen as superior, more important, and of higher literary value. And when we reach the lower levels of canon, we can easily apply to them the same judgement M. R. James had of the Christian Apocrypha: they are theatrical and jejune.⁴⁸ In this way, 'fans themselves often replicate and reinforce these tiers'.⁴⁹

In some ways this reflects the reality of Christian canonicity by the end of the second century. Jens Schröter highlights the shift that happens around this time.⁵⁰ Whereas early to mid-second century Christian authors, such as Justin Martyr, do not seem to have any problem with the existence of several gospels, 'by the end of the second century and the first half of the third, this situation has changed'.⁵¹ Now suddenly, significant Christian thinkers, such as Clement of Alexandria, Irenaeus of Smyrna, and Origen of Alexandria, rigorously defend the canonicity of four and only four gospels. They, like Lucasfilm or Disney, make these authoritative statements in an attempt to control the storyworld, attempting to police which voices can and which voices should not be included. They wish to create 'a clear awareness of the different status of the four gospels of the church on the one hand and of other gospels on the other'.⁵² This is the first step on the path that ultimately led to the canonization of some gospels, and the exclusion of others from the canon.

Early Christian scholar Origen 'Adamantius' of Alexandria (*c.* 185–253), for example, leaves no doubt about which gospels he considers part of the canon and which he does not. In his first sermon on Luke, he writes 'the church has four

---

47. Suzanne Scott, 'Who's Steering the Mothership? The Role of the Fanboy Auteur in Transmedia Storytelling', in *The Participatory Cultures Handbook*, ed. Aaron Alan Delwiche and Jennifer Jacobs Henderson (New York: Routledge, 2013), 46. Scott is citing Geoffrey A. Long, 'Transmedia Storytelling Business, Aesthetics and Production at the Jim Henson Company' (MA thesis, Massachusetts Institute of Technology, 2007).

48. James, *Apocryphal New Testament*, xii.

49. Scott, 'Who's Steering the Mothership?', 46.

50. Jens Schröter, 'Jesus and Early Christian Identity Formation: Reflections on the Significance of the Jesus Figure in Early Christian Gospels', in *Connecting Gospels: Beyond the Canonical/Non-Canonical Divide*, ed. Sarah Parkhouse and Francis Watson (New York: Oxford University Press, 2018), 238–39.

51. Schröter, 'Jesus and Early Christian', 238.

52. Schröter, 'Jesus and Early Christian', 238.

gospels, the heretics have many' (Origen *Homily on Luke* 1.2).[53] Origen, in his attempt to discredit these texts, invokes the term 'heretic', which I will discuss and contextualize in detail in the next chapter. Here it suffices to note the political aspect of Origen's declaration, he invokes a category of otherness to stigmatize both the texts and those reading them. He goes on to name five of these heretical gospels, many of which are unknown to us: potentially as 'heretical' texts they didn't survive or maybe Origen made them up. Origen also admits to having read many more 'so as not to seem ignorant' (*Homily on Luke* 1.2). Origen, then, claims to have read many gospels, but doesn't feel that they all should have the same authority. He advocates discarding these 'heretical gospels' from the authoritative centre of the storyworld. Ultimately, he concludes with an authoritative statement similar to that of contemporary producers: 'many have tried to write Gospels, but only four have been approved' (*Homily on Luke* 1.2).

Clement of Alexandria (c. 150–215), quite probably one of Origen's teachers, allows a more nuanced view on the plurality of gospels. Throughout his books he quotes from gospels besides the four that Origen accepts,[54] potentially showing that he advocates for things being slightly less uncompromising than Origen does. Yet, when disputing a certain Cassian's claims, he discredits those claims by saying that Cassian's citation of Scripture cannot be found 'in any of the four gospels that we have been handed down to us, rather it is in the Gospel according to the Egyptians' (Clement *Miscellanies* 3.93.1).[55] It is peculiar to note that he claims a gospel to be unauthorized to discredit another's opinions, yet himself cites from that gospel in a number of locations.[56] Ultimately, it seems that he advocates for 'a difference between "the four gospels that are delivered to us" and other gospels',[57] but doesn't reject the others in the same way Origen does. Here we see some evidence for something similar to how Lucasfilm attempted to define *Star Wars*'

---

53. The translations of Origen's *Homilies on Luke* are edited versions of Origen, *Homilies on Luke*, trans. Joseph T. Lienhard, The Fathers of the Church 94 (Washington D.C.: Catholic University of America Press, 1996), doi:10.2307/j.ctt32b0dn. Origen, *Homèlies sur saint Luc.*, trans. Henri Crouzel, François Fournier, and Pierre Périchon, Sources chrétiennes 87 (Paris: Cerf, 1962).

54. These include texts Clement calls the 'Gospel according to the Hebrews' and the 'Gospel according to the Egyptians'. See, for a longer list and locations, Schröter, 'Jesus and Early Christian', 239.

55. Translation mine. For an English translation, see Clement, *Stromateis. Books One to Three*, trans. John Ferguson, The Fathers of the Church 85 (Washington, D.C.: Catholic University of America Press, 1991). A copy of the Greek text can be found in Clement, *Clemens Alexandrinus II: Stromata, Buch I–IV*, ed. Ludwig Früchtel and Otto Stählin, Die griechischen christlichen Schriftsteller der ersten drei Jahrhunderte 52 (Berlin: Akademie, 1960).

56. Schröter, 'Jesus and Early Christian', 239 n28.

57. Schröter, 'Jesus and Early Christian', 239.

canon as consisting of a number of tiers. There and in Clement these tiers imply a hierarchy of value and authority. Clement sees some gospels as 'handed down' and others just as gospels. Clement does not define 'who' handed down the texts, presumably he means that these texts have been faithfully transmitted from the first community of Christ-followers. The handed-down gospels are more authoritative, but that does not mean the others are non-authoritative.

The binary differentiation that Clement and Origen create between approved and unapproved gospels (in fan terms: between canon and non-canon) is nuanced in later years. There are a number of early Christian authors that argue for, implicitly or explicitly, three or more tiers of canon. For example, both Cyril of Jerusalem and Eusebius of Caesarea appear to create three categories. Cyril (*c.* 315–387) promotes 'a trifold schema of religious writings: the canonical books, the books of "second rank" (which may also be read or cited in churches), and the heretical apocryphal books'.[58] Eusebius (*c.* 260–339), in his *Ecclesiastical History*, apparently also presses for three categories of texts: agreed upon texts, disputed texts, and counterfeit texts.[59] It is key to remember that these authors are arguing for how *they* imagine Christian texts should be organized, or how they wish these texts were organized. As Hassler-Forest argues, these authorities spend 'most of the energy' trying to create an authoritative and coherent centre for the storyworld. Yet the reality is as the transmedia enterprise grows, it transforms the nature of the narrative, and there is a natural multiplicity of meaning that rejects the prevailing discourses of univocality and coherency.[60] This means that though authorities try to enforce a centripetal meaning, the reality is a centrifugal one. The producer's tiers do not necessarily become the audience's tiers, and individual books regularly move between tiers depending on authorities and communities. In reality these boundaries are porous. But, for our exploration it is the fact that these authors argue for three levels of canonicity or authorization that is important.

François Bovon has long maintained the existence of a three-tiered system of categorizing texts in early Christianity: 'those that were canonical, those that were rejected (apocryphal), and those that were useful for private piety, edification of the community, and a historical understanding of Christian origins'.[61] He has

---

58. Edmon L. Gallagher and John D. Meade, *The Biblical Canon Lists from Early Christianity: Texts and Analysis* (Oxford: Oxford University Press, 2017), 117.

59. Gallagher and Meade, *The Biblical Canon Lists*, 100, 108–9.

60. Hassler-Forest, 'Politics of World Building', 380–81.

61. François Bovon, '"Useful for the Soul": Christian Apocrypha and Christian Spirituality', in *The Oxford Handbook of Early Christian Apocrypha*, ed. Andrew Gregory et al., Oxford Handbooks (Oxford: Oxford University Press, 2015), 185, doi:10.1093/oxfordhb/9780199644117.013.33. Bovon presents this chapter as the culmination of his earlier work on this topic, including François Bovon, 'Beyond the Canonical and the Apocryphal Books, the Presence of a Third Category: The Books Useful for the Soul', *Harvard Theological Review* 105, no. 2 (2012): 125–37, doi:10.1017/S0017816012000466.

pointed out that this third category, standing between canon and non-canon, is often called 'useful' or 'profitable'. These books, though sometimes containing theology that was deemed heretical, were considered suspect, but the 'need for ... memories ... remained too strong to allow simple rejection'.[62] Even among authorities, the fannish love of the characters and their narratives overwhelmed the desire to keep canon univocal and coherent.[63] That is, unless it somehow led Christians astray, as we will see in an example of the bishop Serapion below.

It was Athanasius of Alexandria (*c.* 295–373), pope of what became the Coptic Orthodox Church, who is probably 'the first to develop an explicit schema for a threefold categorization of religious literature'.[64] Athanasius is concerned about apocryphal books, so he proceeds to lists the books he sees as canonical. He then names those that 'have not been canonised, yet have been appointed by the forebears to be read to those who have just joined us and wish to be taught the word of piety' (*Festal Letters* 39.20).[65] Thus he argues that several non-canonical – or dare I say 'semi-canonical' – books can be used for the initiation of new members of the community.[66] At first it may seem counterintuitive to use less accepted works rather than the canon for introducing newcomers. But here we see another similarity with contemporary fan communities, where initiation into them involves much more, or even something completely different than awareness of the canon. As Karen Helleksen argues, becoming part of fandom involves learning the identity of the group. This means that 'learning how to engage is part of the initiation, the *us* versus *them*, the fan versus the nonfan'.[67] New fans need to be introduced to both the fan products and the way fans interact with them. Additionally, it is often fan works, not fandom of the canon itself that carry people 'deeper into the ... community'.[68] In *Enterprising Women: Television Fandom and the Creation of*

62. Bovon, 'Useful for the Soul', 188.

63. Laura Salah Nasrallah, '"Out of Love for Paul": History and Fiction and the Afterlife of the Apostle Paul', in *Early Christian and Jewish Narrative: The Role of Religion in Shaping Narrative Forms*, ed. Ilaria Ramelli and Judith Perkins, Wissenschaftliche Untersuchungen zum Neuen Testament 348 (Tübingen: Mohr Siebeck, 2015), 73–96.

64. Gallagher and Meade, *The Biblical Canon Lists*, 128. See also David Brakke, 'A New Fragment of Athanasius's Thirty-Ninth *Festal Letter*: Heresy, Apocrypha, and the Canon', *Harvard Theological Review* 103, no. 1 (2010): 47–66, doi:10.1017/S0017816009990307.

65. Translation mine. An English translation, and the Greek text can be found in Gallagher and Meade, *The Biblical Canon Lists*, 120–27. See also Brakke's translation of a longer Coptic source, Brakke, 'A New Fragment'.

66. Athanasius doesn't really list any apocryphal books, but makes vague references to some texts, Brakke, 'A New Fragment'. I know of no analogue in fandom, where fan works are highlighted as 'not to be read', similar to how Athanasius does this. The argument in fandom revolves around authority not consumption.

67. Karen Helleksen, 'A Fannish Field of Value: Online Fan Gift Culture', *Cinema Journal* 48 (2009): 114, doi:10.1353/cj.0.0140.

68. Camille Bacon-Smith, *Enterprising Women: Television Fandom and the Creation of Popular Myth* (Philadelphia, PA: University of Pennsylvania Press, 1992), 89.

Popular Myth – published contemporaneously with Henry Jenkins's *Textual Poachers*, and thus one of the first academic works on fandom – Camille Bacon-Smith documents in detail how newcomers to *Star Trek*[69] fandom in the 1970s and 80s were trained in the structures and codes of the community of fans.[70] She notes that many fan writers had only seen 'bits and pieces' of the show before joining the fan community, but that they 'develop a love of the products of the community, especially the fanzines'.[71] In turn, this love of fan fiction leads to attending fan conventions and heightened appreciation of the television show. Kristina Busse notes that in other fan communities, 'some of the readers and writers in these communities have only passing – if any – familiarity with and commitment to the source text'.[72] In this context, Athanasius's insistence that some non-canonical texts are vital to introducing newcomers to the community makes a lot of sense.

Though Athanasius is the first to explicitly write about these three levels of canon (canonical, useful/ecclesiastical/semi-canonical, and apocryphal), he does not claim it as his invention. He attributes it to forebears or ancestors, 'and scholars have been able to locate some antecedents', including Origen of Alexandria.[73] Curiously enough, though there is a distinction into three categories, two of them function in almost exactly the same way. Surely, 'the apocrypha were to be avoided altogether' but 'the other two classes were to be used by the Church, and scholars have, in fact, found little distinction between the way the Fathers used the canonical books and those termed ecclesiastical'.[74] Athanasius suggests using the ecclesiastical texts to instruct new members of the church, and other authors cite from them *as if* they were canon, just less frequently. Thus, even in places where authorities attempt to create clear distinction in canonical lists, the murkiness remains

---

69. *Star Trek* finds it origins in the *Star Trek* TV show (later renamed to *Star Trek: The Original Series*) running on NBC for three seasons from 1966 to 1969. Since the 1970s, a series of 13 films and 11 television series (counting more than 800 episodes) have been produced. The transmedia enterprise includes hundreds of books, comics, games, magazines, and the like.

70. Due to the change in the media landscape, and the shift of fan works from zines to the internet, initiation to fandom nowadays is rather different to what Bacon-Smith describes. See, e.g. Judith Fathallah, *Fanfiction and the Author: How Fanfic Changes Popular Cultural Texts*, Transmedia: Participatory Culture and Media Convergence (Amsterdam: Amsterdam University Press, 2017), 30–31.

71. Bacon-Smith, *Enterprising Women*, 89. Fanzines are magazines produced by fans and for fans of a particular fandom. Before the rise of the internet, they were the primary way fan fiction was distributed and consumed.

72. Kristina Busse, *Framing Fan Fiction: Literary and Social Practices in Fan Fiction Communities* (Iowa City, IA: University of Iowa Press, 2017), 116.

73. Edmon L. Gallagher, *Hebrew Scripture in Patristic Biblical Theory: Canon, Language, Text*, Supplements to Vigiliae Christianae 114 (Leiden: Brill, 2012), 28.

74. Gallagher, *Hebrew Scripture in Patristic Biblical Theory*, 28.

surrounding canonicity, with authors implicitly and explicitly allowing for tiers of canonicity to exist between the two poles of canon and non-canon.

All in all, these early Christians engage in discussion that is both political and authoritative. They, similar to the modern-day franchise holders described by Hassler-Forest, wish to clearly define which texts, stories and thoughts are part of the(ir) authoritative centre of Christianity, and which should be banished to the edges, to the heretical peripheries. Yet, from Irenaeus to Athanasius, there is a long tradition that counteracts this binary, from quoting books they themselves claim are de-authorized to defining intermediate categories between the centre and periphery. Again, we return to the contrast between the desire to create coherent and univocal storyworlds and the multivocal, heteroglossic reality. Throughout the monoglossic pronouncements of these early Christians, the existence, creation, citation and use of works that don't fit this single storyworld destabilize 'any central conception of "unity" or single meaning'.[75] In the rest of this chapter, I will examine this process in more detail, nuancing both the centripetal forces and the centrifugal multiplicities of early Christianity.

Canon Debates and Fan Works

So far, in my example of *Star Wars* canon, I haven't examined how much more complicated canonicity becomes when fan works are introduced into the equation. An excellent example of how we could imagine fan fiction in ancient debates on canon could be to look at the qualification of 'handed down' or 'received' in the historical narrative of how Bishop Serapion dealt with an issue in one of his churches. Serapion was bishop of Antioch (c. 199–211), and church historian Eusebius records this narrative around 100 years later in his monumental *Ecclesiastical History*. Eusebius relates that people have been reading the Gospel of Peter (an apocryphal text) in one of Serapion's churches and have been led astray. Serapion writes to the church, 'Siblings, we have *received* both Peter and the other apostles as Christ, but we reject the writings that falsely bear their names, for we, as people of experience, know that we did not *receive* those' (Eusebius *Ecclesiastical History* 6.12.3).[76] Serapion seems to make the same distinction as Origen and Clement, between texts that have been received and those that have not. But he makes the distinction much more complex. When he first heard of this writing, he hadn't read it. Even though he felt it was not handed down, he let it be read in

---

75. Hassler-Forest, 'Politics of World Building', 380–81.

76. Translation and emphasis mine. For an English translation, see Eusebius, *Ecclesiastical History, Books 6–10*, trans. Deferrari Roy J., The Fathers of the Church 29 (Washington D.C.: Catholic University of America Press, 1969). The Greek can be found in Eusebius, *Ecclesiastical History, Volume II: Books 6–10*, trans. J. E. L. Oulton, Loeb Classical Library 265 (Cambridge, MA: Harvard University Press, 1932).

church. The text fell in a liminal category: Serapion neither received nor rejected it, for him it was neither canon nor non-canon. It was, to borrow Bovon's terminology from above, 'useful'.[77] Later, after seeing that some members, on the basis of the text, had adopted teachings Serapion felt were not correct, he suggests the text be rejected. He considers it now to be non-canon. Yet, having read it and having compared it to other 'heretical' texts, he concludes that 'the most part was in harmony with the teachings of the Saviour' (*Ecclesiastical History* 6.12.6). This 'is especially interesting' notes Jens Schröter, 'because it demonstrates that it was possible in a Christian community to use an additional gospel'.[78] Authoritative statements to discard texts from the storyworld's centre should not be taken to mean that they were discarded by audiences. Schröter emphasizes that, even though more than 100 years earlier major Christian authors argued for a single set of four 'received' gospels, some churches actively read other gospels. And indeed, Serapion only forbids the writing because it is *associated* with heretics, not based on the contents which he judges non-heretical.[79] He assigns the text to the periphery based on its reputation, not on its quality or message. And, for Serapion, whether he feels that the text is authentically received or not doesn't seem to influence the value of the text. Though he considers it a derivative text, that does not disqualify it from being read in church.

Serapion is a useful example of how much more complicated canonicity and authoritative statements about canonicity become once derivative works are included in the discussion. Jason Mittell's analysis of canon on *Lostpedia* is extremely helpful in exploring the introduction of fan works into discussions of canonicity.[80] Created during the second season of hit TV show *Lost*,[81] *Lostpedia* is a community edited encyclopedia that was created 'to allow fans of the show to organize the massive amounts of theories, plotlines and cast information that was

---

77. Bovon, 'Useful for the Soul'.

78. Schröter, 'Jesus and Early Christian', 239. See also Larry W. Hurtado, 'Who Read Early Christian Apocrypha?', in *The Oxford Handbook of Early Christian Apocrypha*, ed. Andrew Gregory et al., Oxford Handbooks (Oxford: Oxford University Press, 2015), 155–56, doi:10.1093/oxfordhb/9780199644117.013.1.

79. See also, Jens Schröter, 'Apocryphal and Canonical Gospels within the Development of the New Testament Canon', *Early Christianity* 7, no. 1 (2016): 26, doi:10.1628/186870316X14555506071137.

80. Jason Mittell, 'Sites of Participation: Wiki Fandom and the Case of Lostpedia', *Transformative Works and Cultures* 3 (2009), doi:10.3983/twc.2009.0118.

81. *Lost* (2004–2010) is a science fiction TV series documenting the lives of the survivors of a plane crash on a mysterious South Pacific island. Core to the show was the slow unveiling of enigmas related to the island. It was created by Jeffrey Lieber, J. J. Abrams, and Damon Lindelof and ran for six seasons. The series became a transmedia enterprise with the publication of books, websites, and video and board games.

generated by the show'.[82] Key features of *Lost* are puzzles and mystery, and '*Lostpedia* has served as a site for mulling possible explanations for the island's enigmas'.[83] The encyclopedia therefore always contained canonical and non-canonical materials, and Mittell has traced the community's development of thinking about canon. Originally the fans only differentiated between 'canon' (endorsed by the show's creators) and 'noncanon'. As the series progressed and the transmedia storyworld became more complex, this differentiation was no longer fit for purpose. The heteroglossic reality of the storyworld no longer consisted of, to borrow Hassler-Forest's words, 'mappable, measurable, and navigable spaces with coherent chronologies, characters, and events'.[84] One suggested solution was to borrow from Christianity and to differentiate between 'Canon, Deuterocanon, Ex cathēdrā, and Apocrypha'.[85] This was judged too complex, and ultimately, the decision was made to follow a simpler model. Many of *Lost*'s transmedia products were delegated to a third category of 'semi-canon'. Developing two tiers of authorized canon removed any doubt towards the veracity and coherence of the producer's canonical material, anything that seemed to contradict established canon could simply be designated semi-canon. Though of course, such decisions to delegate a text to semi-canon were never unanimous or authoritative for all fans. Ultimately, this encyclopedia includes three tiers of canonical authority, and seeks to differentiate between them, 'creating a clear hierarchy between creator-endorsed truth and fan-created para-truth'.[86] Yet, for *Lostpedia* the fan created non-canon was extremely important and could not be removed from the encyclopedia entries. This vital inclusion of non-canonical para-truth is best evidenced by the 'theories'. These are hundreds of fan works that serve to explain the enigmas of *Lost* canon. This means that in the encyclopedia, *Lost* canon is 'supplemented – and made questionably valid – by the associated speculation and theories'.[87] The non-canon in the encyclopedia works to both justify and authorize canon. As *Lost* canon is so enigmatic it would hardly make sense without the theories – the theories function to explain, elucidate and justify canonical characters, events and the like. At the same time, the explicit differentiation between canon and non-canon 'further enshrines the site's authorial-endorsed factual content'.[88]

Including fan works into the discussion of canonicity thus complicates matters but also shows how this can further strengthen the attempts to elevate some texts to canon through discarding others. To return to early Christianity, third- and fourth-century church historian Eusebius makes a similar point to Mittell's:

82. 'About Lostpedia', *Lostpedia*, 24 April 2010, https://lostpedia.fandom.com/wiki/Lostpedia:About.
83. Mittell, 'Sites of Participation', para. 2.31.
84. Hassler-Forest, 'Politics of World Building', 381.
85. Mittell, 'Sites of Participation', para. 2.12.
86. Mittell, 'Sites of Participation', para. 2.13.
87. Mittell, 'Sites of Participation', para. 2.19.
88. Mittell, 'Sites of Participation', para. 2.16.

It was necessary to make a list, distinguishing between the writings, which were – according to the church – received as truthful, authentic, and agreed upon, and the others. These are not agreed upon and disputed, yet known to most of the church. We did this so that we will know the [canonical] ones and those added by heretics under the name of the apostles. (Eusebius *Ecclesiastical History* 3.25)[89]

Eusebius explains that his listing of canonical, semi-canonical and non-canonical texts function to reinforce the value of the canonical ones. We can note that Serapion uses the Gospel of Peter in a potentially similar way. By stating that that he feels that it is not 'received' in the way that other texts are, he creates an opposition that allows him to justify and authorize other 'received' texts. Just as in the *Lostpedia*, Serapion creates a 'marked-out, separate sphere of unofficial knowledge that helps make canon seem more official by comparison'.[90] Yet at the same time, having examined the text he notes that its contents are 'in harmony with the teachings of the Saviour' (Eusebius *Ecclesiastical History* 6.12.6). Though rejecting the text, he doesn't feel it is incorrect or wrong, he simply does not authorize it in the same way other texts are. The text actually supports the contents of canon, in much the same was as theories on Lostpedia support the coherence of the *Lost* television episodes. Serapion's conceptualization of canon is more than simply a dichotomy between what he does and does not authorize, between what he considers received and not-received.

Clearly, apocryphal texts had a place in Christian communities, despite authoritative statements otherwise. Chris Keith's examination of the concept of 'handed down' or 'received' in the context of Christian liturgies elucidates this further. He notes that there were many settings where Christians read Christian texts, from reading alone at home to citing a text as Scripture in church.[91] The religious hierarchy of these settings, argues Keith, creates a hierarchy of texts: some texts could be read at home, but not in a gathering, or not in church. This more closely mirrors the tiers of *Star Wars* canon. Keith examines some of the examples I mention above – and a number that I have not mentioned – but most applicable for this discussion are his conclusions about the so-called Muratorian Fragment. At face value this text appears to be from the second century, yet there is significant debate whether it should rather be dated to the fourth century.[92] The dating is not

---

89. Translation mine. The Greek text and English translation can be found in Eusebius, *Ecclesiastical History, Volume 1: Books 1–5*, trans. Kirsopp Lake, Loeb Classical Library 153 (Cambridge, MA: Harvard University Press, 1926).

90. Mittell, 'Sites of Participation', para. 2.16.

91. Chris Keith, *The Gospel as Manuscript: An Early History of the Jesus Tradition as Material Artifact* (Oxford: Oxford University Press, 2020), 173–74.

92. Clare K. Rothschild, *The Muratorian Fragment: Text, Translation, Commentary*, Studies and Texts in Antiquity and Christianity 132 (Tübingen: Mohr Siebeck, 2022).

necessarily important for our discussion. Rather, it is important to note that the Latin of this text is at times 'wretched' making it 'difficult to know what the writer intended'.[93] This text is at first glance a list of texts that are and are not 'received' by the church; it is a list of which texts are canonical and which are not. More precisely it is the author's attempt to police which texts should be considered canonical and which should be discarded. Closer inspection shows that the author of the fragment distinguishes between several levels of canonicity and authority. The fragment first lists some texts that the author feels are canonical, including many of the books that came to be collected in the New Testament canon. Then four types of texts are mentioned, with varying levels of canonical authority. (1) There are some books, such as the apocryphal letters of Paul to the Laodiceans and Alexandrians, which are called forgeries, and they 'cannot be received into the catholic church' (*Muratorian Fragment* 66).[94] The author non-authorizes these texts; they are non-canon. (2) There are other books, including the canonical Revelation of John and the apocryphal Revelation of Peter, which are 'received ... although some of us do not want [them] to be read in church' (*Muratorian Fragment* 71–73). The author wants these to be received, and thus they appear to be canonical, but admits some people don't think they are worthy of being read in churches. (3) Finally, there are texts like the Shepherd of Hermas, which 'ought to be read, but it cannot come before the people in the church, either among the prophets ... or among the apostles' (*Muratorian Fragment* 77–80). There is some debate whether this means the book cannot be read at all in church, or only not as part as the prophets and the apostles, nevertheless we 'can say confidently at least that the Fragment discourages reading Hermas "in church" in the same way as these other texts'.[95] (4) Finally, the Fragment mentions the writings of the theologians Arsinous, Valentinus, Miltiades and Basilides. The author claims that they accept 'nothing in its entirety' of these writers (*Muratorian Fragment* 81–82). Keith engages with this fragment in detail because it demonstrates that whether someone considered a text to be received or not wasn't the only aspect that affected their authorizing a text; that a text was read in church was often more important He concludes:

> Modern scholarship on the development of the canon has focused heavily upon the content of early Christian texts and their purported authors in explaining the development of the canon. But when Christians such as Justin and the unknown author of the Muratorian Fragment discuss how one would know if a given assembly revered a particular text as authoritative, the litmus test was not exclusively what the text said; it was what the assembly did with that text in its communal meetings.[96]

---

93. Metzger, *Canon*, 305.
94. Translations of the *Muratorian Fragment* are from Rothschild, *The Muratorian Fragment*. That Latin can also be found there.
95. Keith, *The Gospel as Manuscript*, 193.
96. Keith, *The Gospel as Manuscript*, 193.

Discussions of canonicity then revolve around much more than simply the contents or authorship of texts. Indeed, as evidenced in the discussion above, even authoritative statements on the contents of canon and the rejection of certain texts do not completely restrict their consumption, personally or communally. Communities accept and reject texts in complicated ways. Though authorities try to relegate some texts to the periphery and keep others in the centre, communities and individuals do not always follow suit. These individual and communal considerations destabilize authoritative attempts to police a single Christian storyworld. In the following section I will examine this process of how communities construct canon in more detail.

Debating Canon

Paul Thomas spent months doing ethnographic research among the editors of the 'Star Wars canon' Wikipedia page, examining their discussion, debate and thoughts on the Star Wars canon.[97] This was in 2006, before Disney acquired the Star Wars franchise, when canon was still defined and maintained by Lucasfilm. Thomas's research is a useful case study for us because Wikipedia's policies require each page to be a 'monoglossic compendium of knowledge', meaning that the editors needed to reach a single, authoritative interpretation of what constitutes the canon of Star Wars.[98] The basic assumption of the editors – which I will problematize below – is that 'the goings-on in a fictional universe can be objectively and encyclopaedically documented'.[99] Or, to put it in the terms I borrowed from Hassler-Forest above, the heteroglot utterances can (and should) be unified into a stable and coherent whole. These editors, all fans of Star Wars, spent months taking 'part in a complex dialogic and performative process to determine canon'.[100] Though most editors agreed that the creator of the storyworld (i.e. George Lucas) had authority over what should and should not be canon, the situation was complicated by the fact that Lucas had shared his authority with a company, Lucasfilm, and an employee, Leland Chee. Chee 'was charged with stewarding the continuity and cohesiveness of the Star Wars canon'.[101] It was Chee who was responsible for creating and curating the six levels of canon mentioned above. But, Lucas's public statements on canon differ slightly from Chee's, and thus the canonicity of certain texts not created by Lucas became a topic of debate. In their debate, the editors used citations of both Lucas

---

97. Paul Thomas, 'Canon Wars: A Semiotic and Ethnographic Study of a Wikipedia Talk Page Debate Concerning the Canon of Star Wars', The Journal of Fandom Studies 6, no. 3 (2018): 279–300, doi:10.1386/jfs.6.3.279_1.
98. Thomas, 'Canon Wars', 281.
99. Thomas, 'Canon Wars', 285.
100. Thomas, 'Canon Wars', 284.
101. Thomas, 'Canon Wars', 291.

and Chee to argue their points-of-view about the *Star Wars* canon. Thomas calls these citations 'ritualized', because 'by indexing the author's sayings, the fan editor is not only trying to call attention to the "real" canon, but also (by iconizing the author's quotes) attempting to ascribe the authority of that author to him or herself'.[102] The citation is not simply an 'appeal to authority', instead it is an 'attempt to *participate* in that authority'.[103]

Rather obviously, this method of debating canon would be almost impossible in the context of early Christianity. As the writers of the potentially canonical texts had long ago passed away, ancient writers could not appeal to the words of the writers for authority – except of course the words contained in the text under debate.[104] Yet, similar to the example from *Star Wars* canon debates, early Christians did often include ritualized statements about the identity of the authors. Take, for example, what the ancient church historian Eusebius records of Origen of Alexandria's opinions on the four gospels:

> But in the first of his *Commentaries on the Gospel according to Matthew*, defending the canon of the Church, he testifies that he knows only four gospels, writing somewhat as follows: 'For I learned by tradition concerning the four gospels, which alone are indisputable in the church of God under heaven, that first there was written that according to the one-time tax-collector and later apostle of Jesus Christ, Matthew ... secondly, that according to Mark, which he wrote as Peter guided him, whom also Peter acknowledged as son in his catholic epistle, speaking with these words: "The church that is in Babylon, elected together with you, salutes you: and so does my son Mark"; and thirdly, that according to Luke, who composed this Gospel, which was praised by Paul, for Gentile converts; and in addition to them all, that according to John'. (Eusebius *Ecclesiastical History* 6.25.3–6)[105]

Origen cites 'tradition' (i.e. knowledge that has been passed down) that has given him the identities of the four gospel writers, and then cites other authoritative sources to enforce that identification. Tradition and these sources are both silent on the topic of canonicity, yet Origen uses this appeal to tradition and established sources to make authoritative statements on canonicity itself. As in the *Star Wars* canon debate, by citing authoritative statements, Origen is 'attempting to ascribe the authority of that author to him or herself'.[106] As such, his invocation of tradition allows him to appeal to a higher authority than himself, and he uses that authority to make statements beyond what that authority speaks of. Just as the fan editors

---

102. Thomas, 'Canon Wars', 294.

103. Thomas, 'Canon Wars', 294.

104. There is some evidence of early Christians using the words in a text itself to justify the authority of that exact text. See, for example, Eusebius *Ecclesiastical History* 7.25.

105. Translation is a slightly edited version of Eusebius, *Ecclesiastical History, Vol. 2 (Fathers of the Church)*.

106. Thomas, 'Canon Wars', 294.

wish to inhabit and participate in the authority of Lucas or Chee, Origen can 'inhabit the role of an authority' and 'participate in that authority'.[107]

There are also cases where early Christians refer to judgements made about texts by other people, assumed to be experts on the matter. For example, we have a letter that Origen of Alexandria wrote in reply to Sextus Julius Africanus. Here he defends the canonicity of the book of Susanna (one of the Old Testament Apocrypha) and amongst his arguments is that he knows a 'learned Hebrew person' who did not reject the book – thus Christians needn't reject it either (*Letter to Africanus* 7).[108] Similarly, as time progressed, writers could appeal to the authority of Christians that came before them, though admittedly this does not frequently occur. A good example of this is the fifth- or sixth-century Pseudo-Gelasian decree. This (in all probability fake) papal decree contains a list of books that are to be considered canonical, of books that are not forbidden to be received, and of books that should be seen as absolutely not received and to be avoided altogether. Again, we have three tiers of canon. In the middle list, the decree discusses the reception of the works of two Christian writers, Rufinus and Origen:

> Likewise, Rufinus, a pious man, published many books of ecclesiastical works. He also translated some scriptures. But as the reverend Jerome noted that he took some freedoms in decisions, we deem acceptable those books which we know the aforesaid blessed Jerome accepted.... Likewise, some of Origen's treatises, which the most blessed man Jerome does not reject, we receive for reading. But others as well as this author are to be rejected. (*Pseudo-Gelasian decree* 232–41)[109]

Origen was a controversial figure in the fourth to sixth century, with calls for his writings to be banned in the fourth century, and he himself possibly being condemned by a church council in the sixth. The Pseudo-Gelasian decree, from around that time, deals with the acceptability of Origen's work by referring to the judgements of the always authoritative Jerome, and suggests accepting whatever he accepts from among the works of both Rufinus and Origen. As such it too

---

107. Thomas, 'Canon Wars', 294–95.

108. An English translation of this text can be found in Alexander Roberts, James Donaldson, and Cleveland A. Coxe, eds., *Ante-Nicene Fathers 4: Fathers of the Third Century: Tertullian, Part Fourth; Minucius Felix; Commodian; Origen, Parts First and Second*, Ante-Nicene Fathers 4 (Christian Literature Company, 1885).

109. This translation is mine, based on the Latin found in Ernst von Dobschütz, *Das Decretum Gelasianum de libris recipiendis et non recipiendis*, Texte und Untersuchungen zur Geschichte der altchristlichen Literatur, 38.4 (Leipzig: J. C. Hinrichs, 1912). I am unaware of a traditionally published English translation. There is a translation online on the website of the Tertullian Project: https://www.tertullian.org/decretum_eng.htm [accessed 15 September 2023].

'participates in the authority' of Jerome, allowing the decree's judgement of Origen and Rufinus 'to be seen as (more) definitive and thus be taken (more) seriously'.[110] Despite these few examples,[111] early Christians mostly use citations of authority figures sparingly when discussing canon, preferring vaguer terms such as 'tradition'.

Returning to Thomas's ethnographic study of fan editors, we find another key issue about this discussion of canon: the editors of the Wikipedia page do not recognize their role in the construction of the canon. In the debate they attempt to 'locate the "One True Canon" set down by the author. From their perspective, the debate is merely the process of sifting through information to find the "truth" that is assumed to be "out there"'.[112] There is a basic and unchallenged assumption that there is a single canon that can be discovered by doing enough research. The 'Canon' exists in a way similar to a Platonic Form: it's abstract, unchanging, and transcends time and space. All the editors need to do is recognize the form through study, argument, and debate. This conception of canon is commonplace, with both fans *and* authors. When George Lucas released the so-called special editions of the first three *Star Wars* films in the 1990s, there was a lot of pushback from many fans: Lucas had changed the canon. This controversy came to be summarized with a single phrase 'Han shot first', referencing a scene involving a gunfight between protagonist Han Solo and a hostile bounty hunter Greedo. In the original cinematic cut of the film it appears that Han Solo shoots Greedo first, demonstrating his ruthless survivalist nature. Lucas's special edition shows Greedo shooting first, missing, and then only does Han shoot him. This changes Han's ethics significantly. Of particular interest for our discussion is Lucas's justification for these changes. In a 2012 interview he reacts to the 'the who-shot-first, Han Solo or Greedo furor':[113]

> It's a movie, just a movie. The controversy over who shot first, Greedo or Han Solo, in *Episode IV*, what I did was try to clean up the confusion, but obviously it upset people because they wanted Solo … to be a cold-blooded killer, but he actually isn't. It had been done in all close-ups and it was confusing about who did what to whom. I put a little wider shot in there that made it clear that Greedo is the one who shot first, but everyone wanted to think that Han shot first, because they wanted to think that he actually just gunned him down.[114]

---

110. Thomas, 'Canon Wars', 295.

111. A few more examples can be found in Eusebius's *Ecclesiastical History*, where Eusebius or people he cites and paraphrases, quote earlier authors as authoritative on issues of canon. See, e.g. 3.39, 6.16.

112. Thomas, 'Canon Wars', 293.

113. Alex Ben Block, '5 Questions With George Lucas: Controversial "Star Wars" Changes, SOPA and "Indiana Jones 5"', *Hollywood Reporter*, 9 February 2012, https://www.hollywoodreporter.com/movies/movie-news/george-lucas-star-wars-interview-288523/.

114. Block, '5 Questions With George Lucas'.

Lucas admits that people are upset about this new version, but defends the special edition in an important way. 'He denies', notes John Lyden, 'that there *was* any change'.[115] Twice Lucas says that people thought something, but 'actually' that was not the case. As far as Lucas is concerned, Han had always shot second, even if the films up to that point had portrayed the opposite. Lyden continues to argue that 'for someone who claims that "it's just a movie," this seems an oddly *realistic* defense of the alteration, as if to claim that there is some reality "out there" to which the film refers'.[116] In a manner very similar to the editors of the *Star Wars* canon Wikipedia page, Lucas argues that there is a 'reality out there' that the films need to faithfully reproduce, neglecting to note how the films create a storyworld. In his view, there is a pre-existent canonical list of situations and events, and the films must reflect these as well as possible. Changing the films is in Lucas's view perfectly justified, as the canon exists outside of the films themselves and he is simply putting the canon to film.

This is – of course – not how canon comes about. Canon is the result of a subjective negotiation between texts, readers and communities. Yet, like in fan communities, some early Christians appeared to imagine that their role was recognizing canon – not constructing it. It seems that in the minds of these writers, there was a fixed set of writings that could be considered 'handed down' or 'received' and their task was simply correctly identifying that collection. Everett Ferguson gives a number of examples of authors using this terminology with this mindset, including Irenaeus of Smyrna who refers to the gospel 'handed down to us by the will of God'.[117] Irenaeus, then, seems to see this collection as finding its origins in the mind of God. Ferguson's conclusion on early Christians mirrors exactly the same attitude as that of the *Star Wars* Wikipedia page editors: 'the early ecclesiastical writers did not regard themselves as deciding which books to accept or to reject. Rather, they saw themselves as acknowledging which books had been handed down to them'.[118] In fact, early Christians take it even further: they do not simply recognize the pre-existing 'One True Canon', they feel that this canon constructs reality itself. For example, examining how early Christians 'imagined a gospel corpus consisting of precisely four texts', Jeremiah Coogan demonstrates that 'a number of early Christians ... thought that the fourfold Gospel was the *reason* for

---

115. John C. Lyden, 'Whose Film Is It, Anyway? Canonicity and Authority in Star Wars Fandom', *Journal of the American Academy of Religion* 80, no. 3 (2012): 778, doi:10.1093/jaarel/lfs037.

116. Lyden, 'Whose Film Is It, Anyway?', 778.

117. Everett Ferguson, 'Factors Leading to the Selection and Closure of the New Testament Canon: A Survey of Some Recent Studies', in *The Canon Debate : On the Origins and Formation of the Bible*, ed. Lee Martin McDonald and James A. Sanders (Peabody, MA: Hendrickson, 2002), 295.

118. Ferguson, 'Factors Leading', 295.

cosmic quadriformity'.[119] In other words, they started from an observation that the cosmos was quadriform – four winds, four corners of the earth, four parts to a walnut, four primeval rivers, four elements, four virtues, the list goes on. Having ascertained that the number four plays a large role in so much of the natural world, they theorized that the cosmos was made like this precisely *because* there were four gospels. They imagined that there were always four gospels, and that explained why there were so many fours in the world. Thus, their role was not seen to be the creation of a canon – the canon preceded the universe itself – it was simply recognizing the canon as set out by God. This mirrors very closely how Thomas described the *Star Wars* Wikipedia editors: 'from their perspective, the debate is merely the process of sifting through information to find the "truth" that is assumed to be "out there"; in their minds, they are not creating, but merely aggregating'.[120] These early Christians sifted the 'disciplines of meteorology, geography, music, mathematics, and astronomy' to find the truth about the nature of the canon.[121] In these ways, it appears that early Christians imagined their roles very similar to those of contemporary fan editors: 'they, via debate, *can* locate the "One True Canon" set down by the author' or – for early Christians – by God.[122]

Returning to Thomas's analysis of the construction of *Star Wars* canon, he points out that the way the fan editors imagine their role does not reflect reality: 'the reality, however, is that a debate like the one in question is inherently productive, in that it is not merely an objective "sorting" of deposited information, but rather a fairly subjective ritual in which information is cited and a final product created from these citations'.[123] The debate, whether in fandom or early Christianity, is not one of recognizing canon, but rather one of creating a canon. As these curators attempt to create a univocal position from the heteroglossic reality, once again we are reminded that this is a discourse that is both political and authoritative. Though the fan editors and early Christians may feel that they are simply recognizing the canon, in reality they are struggling to reinforce the 'centripetal notion of the "authoritative"' and are actively engaged in a political discussion which works should be 'discarded by the storyworlds' "authoritative" center'.[124] We needn't look much further than Origen's statement that 'the church has four Gospels; heretics have many', to see these polemics in practice.[125] In the case of Coogan's examples, arguing that canon precedes reality, functions as little more than an extremely authoritative argument for one opinion on the contents on the canon.

---

119. Jeremiah Coogan, 'Reading (in) a Quadriform Cosmos: Gospel Books in the Early Christian Bibliographic Imagination', *Journal of Early Christian Studies* 31, no. 1 (2023): 102–3, doi:10.1353/earl.2023.0004, original emphasis.
120. Thomas, 'Canon Wars', 293.
121. Coogan, 'Reading (in) a Quadriform Cosmos', 85.
122. Thomas, 'Canon Wars', 293, emphasis mine.
123. Thomas, 'Canon Wars', 293.
124. Hassler-Forest, 'Politics of World Building', 381.
125. Coogan, 'Reading (in) a Quadriform Cosmos', 86.

Conclusions

In this chapter I have looked at how fan studies can inform our discussions of canon in early Christianity. Fan communities show surprising similarities with early Christian ones when it comes to discussions of authority and (interpretations of) canon, and support contemporary portrayals of early Christianity as highly diverse. Studies of contemporary fans and their communities allowed me to analyse the way early Christians attempted to claim authority, and police meaning. In the vast Christian transmedial universe a hierarchy of texts was enforced and reinforced, maintained and policed. Christians created hierarchies of authority. In this way they attempted to clearly define which texts, which stories and – most importantly – which ideas and thoughts are part of the authoritative centre of Christianity. Fan studies assists in identifying the political aspects at play in the creation and policing of canon. The authorizing process, where texts are approved and denounced, attempts to create a coherent and univocal storyworld out of the multivocal, heteroglossic reality of early Christianity. At the same time, individual and communal reading practices destabilize these authoritative attempts to police a single Christian storyworld.

When it comes to accepting texts as authoritative, there is no recognition of the subjectivity of this process. Many ancient Christians imagine that they are simply recognizing the list of canonical texts as given by God, not actively reinforcing their own interpretations. There is little appreciation that they are actively policing the storyworld of early Christianity by reinforcing the centripetal notion of the authoritative: they themselves are the authorities authorizing certain texts, defining what lies at the heart of the Christian storyworld and what should be discarded by the storyworld. Though the stigmatization of texts in this debate is strong, there *is* recognition among authors that the binary canon–non-canon does not hold. Fans and early Christians allow texts to exist in categories between acceptance and rejection, and the reality is that though certain texts are demonized, they remain influential and are read in various communities. Some rejected texts even become required reading for initiates to the community. Though there is an attempt to police a univocal storyworld, the reality is that great diversity exists.

Chapter 4

GATEKEEPING, HERESY, INFANTILIZATION, AND FEMINIZATION: HOW DO PEOPLE POLICE DERIVATIVE WORKS?[1]

In this chapter I will continue my exploration of how people react to the existence of derivative works. Whereas in the previous chapter my focus was on how texts are regulated to create canons of authorized and un-authorized texts, in this section I will look at how interpretations of texts are regulated. I will look at how communities arrive at authoritative interpretations of texts, and how these interpretations are reinforced and policed by these very same communities.

In the previous chapter I discussed how reviewers of Anne Rice's *Christ the Lord* criticized her use of non-canonical texts due to their alleged historical inaccuracy.[2] This helped introduce how people react to derivative works by gatekeeping a collection of canon – to which many positive characteristics are ascribed – and non-canon. But criticizing the choice of which texts are authoritative and aesthetically pleasing is not the only way audiences responded to her work. Esther Spurrill-Jones reflects in a blog post on how her own religious context reacted to the publication of the book:

> I was in university when *Out of Egypt* was published in 2006. I remember it caused an uproar in the church circles I was part of at the time. Christians were aghast that the vampire lady had written a book about Jesus. Some assumed the fictional Jesus in the book was a vampire. Everyone was certain it was blasphemous. I'm sure none of them bothered to read it.[3]

In the religious contexts that Spurrill-Jones was part of, the book caused quite a stir. Rice's reputation preceded her, and her work was automatically assumed to be

---

1. As for many chapters in this book, I'm highly indebted to Kelsie Rodenbiker for her extensive feedback on a draft of this chapter.
2. Anne Rice, *Christ the Lord: Out of Egypt* (London: Arrow, 2007).
3. Esther Spurrill-Jones, 'Anne Rice's Out of Egypt Is Not About a Vampire Christ', *The Book Cafe* (blog), 21 January 2022, https://medium.com/the-book-cafe/anne-rices-out-of-egypt-is-not-about-a-vampire-christ-9cef0f602ea4.

highly problematic. Comments from the time of publication can still be found on Christian discussion boards and blogs, calling the work 'heretical' and attributing 'doctrinal error' and 'heresy' to Rice herself.[4] And Christian apologetic websites include several thousand word articles addressing how to 'recognize truth or heresy', naturally concluding that Rice's work is heresy.[5]

At stake in this discussion is the interpretation of canon. Berit Kjos, in her four-thousand-word refutation of Anne Rice's book, makes exactly this point, rhetorically asking 'will it introduce people to the Biblical Jesus or to a heart-warming counterfeit?' Rice's work, she argues, 'clashes with God's revealed Word', and she highlights a number of ways to recognize heresy; in general and in Rice's work.[6] Kjos engages in a discussion on the interpretation of canon in a specific way. Any interpretation that does not match hers is automatically assumed to be in contradiction to the canon, and those other interpretations are immediately maligned as 'imagination', 'heretical', and a 'seductive illusion'.[7] This chapter will explore similar discussions in early Christianity and contemporary fan communities.

Creating Canon, Creating Heresy

The discussion in the previous chapter focussed on one definition of canon – the collection of authoritative writings. Within fandom, however, canon usually refers to the interpretation of events laid out in these writings. Let me now move from canon as a list of authoritative books, to canon as the common interpretation of said books. Kristina Busse explores the process of how a text leads to interpretative canon.[8] She notes that as soon as a reader begins to consume the collections of texts they consider canon, 'they produce a personal and idiosyncratic reading ... that then becomes the basis for their interpretation and writing'.[9] This reading can be very minor, from focussing on (or rejecting) one character or event over others, to excluding entire sections of texts, or even entire texts. Readers are generally not aware of this process and consider their recollection of canon to be canon itself. Ultimately, as Busse summarizes:

> The fan fiction writer is constantly engaged in creating her own individualized version of canon: she foregrounds certain facts and scenes and overlooks others;

---

4. See, e.g. https://www.puritanboard.com/threads/anne-rice-ill-wait-and-see-the-fruit-of-this-one.9755/ [accessed 15 September 2023]; http://introiboadaltaredei2.blogspot.com/2016/03/the-young-false-messiah.html [accessed 15 September 2023].

5. Berit Kjos, 'Anne Rice Re-Imagines Jesus and Christian Leaders Applaud', *Kjos Ministries*, January 2006, http://www.crossroad.to/articles2/006/anne-rice.htm.

6. Kjos, 'Anne Rice'.

7. Kjos, 'Anne Rice'.

8. Kristina Busse, *Framing Fan Fiction: Literary and Social Practices in Fan Fiction Communities* (Iowa City, IA: University of Iowa Press, 2017), 108–13.

9. Busse, *Framing Fan Fiction*, 108.

she makes some aspects of the story much more central to her reading than they may be in the source text; and she reads the text within her own cultural context, thus affecting her very individual responses.[10]

Each individual engaging with the texts of canon thus creates their own canon (of interpretation). Combining these idiosyncrasies with each person's 'own literary and personal background' – and let me add, for early Christianity this includes the very important 'theological background' – leads to highly individualized interpretations of canon. Yet, as 'fandom communities form, some readings of the source text become privileged among certain groups of fans'.[11] These privileged readings can become fanon (fan canon) or even ascend to become included in future 'official' canon.[12] In this chapter, I am most interested in the various communities that form around common interpretations of canon. Busse gives a number of examples of contemporary fan communities gathered around a similar reading of canon.[13] Some communities are heavily invested in (erotic) relations between fictional characters; others congregate around a specific 'focus or approach to the text';[14] some even form around grammatical or stylistic preferences. These communities, 'agree on particular events, characteristics, and interpretations of the actual texts and will read certain canonical events with a particular lens'.[15] Thus each community implicitly forms its own commonly agreed on (interpretation of) canon and hermeneutical strategies.

Busse's analysis of contemporary fan communities resonates strongly with the so-called Bauer thesis about early Christian communities. In 1933, Walter Bauer published *Rechtgläubigkeit und Ketzerei im ältesten Christentum* (Orthodoxy and Heresy in Earliest Christianity), which has become a landmark in the study of early Christianity.[16] Bauer's thesis was a major reconfiguring of the history of early Christianity.[17] Up to that point there was a general consensus that there had always been an original, orthodox Christianity, with many secondary heresies branching off from this correct understanding of Christian theology. Bauer summarizes this as 'Jesus reveals the pure doctrine to the apostles' and 'each takes

10. Busse, *Framing Fan Fiction*, 108.
11. Busse, *Framing Fan Fiction*, 109.
12. See pp. 162–63.
13. Busse, *Framing Fan Fiction*, 110–13.
14. Busse, *Framing Fan Fiction*, 112.
15. Busse, *Framing Fan Fiction*, 110.
16. Walter Bauer, *Rechtgläubigkeit und Ketzerei im ältesten Christentum*, Beiträge zur historische Theologie 10 (Tübingen: Mohr, 1933). The first edition remained relatively unknown outside of Germany. Only the 1964 second edition of this book was translated into English: Walter Bauer, *Orthodoxy and Heresy in Earliest Christianity*, ed. Robert A. Kraft and Gerhard Krodel, 2nd ed. (Philadelphia, PA: Fortress, 1971).
17. A good introduction to Bauer's work and influence can be found in David W. Jorgensen, 'Approaches to Orthodoxy and Heresy in the Study of Early Christianity', *Religion Compass* 11, no. 7–8 (2017): 1–14, doi:10.1111/rec3.12227.

the unadulterated gospel' with them. Later 'true Christians blinded by [Satan] abandon the pure doctrine', but ultimately the 'right belief' wins out.[18] Bauer fundamentally questioned this understanding of history and – to quote the first sentence of the foreword to the second edition – argued that 'in earliest Christianity, orthodoxy and heresy do not stand in relation to one another as primary to secondary, but in many regions heresy is the original manifestation of Christianity'.[19] Bauer's phrasing here highlights how this conception of early Christianity intersects with the concerns of this book: heresy is framed as derivative and secondary, orthodoxy is original and primary.

While most of the details of Bauer's work have been challenged, 'Bauer's central insights ... are now accepted as the basis for understanding Christianity in the early centuries'.[20] Paul Hartog summarizes Bauer's argument as:

1) In many geographical regions, what came to be deemed as 'heresy' was the original form of Christianity. 2) In many locales, the 'heretical' adherents often outnumbered the 'orthodox' adherents. 3) As one form of Christianity among many, 'orthodoxy' suppressed 'heretical' competitors, often through ecclesiastical machinations and coercive tactics, and especially through the powerful influence of the Roman church. 4) The 'orthodox' parties then revised the church's collective memory by claiming that their views had always been the accepted norm.[21]

Basically, Bauer portrays early Christianity as loosely connected communities with competing interpretations, which in hindsight have been refigured – or to use fan parlance *retconned*[22] – to allow for one interpretation to always have been the original and correct one. Bauer's first two points relate strongly to Busse's examination of how fan groups originate. Let me examine these two first, before looking at Bauer's last two points.

Bauer argues, simply put, that heresy is not formed by a group splitting off from an original, orthodox group, but that these heresies always existed from the earliest Christian communities. This is what Busse argues about fans interacting with texts: that they create idiosyncratic readings which become influential for themselves, and naturally form communities. She reflects that 'fans spontaneously articulate their reader responses in writing, and they offer myriad interpretations

---

18. Bauer, *Orthodoxy and Heresy in Earliest Christianity*, xxiii–xxiv.
19. Georg Strecker, introduction to Bauer, *Orthodoxy and Heresy in Earliest Christianity*, xi.
20. David Brakke, *The Gnostics: Myth, Ritual, and Diversity in Early Christianity* (Cambridge, MA: Harvard University Press, 2010), 6.
21. Paul A. Hartog, 'Introduction', in *Orthodoxy and Heresy in Early Christian Contexts: Reconsidering the Bauer Thesis*, ed. Paul A. Hartog (Cambridge: James Clarke, 2015), 2.
22. The concept 'retcon', or retroactive continuity, is probably most well-known in the context of comic books, were later installments of a series adjust, supplement or even contradict earlier established canon.

that … are shared by a sizable number of readers'.²³ These communities do not form by a group of people disagreeing with a commonly accepted, orthodox reading, and looking for an alternative, heretical one. As Busse demonstrates, the idiosyncrasies and backgrounds of readers create these readings, and communities form. Inside a community there is a tendency to maintain the status quo of what brought the community together, which is done by repetition of shared interpretation: 'any time a shared interpretation reverberates through the community, it is repeated and becomes reinforced'.²⁴ As shared interpretations are repeated – in fan communities through fan fiction and other fan products, in early Christianity through writings, liturgies, sermons, and art – these naturally become more normative. Each new work exists as part of an ever-growing collection of canon. Busse explains that 'as more stories appear within a certain community, fans read and write against not just the source text and what they themselves bring to it via their personal interpretations but against a vast corpus of other fan fiction'.²⁵ As these communities form and develop, they develop community norms that 'restrict individual readings'.²⁶ These norms are more than just an agreed upon interpretation, but consist of the totality of fandom: producing and consuming fan productions, commenting, sharing, gifting.²⁷ In this respect they are extremely similar to how David Brakke, building on Bauer's thesis, portrays the 'cohesion' of early Christian groups, as 'not just a function of shared ideas; it was also the effect of such practices as repeated rituals, exchange of letters and gifts, and patronage'.²⁸

So far, this discussion has been focussed on internal forces, on each individual community of mostly like-minded fans or Christians. But these communities also co-exist and – in some respects – compete on a larger scale. Here we return to the third and fourth parts of Bauer's thesis, that ultimately one community ruled them all. Though Bauer's ideas of competition or even differentiation between groups of Christians have come to be increasingly criticized,²⁹ 'boundaries among early Christian groups', Brakke argues, 'may have been porous and in constant need of reassertion, but sometimes they did exist'.³⁰ Some early Christians called other

---

23. Busse, *Framing Fan Fiction*, 109.

24. Busse, *Framing Fan Fiction*, 113.

25. Busse, *Framing Fan Fiction*, 113.

26. Busse, *Framing Fan Fiction*, 116.

27. Karen Hellekson, 'A Fannish Field of Value: Online Fan Gift Culture', *Cinema Journal* 48 (2009): 113–18, doi:10.1353/cj.0.0140.

28. Brakke, *The Gnostics*, 15.

29. See, for example, Paul A. Hartog, ed., *Orthodoxy and Heresy in Early Christian Contexts: Reconsidering the Bauer Thesis* (Cambridge: James Clarke, 2015), doi:10.2307/j.ctt1cgfl4m; Brakke, *The Gnostics*, 6; Michel Desjardins, 'Bauer and Beyond: On Recent Scholarly Discussions of Αἵρεσις in the Early Christian Era', *Second Century: A Journal of Early Christian Studies* 8, no. 2 (1991): 65–82; Daniel J. Harrington, 'The Reception of Walter Bauer's *Orthodoxy and Heresy in Earliest Christianity* during the Last Decade', *Harvard Theological Review* 73, no. 1–2 (1980): 289–98, doi:10.1017/S0017816000002170.

30. Brakke, *The Gnostics*, 15.

Christians heretics, and their thoughts and writings were deemed heretical. Again, this reflects contemporary fan communities. Busse cites Stanley Fish in her discussion of how fan communities view one another: 'the assumption in each community will be that the other is not perceiving the "true text," but the truth will be that each perceives the text (or texts) its interpretive strategy demands and calls into being'.[31] As each community interprets the text in their own idiosyncratic way, they assume that their way is the only (correct) way. Any reading that falls outside the norms of the group is thus automatically seen to be incorrect, and therefore heretical. It is these competing truths that are key to the struggles between both fan and Christian communities, they 'can easily cause conflicts, online arguments, and even flame wars when the respective supporters differ sharply over acceptable readings of the source texts'.[32] Busse's invocation of fan term 'flame war', for a prolonged exchange of angry or even abusive messages in an online forum, demonstrates how strong competition can be between two groups that both feel their interpretation is the only correct, canonical one.

Derek Johnson has analysed competition between interpretative communities in detail. 'Divergent fan interests', he argues, 'cannot ... be met by any singular, canonical iteration'.[33] The diversity of fan groups with competing interests ultimately requires a diversity of canonical interpretations. Thus, antagonism between groups with competing interpretations is constitutive to interpretive communities, including groups of fans and Christians. Calling intracommunity rivalry 'fantagonism', he argues that these 'ongoing struggles for discursive dominance' are at the very core of fan communities and fan identity.[34] Fans are passionate about their fandom, which revolves around their and their community's engagement with canon. From this passion arises the necessity of defending that engagement with and that interpretation of canon. It is core to the fan identity. When many sides of a debate all define their own interpretation as the only correct one, they define 'true fan' as 'one prescribed evaluative relationship to the text'.[35] Thus they link one's very identity as a fan to a certain interpretation, and police the identity.

As interpretative communities debate the meaning of the text, usually a '"commonsense" consensus' is found that spans fandom as a whole.[36] This means

---

31. Busse, *Framing Fan Fiction*, 109–10. Busse is citing Stanley Fish, *Is There a Text in This Class? The Authority of Interpretive Communities* (Cambridge, MA: Harvard University Press, 1980), 171–72.

32. Busse, *Framing Fan Fiction*, 111.

33. Derek Johnson, 'Fantagonism: Factions, Institutions, and Constitutive Hegemonies of Fandom', in *Fandom: Identities and Communities in a Mediated World*, ed. Jonathan Gray, Cornel Sandvoss, and C. Lee Harrington, 2nd ed. (New York: New York University Press, 2017), 370, doi:10.18574/nyu/9781479845453.003.0025.

34. Johnson, 'Fantagonism', 370.

35. Johnson, 'Fantagonism', 374.

36. Johnson, 'Fantagonism', 375.

that one group of fans' idiosyncratic interpretation has become normative for the entire fandom. Pointing out that a unified interpretation requires policing, Johnson argues that 'alternative positions and tastes must somehow be silenced so that divergent interests within a community can be unified as hegemonic interpretative consensus'.[37] As a hegemonic interpretation becomes seen as commonsense, other interpretations are no longer welcome. Dissidents either fall in line or are forced to leave the community. Thus, to use the terms common in Christianity, orthodoxy has been created and those who disagree are deigned to be heretics.

Johnson's portrayal of fantagonism as a fundamental aspect of fannish identity is extremely similar to that found in early Christianity. Take, for example, how Matthijs den Dulk places antagonism towards rival theologies at the very core of the writings of early Christian author Justin Martyr (c. 100–165):

> Justin's *Dialogue with Trypho* sits at the crossroads of various discursive developments central to the formation of early Christianity. At the time of its composition in the mid-second century CE, many of the constitutive parts of what would eventually become 'orthodox' Christianity were still being negotiated and the boundaries between Christianity and Judaism as well as between various rival 'Christianities' remained in flux and permeable. ... Justin is arguing for a particular interpretation and positioning of Christianity vis-à-vis Judaism, and he is doing so in constant negotiation with rival Christian theologies. He develops his particular account of Christianity's relation to Jewish as well as Greco-Roman philosophical traditions in response to, and with a constant eye on, Christian opponents who construed these relations very differently. Justin's concern with such 'other' Christians ... has deeply impacted the *Dialogue*.[38]

Den Dulk's description of both second century Christianity and Justin Martyr's discursive goals resonate strongly with Johnson's concept of fantagonism. Justin's theological position is 'taken in opposition',[39] in almost exactly the same way Johnson argues contemporary fan positions are assumed. While for contemporary fans these factions are other fans and producers,[40] for Justin these factions are other Christians, Jewish communities, and Greco-Roman philosophers. As Den Dulk argues, core to Justin Martyr's *Dialogue with Trypho* is the opposition between Justin's interpretation of Christian texts and competing interpretations: 'at the heart of the *Dialogue* is Justin's attempt to demonstrate the truth of his claims

---

37. Johnson, 'Fantagonism', 372.

38. Matthijs den Dulk, *Between Jews and Heretics: Refiguring Justin Martyr's Dialogue with Trypho*, Routledge Studies in the Early Christian World (Abingdon: Routledge, 2018), 139, doi:10.4324/9781351243490.

39. Derek Johnson, 'Fantagonism, Franchising, and Industry Management of Fan Privilege', in *The Routledge Companion to Media Fandom*, ed. Suzanne Scott and Melissa A. Click (New York: Routledge, 2018), 397, doi:10.4324/9781315637518-47.

40. See Johnson, 'Fantagonism', 375–83.

about Jesus *on the basis of Scripture*'.[41] As Justin creates these truth claims, he embarks on a long 'process of creating a unified Christian identity',[42] which Bauer identified as ultimately the orthodox position. Absolutely vital to this process is Justin's 'invention and implementation of the orthodoxy–heresy binary'.[43] As Justin places interpretive communities into these stigmatized categories, we can recognize that early Christianity was similar to how Johnson portrays contemporary fandom 'as a hegemonic struggle over interpretation and evaluation'.[44] In this struggle alternate voices need to be silenced and Justin does so by stigmatizing others as heretics, whom he tells us – in language not unsuited for a flame war – are blaspheming atheists, and impious, unjust lawbreakers (*Dialogue with Trypho* 35.5). Indeed, Justin's heretics are 'among the most "urgent" kinds of "other," because ... deviance of the "heretic" is of such a nature that it precludes the possibility of a person's ongoing membership in a group ... being a "heretic" and being a "Christian" are mutually exclusive'.[45] In this way Justin seeks to, to borrow Johnson's description of contemporary fandom, 'install certain evaluations as hegemonic common sense through antagonistic, intracommunity discourse'.[46] Furthermore, as Den Dulk argues, Justin's work seeks to argue that this antagonist discourse is a useful method of policing theological interpretation among early Christians. Justin sets out to 'to convince [his audience] of the expediency and feasibility of this aggressive response to self-identified Christians whose views differed from his own'.[47] In arguing for his canon, his interpretation of Christianity, Justin creates and enforces a new category of (non-)Christian: the heretic.

As Christian interpretative communities vie for dominance in the canon debate, we should once again return to the politics of the issue. Authority is used and even a new category of (non-)Christian is created in order to centre a certain unified interpretation over the multivocality of reality. In her discussion of canon in a contemporary fandom and Jewish and Christian canons, Meredith Warren argues that 'because canonical literature becomes so based on reader-response and the support of a community, the difference between canon and "uncanon" is a difference in power'.[48] Though certain aspects of Bauer's thesis have been challenged, this discussion reminds us that the communal orthodoxy that arose in Christianity was indeed the outcome of power and politics. Just as contemporary media conglomerates work to 'identify clearly which texts are considered part of the "real" imaginary world and that are discarded by the storyworlds' "authoritative"

41. den Dulk, *Between Jews and Heretics*, 52.
42. den Dulk, *Between Jews and Heretics*, 2.
43. den Dulk, *Between Jews and Heretics*, 2.
44. Johnson, 'Fantagonism', 370.
45. den Dulk, *Between Jews and Heretics*, 106.
46. Johnson, 'Fantagonism', 375.
47. den Dulk, *Between Jews and Heretics*, 143.
48. Meredith Warren, 'My OTP: Harry Potter Fanfiction and the Old Testament Pseudepigrapha', *Scriptura* 8 (2006): 64.

center',[49] ancient Christians did the same. 'It takes power', concludes Warren, 'to establish a canon as closed ... It took many centuries of forceful writing and even more forceful treatment of "heretics" to stamp out heterodox canons in Christianity'.[50] Though, of course, no matter the force used, this has never actually been successful – the heteroglossic reality endures. In the next section I will examine this process of policing the boundaries of Christianity, of creating heretics and excluding them, and gatekeeping the community.

Heretics, Gatekeeping and Bad Fans

The multiplicity of interpretations and interpretative communities in constant (f)antagonism necessitates the creation and policing of boundaries. These boundaries, as Judith Fathallah argues, 'are always in tension', which is why 'all fandoms engage in gatekeeping'.[51] This practice occurs when 'a group member determines the conditions upon which group membership is contingent, often to keep out those considered undesirable'.[52] Justin Martyr's 'heresiological approach',[53] discussed in the previous section, is an ancient example of the same process. By calling some Christians 'heretics', Justin indicates that they do not belong in his interpretative community. This derogatory name, I argue, maps onto the concept of a Bad Fan in contemporary fan circles.

The academic concept of a Bad Fan, as the counterpart to a Good Fan, finds its origins in Matt Hills's influential monograph *Fan Cultures*.[54] In this book, Hills examines discourses in both fan cultures and fan studies, 'cautioning against repetitive moral dualisms – fans versus producers, fans versus academics, active audiences versus passive consumers'.[55] Reacting to Jenkins's original positive reframing of typically maligned fans,[56] Hills problematizes the framing of the discourse. He argues

---

49. Dan Hassler-Forest, 'The Politics of World Building: Heteroglossia in Janelle Monáe's Afrofuturist WondaLand', in *World Building. Transmedia, Fans, Industries*, ed. Marta Boni, Transmedia: Participatory Culture and Media Convergence (Amsterdam University Press, 2017), 381, doi:10.5117/9789089647566/ch21.

50. Warren, 'My OTP', 64.

51. Judith Fathallah, '"BEING A FANGIRL OF A SERIAL KILLER IS NOT OK": Gatekeeping Reddit's True Crime Community', *New Media & Society*, 2022, 1–2, doi:10.1177/14614448221138768.

52. Courtney N. Plante et al., '"Get out of My Fandom, Newbie": A Cross-Fandom Study of Elitism and Gatekeeping in Fans', *Journal of Fandom Studies* 8, no. 2 (2020): 125, doi:10.1386/jfs_00013_1.

53. den Dulk, *Between Jews and Heretics*, 143.

54. Matt Hills, *Fan Cultures* (London: Routledge, 2002).

55. Rukmini Pande, *Squee from the Margins: Fandom and Race*, Fandom & Culture (Iowa City, IA: University of Iowa Press, 2018), 3.

56. See pp. 30–32.

that when Jenkins attempts to overcome the 'stereotypical conception of the fan as emotionally unstable, socially maladjusted, and dangerously out of sync with reality',[57] he creates a 'moral dualism' where 'the "good" fan is cleansed of aberrant psychology while the "bad" non-fan responsible for reproducing negative stereotypes of fandom' is pathologized instead.[58] In other words, as Jenkins tries to argue that the fans he examines are 'good', he simply shifts the common stereotypes used against fans onto others, who become 'bad'. As Hills continues to examine this shifting of moral pathologization, he notes that this is prevalent inside of fandoms as well. Examining *Twilight* fandom,[59] he demonstrates the same 'pathologizing stereotypes of fans' but this time the stereotypes are enforced 'by fans' themselves.[60] Hills shows that some fans use common stereotypes of fans against other fans to exclude them from their community. Some fans are 'repurposing ... negative fan stereotypes' for gatekeeping purposes.[61]

A key issue here, as evidenced by the weaponization of fan stereotypes against certain fans, is the idea that certain fan behaviours make the fandom look bad. Fans behaving like stereotypical fans works against the counternarrative that tries to redeem fans' image. Kathryn Dunlap and Carissa Wolf note a frequently used phrase in this context 'Get out of my fandom, you make my fandom look stupid'.[62] Fan gatekeeping, on the surface, takes the form of 'accusing others of bringing fandom into disrepute'.[63] The policing of the members of fandom appear to serve – at the surface – to maintain a certain reputation for the fandom. This reflects the reality of heresiology in early Christianity. Geoffrey Smith, in his analysis of heresy catalogues in early Christianity, concludes that 'heresiological efforts likely grow out of the insecure suspicion that those who are not properly informed might confuse followers of Jesus for Jews or philosophers'.[64] These thinkers, like fan

---

57. Henry Jenkins, *Textual Poachers: Television Fans & Participatory Culture* (London: Routledge, 1992), 13.

58. Hills, *Fan Cultures*, xxiv.

59. *Twilight* started as a novel by Stephanie Meyer in 2005. The book is a teen romance novel, where some characters (including the major love interests) are vampires and werewolves. Three sequels followed in the next few years, and two more, a decade later. The books were made into five blockbuster films (2008–2012).

60. Matt Hills, '"Twilight" Fans Represented in Commercial Paratexts and Inter-Fandoms: Resisting and Repurposing Negative Fan Stereotypes', in *Genre, Reception, and Adaptation in the 'Twilight' Series*, ed. Anne Morey, Ashgate Studies in Childhood, 1700 to the Present (London: Routledge, 2016), 121, doi:10.4324/9781315584331-8.

61. Hills, '"Twilight" Fans Represented', 126.

62. Kathryn Dunlop and Carissa Wolf, 'Fans Behaving Badly: Anime Metafandom, Brutal Criticism, and the Intellectual Fan', *Mechademia* 5 (2010): 279.

63. Fathallah, 'BEING A FANGIRL', 3.

64. Geoffrey S. Smith, *Guilt by Association: Heresy Catalogues in Early Christianity* (Oxford: Oxford University Press, 2014), 175, doi:10.1093/acprof:oso/9780199386789.001.0001.

gatekeepers, *appear* to be concerned about the public reputation of their religious group, and call those they think bring the group into disrepute 'heretics' to signal their exclusion from the community. Den Dulk gives useful examples of this same concern in his discussion of Justin's *Dialogue with Trypho*, under the heading 'the poisonous influence of the "heretics"'.[65] He notes Justin's argument that one of the reasons many Jews have not accepted Christianity is because they have encountered the wrong type of Christians. Justin specifically highlights ideas as heretical that would have been offensive to Jewish believers, such as the eating of meat sacrificed to idols (*Dialogue with Trypho* 35.1) and blaspheming the God of Abraham, Isaac and Joseph (*Dialogue with Trypho* 80.4). Den Dulk argues that 'eating such meat was anathema to most Jews, and their association of such practices with Christian teaching would certainly have contributed to the disrepute in which the Christian message was held'.[66] In other words, Justin accuses other Christians of being Bad Fans, who bring the fandom into disrepute.

At the surface, gatekeeping often takes place on the basis of perceived public opinion and reputation, yet further analysis shows that there are other forces underlying this gatekeeping. A core aspect of negative fan stereotypes is gendering and infantilizing their behaviours. Jenkins listed these as key aspects of fan stereotypes – they are 'feminized and/or desexualized' and 'infantile, emotionally and intellectually immature'.[67] And other researchers emphasized that it is exactly these aspects that are weaponized to gatekeep fan communities. Hills demonstrates that older, predominantly male fans excluded young, female fans of *Twilight* from fan communities, and called this 'gender plus', that is, 'gender plus age or generation'.[68] Busse refers to gatekeeping along the same lines in fandoms of *The Beatles* and boy bands: fans must not be 'too attached, too obsessed, too invested … and all too often such affect is criticized for being too girly or too juvenile'.[69] Fathallah's research into fans of emo music and true crime enthusiasts emphasized the same aspects: 'denigration and distaste for feminine-coded behaviours associated with physicality, sexuality and excess of emotion' for the music fans, and 'maintaining masculinist gendered norms' for the crime fans.[70] Indeed, this gendered dismissal of certain fans is so ubiquitous that a shorthand has been created: 'fake geek girl', with the term 'girl' serving to both feminize and infantilize.[71]

---

65. den Dulk, *Between Jews and Heretics*, 80–81.
66. den Dulk, *Between Jews and Heretics*, 80–81.
67. Jenkins, *Textual Poachers*, 10.
68. Hills, '"Twilight" Fans Represented', 123.
69. Kristina Busse, 'Geek Hierarchies, Boundary Policing, and the Gendering of the Good Fan', *Participations: Journal of Audience and Reception Studies* 10, no. 1 (2013): 76.
70. Fathallah, 'BEING A FANGIRL', 3.
71. See, for example, Suzanne Scott, *Fake Geek Girls: Fandom, Gender, and the Convergence Culture Industry*, Critical Cultural Communication (New York: New York University Press, 2019).

Infantilizing Fans

Let me focus on infantilization first. Matt Hills, as briefly mentioned above, discusses the reactions of established horror and vampire fans to the rise of *Twilight* fandom, which mainly consisted of teenage girls.[72] Media often portrayed these fans as rabid, fevered, and hysterical,[73] and many fans felt that these 'feral' *Twilight* fans were invading 'their' fan spaces. Add to this that established fans saw the *Twilight* films as 'a "bad" vampire text',[74] which was 'facile and banal',[75] and it is easy to see that these newer fans were denigrated by various groups from many points of view. A key issue in how established fans reacted these newer fans, besides the feminization and pathologization of these fans' emotional attachment, was the age politics. Hills argues that by using the term 'feral' with respect to these fan's fandom, the implication was made that they were 'untutored and unsocialized as a result of age and newness to the scene'.[76] Senior fans felt that these new fans needed to mature and grow up before they could take part in fan communities. Describing this view of the female *Twilight* fan, Lisa Bode summarizes that 'her movement to adulthood will bring appropriate adult tastes and desires ... she will both come to make distinctions between good and bad vampire texts, and leave *Twilight* behind'.[77] The resonances this has with Paul's iconic sentence chastising the church in Corinth are plain: 'When I was a child, I spoke like a child, I thought like a child, I reasoned like a child; when I became an adult, I put an end to childish ways' (1 Corinthians 13:11).

Other examples of infantilization are not hard to find in early Christianity, but let me remain in Corinth. Near the end of the first century the Roman bishop Clement wrote a letter to that church in Corinth, apparently to address recent upheaval there. 'The church in Corinth', summarizes Bart Ehrman, 'had experienced a turnover in leadership, which the author of the letter considered a heinous grab for power by a group of jealous upstarts, who had deposed the ruling group of presbyters and assumed control of the church for themselves.'[78] Ehrman's use of 'jealous upstarts' hints at the age dynamics at play here, especially when we consider that presbyter is simply the transliteration of the Greek word for senior or elder.[79]

---

72. Hills, '"Twilight" Fans Represented'.

73. Jacqueline Marie Pinkowitz, '"The Rabid Fans That Take [Twilight] Much Too Seriously": The Construction and Rejection of Excess in Twilight Antifandom', *Transformative Works and Cultures* 7 (2011), doi:10.3983/twc.2011.0247.

74. Hills, '"Twilight" Fans Represented', 124.

75. Lisa Bode, 'Transitional Tastes: Teen Girls and Genre in the Critical Reception of Twilight', *Continuum* 24, no. 5 (2010): 716, doi:10.1080/10304312.2010.505327.

76. Hills, '"Twilight" Fans Represented', 124.

77. Bode, 'Transitional Tastes', 716.

78. Apostolic Fathers, *The Apostolic Fathers I*, trans. Bart D. Ehrman, Loeb Classical Library 24 (Cambridge, MA: Harvard University Press, 2003), 18.

79. Consider John Barclay's analysis of the usage of elder in this work. 'Even if the term *presbuteros* refers to an "office", it is clear that only "older" people are expected to wield this

In Corinth, similar to contemporary fan spaces, senior members of the church felt disenfranchised by actions of a younger group. 'Apparently a group of younger members', explains Theodore Bergren, 'had succeeded in marginalizing ... some of the older members'.[80] It is generally assumed in scholarship that there was a leadership coup of sorts in the Corinthian church, that is, that Clement's letter represents a fair description of events.[81] Yet, the comparison with how established fans felt disenfranchised by the existence of *Twilight* fans may cast some doubts on that assumption.

In the case of *Twilight*, established (horror) fans felt threatened by the rise of *Twilight* fandom consisting of a different demographic: the new fans were generally young and female. As the demographic of fan spaces significantly changed both in age and gender, long-standing fans felt disenfranchised.[82] At the most iconic annual fan convention in San Diego, they began to produce 'Twilight ruined Comic-Con signs and t-shirts' to protest these changes.[83] In other spaces, on and off-line, anti-*Twilight* propaganda rose, including entire websites devoted to *Twilight* anti-fandom.[84] Of course *Twilight* didn't ruin Comic-Con – it's bigger and more popular than ever – but that narrative remains. Probably because the event has changed. Suzanne Scott, in *Fake Geek Girls*, discusses this phenomenon.[85] She describes the common narrative that 'the invasion of properties like *Twilight* and *Glee* (both marked by adolescent female fan bases) [are] key signifiers of "How

authority, for the corresponding injunction is to "the younger" ... which is not a junior "office", but an age-category, the younger people in the churches ... It is not quite clear here whether the *presbuteroi* represent an informal age-group or a formal office. But that suits Clement's rhetoric well: respect for the office of "elder" is boosted by its association with "old age", while respect for the older members of the congregation is boosted by their association in nomenclature with the emerging office of "elder"'. John M. G. Barclay, 'There Is Neither Old Nor Young? Early Christianity and Ancient Ideologies of Age', *New Testament Studies* 53, no. 2 (2007): 235, doi:10.1017/S0028688507000136.

80. Theodore A. Bergren, *1 Clement: A Reader's Edition* (Washington, D.C.: Catholic University of America Press, 2020), vii, doi:10.2307/j.ctv104tb3c.be

81. David G. Horrell, *The Social Ethos of the Corinthian Correspondence: Interests and Ideology from 1 Corinthians to 1 Clement*, Studies of the New Testament and Its World (Edinburgh: T & T Clark, 1996), 244–50.

82. Melissa A. Click, Jennifer Stevens Aubrey, and Elizabeth Behm-Morawitz, 'Introduction', in *Bitten by Twilight: Youth Culture, Media and the Vampire Franchise*, ed. Melissa A. Click, Jennifer Stevens Aubrey, and Elizabeth Behm-Morawitz, Mediated Youth 14 (New York: Peter Lang, 2010), 6.

83. Jessica Sheffield and Elyse Merlo, 'Biting Back: Twilight Anti-Fandom and the Rhetoric of Superiority', in *Bitten by Twilight: Youth Culture, Media and the Vampire Franchise*, ed. Melissa A. Click, Jennifer Stevens Aubrey, and Elizabeth Behm-Morawitz, Mediated Youth 14 (New York: Peter Lang, 2010), 207.

84. Pinkowitz, 'The Rabid Fans That Take [Twilight] Much Too Seriously'.

85. Scott, *Fake Geek Girls*, 66–68.

the Nerds Lost Comic-Con"', and cites a *Vanity Fair* article from 2017 that claims 'since *Twilight* invaded in 2008, the San Diego Comic-Con fandom has been exploited and overrun'.[86] Again, note the words used – these young female fans are portrayed as invading this fan space and overrunning the established fans. Showing that these opinions are facetious, Scott argues that by falsely maintaining this narrative, even ten years later, these publications validate the bias that incited the disdain of teenage *Twilight* fans. Additionally, even publications 'that actively attempted to celebrate female fans ... position women as an unexpected ... fan demographic, emphasizing novelty and anthropological discovery', rather than a traditionally disenfranchised part of fan communities.[87] Through all these publications, the conclusion is reinforced that those original, established fans protesting these new, young, female fans were right all along – *Twilight* did indeed ruin Comic-Con.

Returning to Clement's letter to the church in Corinth, we can ask similar questions to those Suzanne Scott brought up. Clement addresses what he sees as the issue in the very first section:

> We realize that we have been slow to turn our attention to the matters causing disputes among you, loved ones, involving that vile and profane faction that is alien and foreign to God's chosen people – a faction stoked by a few reckless and headstrong persons to such a pitch of madness that your venerable and renowned reputation, worthy of everyone's love, has been greatly slandered. (1 Clement 1.1)[88]

Clement paints a picture of a (small) group roughly disturbing the status quo in the church. This group is strongly Othered and pathologized, while the establishment is celebrated and complimented. Clement's praise continues when he describes the status quo a few lines further with many positive terms – such as having 'virtuous and stable faith', 'temperate and gentle piety', 'magnificent hospitality', and 'perfect and unwavering knowledge' (1 Clement 1.2). Out of this seemingly utopic state of being, resentment arose:

> All glory and enlargement was given to you ... From this came jealousy and envy, strife and faction, persecution and disorderliness, war and captivity. And so the dishonorable rose up against the honorable, the disreputable against the reputable, the senseless against the sensible, the young against the old. (1 Clement 3.2)

Clement builds up a series of four opposites (borrowing from Isaiah 3:5). The dishonorable, disreputable, senseless, young people rose up against the established

---

86. Scott, *Fake Geek Girls*, 67.
87. Scott, *Fake Geek Girls*, 68.
88. The translations of 1 Clement are a lightly edited version of Bart D. Ehrman, ed., *The Apostolic Fathers*, Loeb Classical Library 24 (Cambridge, MA: Harvard University Press, 2003), which also contains the Greek text.

order, against a group of people that represented everything these youngsters were not ... at least according to Clement. The opponents to the status quo are not just described with negative characteristics, they are infantilized as well. It is rather important to note that Clement doesn't address why part of the church rebelled against the other part at all. Bergren states that 'the issue or issues that motivated the rebellion are uncertain; the letter is conspicuously reticent in this regard'.[89] Clement does not appear to be interested in counteracting interpretations that he disagrees with. He does not dispel heretical teachings; he simply does not want the church community to be in the situation it currently is.

The identities of both the newcomers and established leaders remain veiled. David Horrell argues that it's safe to assume that 'the deposed elders were among the socially prominent members of the community, heads of households' and that 'it is probable that the rebels were those of lower social position'.[90] In other words, socially marginalized people were those standing up against those with more hegemonic positions. Clement seems to openly admit – and praise! – ongoing marginalization in the church. In the days before the rebellion, submission was expected from young people (and women):

> For you used to act impartially in all that you did, and you walked according to the ordinances of God, submitting yourselves to your leaders and rendering all due honor to those who were older among you. You instructed your young people to think moderate and respectful thoughts. You directed women to accomplish all things with a blameless, respectful, and pure conscience, dutifully loving their husbands. And you taught them to run their households respectfully, living under the rule of submission, practicing discretion in every way. (1 Clement 3.3)

Women were directed to be blameless, respectful and pure of conscience, young people were told to think moderate thoughts, and everyone was to render due honour to and submit themselves to the older members.[91] The young, argues John Barclay, 'are classed alongside the "disreputable" and the "senseless" – presumably because they lack the age-entitlement to honour and wisdom.'[92] And, drawing the analogy from *Twilight* fandom, disenfranchised elders are holding up signs that these new, young – 'frenzied and foolish' (1 Clement 46.7, 47.6) – people have 'ruined' Corinth. If only we could go back to Comic-Con before all these young fans showed up. 'Let us honor the elderly' commands Clement, 'Let us discipline our youth in the reverential fear of God; Let us set our wives along the straight path that leads to the good' (1 Clement 21.6). Or, to quote Horrell, 'Clement's primary concern is that the *church* should be a harmonious and peaceful community, but his instructions require that this be attained through the maintenance of the established

---

89. Bergren, *1 Clement*, vii.
90. Horrell, *Social Ethos*, 250.
91. See also 1 Clement 21.6–8, see Horrell, *Social Ethos*, 264.
92. Barclay, 'There Is Neither Old Nor Young?', 236.

hierarchical roles'.[93] Clement's letter works to further the same goal that the articles about *Twilight* and Comic-Con do: it serves to validate the bias that created the narrative in the first place.

Clement proposes a solution to the problem that further resonates with the way established fans reacted to *Twilight* fandom. Throughout the letter he cites his care for the church community, with a 'repeated insistence upon harmony, order, humility, and love'.[94] Like fan gatekeepers, he is ostensibly interested in the community, and thus his solution is the usual one for heretics and Bad Fans: he wants them to leave. They are making his fandom look stupid. Throughout the letter he infantilizes and pathologizes these newcomers, and finally, citing care for the church community, he suggests these young members go away. He has even written their farewell speech:

> If I am the cause of faction, strife, and schisms, I will depart; I will go wherever you wish and do what is commanded by the congregation. Only allow the flock of Christ to be at peace with the elders who have been appointed. (1 Clement 54.2)

Having brought the community into disrepute – at least from Clement's point of view – these newcomers should leave. Clement's gatekeeping resonates strongly with forces in contemporary fandom. The parallels with fandom highlight the 'iniquities, prejudices, and power relations', reminding us to critically consider the political and rhetorical goals of the authors of the texts we read. Ancient authors, like established fans 'elevate their own cultural status at the expense of pathologizing … hence recirculating negative stereotypes'.[95] As Bode argues for *Twilight* 'references in reviews to girls as a dehumanized swarming mass or as the giggling bearers of complex longing, reveal more about the cultural values and social position of the film reviewer than that of actual adolescent girls'.[96] Clement's letter reveals more about his cultural values and social position than the actual church in Corinth and its young rebels.

Feminizing Fans

Moving from infantilization to feminization, Fathallah's examination of gatekeeping in true crime fandom is most illustrative for our examination of early Christianity. True crime fandom can easily be viewed as highly problematic, from 'girls who

---

93. Horrell, *Social Ethos*, 265.

94. Larry L. Welborn, 'Voluntary Exile as the Solution to Discord in 1 Clement', *Zeitschrift für Antikes Christentum / Journal of Ancient Christianity* 18, no. 1 (2014): 8, doi:10.1515/zac-2014-0002.

95. Hills, '"Twilight" Fans Represented', 127.

96. Bode, 'Transitional Tastes', 717.

profess their love for Ted Bundy and Jeffrey Dahmer, boys who admire the "accomplishments" of Richard "The Nightstalker" Ramirez' to the 'collection of mementoes associated with murder ("murderabilia") [and] tourism of murder sites'.[97] True crime fandom feels the need to constantly gatekeep itself to avoid being associated with these types of fandom. And indeed, it prefers the terminology of 'community' over 'fandom'. Gatekeeping here, like in most fan communities, 'involves one fan accusing another person of making the fandom look bad and insisting that they do not belong'.[98] Ironically, what underlies this issue is that parts of the fandom appear to be afraid that common stereotypes of fans are valid, thus they police the fandom accusing some fans of fulfilling the stereotypes. Because the stereotypes are gendered, the gatekeeping is gendered – but not explicitly so. As the true crime community polices the difference between appropriate academic interest in crime, and inappropriate fannish interest, they end up discouraging 'behaviours and expressions associated with stereotypical femininity'.[99] Though the argument is veiled in discussions of suitability, objectivity and distance, the argument is actually about maintaining accepted gender norms. Ultimately, as Fathallah concludes, 'the Bad Fan is definable in terms of the stereotypes that were once applied to fandom more broadly – feminine, insane, irrational, sexual in the wrong way, hysterical and young'.[100]

Using gender to gatekeep the community was also extremely common in early Christianity. Kimberly Stratton gives several examples of this, including Firmilian, bishop of Cappadocia (died c. 269), who claims that a certain unnamed woman's 'sacraments are invalid because she accomplishes them with demonic rather than divine power'.[101] Just as in the true crime community, the argument is veiled in an authentic concern: demonic power has no place in Christian communities. Firmilian appears to be having a theological discussion, yet the argument itself is actually about gender. Initially he admits that this woman performs rituals according to orthodox practice, and this leads one to wonder how her sacraments use demonic power. 'Given the perceived orthopraxy of her rituals', argues Stratton, 'one has to assume that the single problem with her miracles and sacraments is her sex'.[102] Indeed, in Christianity, the trope of the 'heretical woman' is commonplace,[103]

97. Fathallah, 'BEING A FANGIRL', 3.
98. Plante et al., '"Get out of My Fandom, Newbie"', 125.
99. Fathallah, 'BEING A FANGIRL', 6.
100. Fathallah, 'BEING A FANGIRL', 17.
101. Kimberly B. Stratton, 'The Rhetoric of "Magic" in Early Christian Discourse: Gender, Power and the Construction of "Heresy"', in *Mapping Gender in Ancient Religious Discourses*, ed. Todd Penner and Caroline Vander Stichele, Biblical Interpretation Series 84 (Leiden: Brill, 2006), 113, doi:10.1163/ej.9789004154476.i-582.21.
102. Stratton, 'Rhetoric of Magic', 113.
103. See, e.g. Virginia Burrus, 'The Heretical Woman as Symbol in Alexander, Athanasius, Epiphanius, and Jerome', *Harvard Theological Review* 84, no. 3 (July 1991): 229–48, doi:10.1017/S0017816000024007; Christine Trevett, 'Spiritual Authority and the "Heretical"

and Elizabeth Clark shows many ways in which "'orthodoxy" was secured by aligning female gender and heresy'.[104]

A couple of good examples of aligning gender to heresy can be found in prolific Christian writer Tertullian of Carthage's (c. 160–220) heresiology: *Prescription Against Heretics*. In the second chapter of this work, Tertullian introduces an analogy between heresy and a fever:

> We shouldn't be surprised to find fever amongst the deadly and painful issues that destroy human life. For fever exists. And we shouldn't be surprised that it destroys human life, that is why it exists. The same is true of heresies. While we might be afraid to discover that heresies, which exist to weaken and destroy faith, actually do destroy faith. Instead we should be afraid they exist at all. (*Prescription Against Heretics* 2.1–2)[105]

Tertullian portrays heresy as a powerful message that is designed to attack faith, just like fever attacks the body. He admits that there is no way to obliterate a fever, so we must protect ourselves from it. Heresy must be quarantined so that we can keep safe from it. I'd like to put Tertullian's portrayal of heresy in conversation with how Suzanne Scott discusses misogyny in fan communities, and her suggestion that misogyny in fan communities has 'viral qualities':[106]

> misogyny is viral in the sense that these messages are designed to attack particular, predominantly marginalized bodies, but more to the point, those fans doing the spreading or 'infecting' position themselves as antibodies. Herein lies the paradoxical nature of spreadable misogyny, which strives to virally poison the communal body of fan culture against women, who are themselves presented as a virus that must be quarantined or eradicated.[107]

Scott's argument is that in fan communities misogyny is similar to a virus, with an interesting dichotomy when it comes to the discussion of spreading agent and

---

Woman: Firmilian's Word to the Church in Carthage', in *Portraits of Spiritual Authority*, ed. Jan Willem Drijvers and John Watt, Religions in the Graeco-Roman World 137 (Leiden: Brill, 1999), 45–62, doi:10.1163/9789004295919_004; Jennifer Lassley Knight, 'Herodias, Salomé, and John the Baptist's Beheading: A Case Study of the Topos of the Heretical Woman', *International Social Science Review* 93, no. 1 (2017): 1–15.

104. Elizabeth A. Clark, 'Women, Gender, and the Study of Christian History', *Church History* 70, no. 3 (2001): 414, doi:10.2307/3654496.

105. The translation of *Prescription Against Heretics* is mine. An English translation can be found in Alexander Roberts, James Donaldson, and Cleveland A. Coxe, eds., *Ante-Nicene Fathers 3: Latin Christianity: Its Founder, Tertullian*, Ante-Nicene Fathers 3 (Christian Literature Company, 1885). The Latin can be found in Tertullian, *Traité de la prescription contre les hérétiques*, trans. R. F. Refoulé, Sources chrétiennes 46 (1957; repr., Paris: Cerf, 2006).

106. Scott, *Fake Geek Girls*, 81.

107. Scott, *Fake Geek Girls*, 84.

antibody. Gatekeepers spread misogyny and thus infect communities, but portray themselves as antibodies. Their false narrative, their virus, is that it is women who should be seen as the real threat. Tertullian's portrayal of heresies, of interpretations that he disagrees with, shares much with how Scott describes misogynist gatekeeping in fandom. Tertullian wishes heresies to be quarantined, kept far away from the community, suggesting 'shunning them' (*Prescription Against Heretics* 4.1). He, clearly, is the antibody to these heretical interpretations, and in his several-thousand word book he will demonstrate why.

In places Tertullian's argument against heresy is also explicitly misogynist and gendered. In a well-known passage, Tertullian describes what he feels is going on among the heretics.

> I can't not speak about how the heretics live: so vain, so earthly, so human. No gravitas, no authority, no discipline.... And the heretical woman – so shameless! They are eager to teach, to argue, to exorcize, to heal, maybe even to baptize. Their ordinations are reckless, trifling, wavering. (Tertullian, *Prescription Against Heretics* 41.1,5,6)

Tertullian's gatekeeping here works hard to disenfranchise these people. Their way of life is denigrated through emasculation. They are vain and earthly, without authority and discipline – the opposite of the stoic ideal of masculinity so pervasive in the time.[108] And to make matters worse, while the men are soft and weak, the women are too powerful. 'His outrage', writes Blossom Stefaniw, 'creates heresy out of excess female agency, instantiating an order of knowledge and practice in which a woman must not teach, argue, heal or baptise unless she does so in agreement with him'.[109] Tertullian's policing is supremely gendered. As far as he is concerned heretics, both men and women, do not keep to the accepted gender norms.

A second example of how Tertullian aligns gender with heresy is discussed by Brad Windon.[110] In his definition of heresy, Tertullian mirrors the narrative prevalent before Bauer's work: 'our authorities are the Lord's apostles, who themselves never chose to introduce anything, but faithfully distributed the doctrine they received from Christ to the nations' (Tertullian *Prescription Against*

---

108. Colleen M. Conway, *Behold the Man: Jesus and Greco-Roman Masculinity* (Oxford: Oxford University Press, 2008); Peter-Ben Smit, 'Masculinity and the Bible: Survey, Models, and Perspectives', *Brill Research Perspectives in Biblical Interpretation* 2, no. 1 (2017): 1–97, doi:10.1163/24057657-12340007; Tom de Bruin, 'Joseph the Good and Delicate Man: Masculinity in the *Testaments of the Twelve Patriarchs*', *Lectio Difficilior* (2020).

109. Blossom Stefaniw, 'Masculinity, Historiography, and Uses of the Past: An Introduction', *Journal of Early Christian History* 11, no. 1 (2021): 4, doi:10.1080/2222582X.2021.1931903.

110. Brad Windon, 'The Seduction of Weak Men: Tertullian's Rhetorical Construction of Gender and Ancient Christian "Heresy"', in *Mapping Gender in Ancient Religious Discourses*, ed. Todd Penner and Caroline Vander Stichele, Biblical Interpretation Series 84 (Leiden: Brill, 2006), 457–78, doi:10.1163/ej.9789004154476.i-582.83.

Heretics 6.4). Tertullian claims that his interpretive community maintains the 'true' interpretations of Jesus, handed down through the centuries. Heresy, then, is the introduction of new teachings. In his discussion of heretical introductions, Tertullian gives the example of a heretic he wishes to renounce: Apelles, who was led by the miracles and illusions of a woman named Philumene (*Prescription Against Heretics* 6.5). He, writes Tertullian, 'clung to another woman, the virgin Philumene ... who afterwards became an extreme prostitute. Being overwhelmed by her diabolical spirit, he committed to writing *Revelations* which he had learned from her' (*Prescription Against Heretics* 30.6). There are some extremely obvious gender politics here – Philumene is defamed 'on sexual grounds: though shortly before still a virgin'[111] – but also some more subtle ones. Tertullian's focus is delegitimizing Apelles, the heretic introducing new teachings to the community. He is portrayed as weak, easily overwhelmed, and passive – feminine traits. 'Apelles is depicted', writes Windon, 'as lacking the quintessence of masculinity – self-mastery (both cognitive and physical). He embraces the revelations of Philumene, which are ultimately derived from evil spirits and packaged in the seductive form of a woman'.[112] Tertullian is gatekeeping in the same way as contemporary fan communities, through accusations of stereotypical femininity. Apelles is a Bad Fan, whereas Tertullian is a Good Fan, managing 'his own self-identity as one who exercises the cognitive competence and subsequent self-mastery both to resist the emptiness of seduction and to receive only the "pure doctrine"'.[113] In early Christianity, as in contemporary fandom, 'while gatekeepers often claim to be acting in the name of quality, rationality or other supposedly neutral values, fan gatekeeping is often intensely gendered'.[114]

Though these two examples show female agency among heretics, Tertullian, and other early Christian authors, usually associate female gender with heresy in another way. Silke Petersen has performed statistical analysis of early Christian writings, and concludes that '"heretical" female leaders are all but absent in the patristic sources – at least in the texts of the second and third centuries'.[115] Rather, women are usually associated with heresy because of what she calls the 'seduction stereotype'. Women are gullible and much more likely to be seduced by heresies than men, thus many more women are heretical. Tertullian feels that women succumb to the 'fever' of heresy more easily. But ultimately, 'the issue is not only the defamation of "heresy", but also the preservation of male power by means of a derogatory depiction of women'.[116] Tertullian, like Clement, is gatekeeping his

---

111. Silke Petersen, '"Women" and "Heresy" in Patristic Discourses and Modern Studies', in *Women and Knowledge in Early Christianity*, ed. Ulla Tervahauta et al., Vigiliae Christianae Supplements 144 (Leiden: Brill, 2017), 194, doi:10.1163/9789004344938_011.

112. Windon, 'Seduction of Weak Men', 474.

113. Windon, 'Seduction of Weak Men', 474.

114. Fathallah, 'BEING A FANGIRL', 3.

115. Petersen, 'Women and Heresy', 197.

116. Petersen, 'Women and Heresy', 204.

community to ensure that the current power balance and marginalization remains. Returning to the viral misogyny that Scott describes in contemporary fandom, we see that the misogyny here 'attacks marginalized bodies', and 'strives to virally poison the communal body of fan culture against women'.[117] And Tertullian, spreading viral misogyny, portrays himself as the antibody.[118]

I have explored the tension between the authoritative desire to unify and the hybrid, multivocal nature of both fan and early Christian communities. The creation and policing of the boundaries of interpretative communities is a common practice, which is driven by political forces. The concept of a Bad Fan, seen as the counterpart to a Good Fan, has led to the pathologization of certain fans and the enforcement of negative fan stereotypes by fans themselves. The concern for the public reputation of fandoms, similar to heresiological efforts in early Christianity, often serves as a surface-level justification for gatekeeping. However, further analysis shows that there are other underlying political forces in gatekeeping. Negative fan stereotypes are gendered, and these aspects are weaponized to exclude certain fans from fan communities.[119] While gatekeeping is necessitated by the multiplicity of interpretations among different communities and the constant antagonism between these, the political forces are foregrounded in the gendered dismissal of certain community members and the denigration of feminine-coded behaviours. It is essential to recognize the politics at play here, and the way marginalized identities are weaponized to marginalize texts, interpretations and beliefs.

Conclusions

Early Christians were engaged in discussions of orthodoxy and heresy. In this chapter I explored how fan studies can inform our analyses of these discussions. As

---

117. Scott, *Fake Geek Girls*, 84.

118. There are also antibodies to misogyny in early Christianity. Sarah Parkhouse gives the example of the apocryphal Gospel of Mary, which self-consciously portrays itself as counter to the gender roles and theology that is represented in the 'common sense' hegemonic interpretation. While gender is usually weaponized as a way to police and gatekeep, the gospel specifically undermines gender roles. The male disciples are portrayed as ignorant, whereas Mary has access to hidden teachings. In this way the gospel hits back against gendered gatekeeping, in order to 'oppose the dominant or normative' narratives, claiming that 'were wrong not only about apostolic authority and how to read scripture but also about fundamentals of Jesus's teachings'. Sarah Parkhouse, '"Surely These Are Heterodox Teachings": The Gospel of Mary and Tertullian in Dialogue', in *Telling the Christian Story Differently: Counter-Narratives from Nag Hammadi and Beyond*, ed. Sarah Parkhouse and Francis Watson, The Reception of Jesus in the First Three Centuries 4 (London: T&T Clark, 2020), 93.

119. Though my discussion focussed on gender, a similar argument can be made about race. See, Pande, *Squee from the Margins*.

these early Christians attempt to agree on interpretations of Christianity (i.e. theology) and which texts support these interpretations (i.e. the canon), analogies with fan studies demonstrates that they enter into a dialogical and sociological process. While the process is one of a subjective negotiation between texts, readings and communities, often individuals and their interpretative communities do not necessarily recognize it as such. Individuals do not acknowledge that their readings of texts, their interpretations of canon are subjectively defined. Neither do they appreciate that their readings have become authoritative because they are reinforced by their interpretative community. They assume their reading is the only one, and exclude other readings as incorrect, wrong or heretical. Just as fans claim that their (interpretation of) canon is straight from the author, these Christians each assume that their interpretation is the true interpretation straight from the mind of God and/or the mouth of Jesus, and do not see their role in creating this interpretation. It is these competing truths that are key to the arguments between fan and early Christian communities, causing debates, conflicts, and exclusionary gatekeeping.

Contemporary analyses of how fan communities police and gatekeep canon and canonicity shed productive and useful light on similar debates in early Christianity. As Christian authors attempt to police their single interpretation of Christianity, they forcefully exclude interpretations, texts, and people. In early Christianity this process of gatekeeping, where the opinions of others are denigrated, predominantly takes place through heresiology. Other voices are silenced by stigmatizing them as heretical, and thus a new type of (non-)Christian is invented: the heretic. Such a person, though claiming to be a Christian, is forcefully excluded on account of their interpretations. The discourse here is often one of pathologization. All manner of negative stereotypes are attributed to the other. The Other is feminized and infantilized. Though this gatekeeping process presents itself as objective and unbiased in both fandom and early Christianity, in reality it is anything but. Stereotypes of age and gender are weaponized to exclude undesirable interpretations and people alike.

Chapter 5

HEADCANON, FANON, AND THE CHRISTIAN TRANSMEDIA STORYWORLD: WHY DO DERIVATIVE WORKS MATTER?[1]

Having come to the final chapter of this monograph, I'd like to turn to a more conceptual point. I wish to move the focus from the derivative texts themselves to how we think about these texts and to their enduring influence. Why do these texts matter, and why is it vital that we study them both as derivative texts *and* as authoritative texts? Many Christian Apocrypha were penned centuries after the earliest Christian texts, and they are but one part of a vast and ever-expanding world of Christian writings, liturgy, art, pilgrimage, and other traditions. Inhabiting such a world has complex and far-ranging political implications. In this chapter, I will look at how the experience of inhabiting such a world influences the reception and reading of the earliest texts. Or, to phrase it as a question, how does the existence of parabiblical texts influence (the understanding of) the biblical ones?

After introducing some examples of how influential non-authorized texts can be on audiences, I will introduce theory on so-called 'storyworlds'. I will examine what the implications are of thinking of early Christianity as a storyworld. I will explore the political implications through an engagement with Sarah Iles Johnston's similar interpretive step for Greek mythology, where she speaks of the Greek mythic storyworld.[2] I will extend this exploration by including the thousands of non-written texts that are also part of Christianity's *transmedia* storyworld, and finally explore how this storyworld influences readings of some of the earliest Christian texts. Specifically, I will explore how the Christian storyworld influenced readings of the earliest writings, primarily the Christmas narratives in Matthew

---

1. I'd like to thank the organizers of the *Tracing Global Christianity in Late Antiquity* conference, the Society of Biblical Literature's *Apocrypha and Pseudepigrapha* program unit and the Bible, Critical Theory and Reception Seminar where I presented versions of this chapter. The discussion we had following my paper was extremely useful in developing my ideas! I'm also highly indebted to Kelsie Rodenbiker for her extensive feedback on a later draft of this chapter.

2. Sarah Iles Johnston, *The Story of Myth* (Cambridge, MA: Harvard University Press, 2018).

and Luke.³ Throughout all of this I will demonstrate that when we think of Christianity as a vast storyworld, we can see that ultimately *all* texts are authoritative.

By way of example, let me return for a moment to Anne Rice's book on the life of Jesus. In the early twenty-first-century Christian culture in which she was writing, the Apocrypha are overwhelmingly seen as derivative and non-canonical. Rice at first calls the stories from the Apocrypha 'legends' and 'fanciful'. Explicitly asserting that they are not part of the canonical account of Jesus, she claims that they should not be part of her project, which aims to present 'the Jesus of the Gospels'.⁴ Though she clearly understands the apocryphal gospels to be derivative, she notes:

> I'd stumbled on them very early in my research, in multiple editions, and never forgotten them. And neither had the world. They were fanciful, some of them humorous, extreme to be sure, but they had lived on into the Middle Ages, and beyond. I couldn't get these legends out of my mind. Ultimately I chose to embrace this material, to enclose it within the canonical framework as best I could. I felt there was a deep truth in it, and I wanted to preserve that truth as it spoke to me.⁵

Though she maligns them as not serious historical sources – they are legends: fanciful, humorous, extreme – Rice includes these narratives in her work. Freely admitting their status and compartmentalizing them as non-canonical, she acknowledges that they still influence her reading of canon. Even these *fanciful* legends are authoritative to her, in some way. Though the four canonical Gospels don't mention it, she still imagines that 'Jesus did manifest supernatural powers at an early age'.⁶ Many of her episodes and details about Jesus in her book repeat common parabiblical innovations: the child Jesus makes clay doves and brings them to life, he is accused of killing a person, he is born in a cave, and Salome serves as a midwife – to name but a few.⁷ Her experience of a Christian storyworld, one that goes far beyond the books of the canon, influences her reading and reception of the canon. Indeed, Anne Rice, in her preface to the paperback reprint, defends her use of narratives from the Apocrypha by pointing to this vast world:

---

3. Matthew and Luke are the earliest Christian writings that discuss the birth of Jesus in detail. This should be a relatively uncontested historical claim. Other writings might well be witness to older narratives or traditions – that is hard to judge.
4. Anne Rice, *Christ the Lord: Out of Egypt* (London: Arrow, 2007), 451.
5. Rice, *Christ the Lord*, 451.
6. Rice, *Christ the Lord*, 451–52.
7. See, for a longer list, see p. 3 or Tony Burke, 'Early Christian Apocrypha in Popular Culture', in *The Oxford Handbook of Early Christian Apocrypha*, ed. Andrew F. Gregory et al., Oxford Handbooks (Oxford: Oxford University Press, 2015), 432–33, doi:10.1093/oxfordhb/9780199644117.013.29.

> Since the book was published there has been talk in some circles about my use of 'the apocrypha.' I now feel that 'apocrypha' is a very poor word for the material I used. Apocrypha means too many things to too many people.... I would like to make clear here: the material I used in this novel, pertaining to Our Lord's childhood and the life of His Mother, has nothing, absolutely nothing, to do with these late date Gnostic gospels. Nothing at all. What I used was material that is best referred to as 'early legends' pertaining to the life of Christ—and these legends have indeed been used by Christian artists for two thousand years. These stories have been the source for Christians of devotion.[8]

I cited this same section in Chapter 3 to illustrate how Rice defends her use of these narratives, but here I want to further reflect on the fact that she sees these narratives in a variety of media. In contemporary media studies, as I will discuss, we might call this a transmedia storyworld – a world of interconnected and interdependent narratives engendered by a variety of media. These fannish innovations extending canon, the ones Rice finds in apocryphal narratives and repeats in her book, might be called 'fanon' (a portmanteau of fan and canon) or 'headcanon'. Though fanon and headcanon are not authorized they are authoritative. In this chapter, I will explore these phenomena in conversation with parabiblical texts.

The Power of Headcanon

The subconscious influences of non-canon on canon can be extremely personal. Christian Apocrypha scholar Brandon Hawk – in a blog post on canon and Apocrypha in the Bible and the *Star Wars*[9] universe – describes how the non-canonical *Star Wars Customizable Card Game* affects his consumption of *Star Wars*:[10]

> It's hard to imagine that the details I gleaned from those cards will ever leave my memory, though. Whenever I watch the scene in the Mos Eisley Cantina, my mind recalls details about characters like the Tonnika Sisters (Brea and Senni), Ponda Baba, and Dr. Evazan. They're all headcanon to me.[11]

---

8. Rice, *Christ the Lord*, 462–63.

9. *Star Wars* is a multi-billion-dollar multimedia franchise, currently owned by Disney. It finds its origins in the 1977 film *Star Wars* (retroactively renamed *Star Wars: Episode IV – A New Hope*) created by George Lucas. Lucas's Lucasfilm was the copyright holder for decades, maintaining an ever-increasing transmedia world. The transmedia enterprise includes films, books, videogames, board games, toys, TV shows, and theme park attractions.

10. See pp. 93–102 for my discussion of canon in *Star Wars*.

11. Brandon W. Hawk, 'Canonizing Star Wars', *Brandon W. Hawk* (blog), 1 May 2022, https://brandonwhawk.net/2022/01/05/canonizing-star-wars/.

Referring to extremely minor characters from a single scene in the first *Star Wars* movie, Hawk invokes a fan term for personal interpretations of source texts: 'headcanon'. Here we are talking about elements of the universe that are not canon, not even generally accepted fan interpretations, but much more personal. Headcanon is an interpretation 'by an individual fan that does not have a concrete canonical basis – that is, it's in the fan's head'.[12] Usually headcanon is the invention of a single fan. Sometimes the invention gains traction among other fans, but sometimes it just keeps affecting a single fan's experience of the narrative. Yet though the headcanon is extremely personal, that does not mean it is insignificant. Headcanon, as Hawk explains, fundamentally influences the way a single fan interprets a text, but it also affects the fan works that fan produces. Rice's book on Jesus is affected by her headcanon of Jesus's extra-canonical miracles, and her book shows the evidence of that affective relationship.

In the *Star Wars* fandom there is a recent example of a piece of headcanon becoming hugely influential. On 6 February 2016 Pablo Hidalgo, *Star Wars* fan and LucasFilm employee working on maintaining canon, jokingly tweeted 'That dust that Kylo puts his helmet into? Litter box for Hux's cat, Millicent'.[13] In this tweet, Hildalgo flippantly publicized a personal interpretation about an item in the film *Star Wars: The Force Awakens* (2015): in his interpretation the villainous general Armitage Hux has a cat, Millicent. This interpretation is in no way authorized. No cat appears or is mentioned in the film and there is no reason to expect one exists. Hildalgo is making a joke about set and prop design and the unintentional similarity between Kylo Ren's helmet box and a box of cat litter. Within days there were scores of fan products featuring Hux and Millicent – who is a ginger cat.[14] Seven years later there are thousands of fan fictions featuring Millicent the Cat.[15] This process is important because a made-up event, for which we have no authoritative source, has become part of the material culture of the fandom. The topic I am interested in exploring here is the effect of and ethics associated with this non-authoritarian, non-canonical addition. Millicent might seem like an

---

12. Rukmini Pande, *Squee from the Margins: Fandom and Race*, Fandom & Culture (Iowa City, IA: University of Iowa Press, 2018), 97.

13. The tweet has been removed since then. News articles around the date still preserve the tweet, see e.g. Dunc, 'Pablo Made a Funny and Now General Hux Has a Cat Named Millicent (at Least on Tumblr)', *Club Jade*, 2 August 2016, https://clubjade.net/pablo-made-a-funny-and-now-general-hux-has-a-cat-named-millicent-at-least-on-tumblr/.

14. Dunc, 'Pablo Made'.

15. See, for example, *Club Jade*'s follow-up piece a year after the tweet. Dunc, 'The Continuing Adventures of Millicent the Cat (on Tumblr)', *Club Jade*, 2 June 2017, https://clubjade.net/the-continuing-adventures-of-millicent-the-cat-on-tumblr/. Or more than a thousand fan fictions with a 'Millicent the Cat (Star Wars)' tag on a single fan fiction website *Archive of our Own*, Organization for Transformative Works, https://archiveofourown.org [accessed 15 September 2023].

innocent joke, but as Elaine Tveit points out, the cat humanizes the General Hux,[16] who is obviously 'Hitlerian'.[17] *Star Wars* fandom already has a history of right-wing, white supremacist and neo-Nazi influences,[18] with groups of fans claiming more contemporary instalments promote 'white genocide'.[19] Even though Millicent appears as a funny joke, and the fans engaging with Millicent may not identify with the problematic, right-wing parts of *Star Wars* fandom, she still contributes to a right-wing agenda. Millicent is not canon and fans do not seriously consider her part of the *Star Wars* universe, but she has still become a major part of that universe. And through fanart, fans are able to explore Millicent's role and identity, and look at a different, more human side to the Hux 'the intergalactic Hitler'.[20]

With this in mind, let me quickly reflect on Wilhelm Schneemelcher's editions of the Christian Apocrypha, originally dating from 1964, which are one of the few collections that contain a discussion of the motives that drive the creation and rise of the Apocrypha. He argues that 'the motives which were operative in the origin of the apocrypha cannot be answered in a single sentence', and sets out six 'summary remarks'.[21] The six motives Schneemelcher gives resonate with the discussion in the previous chapters regarding fan creativity and fan fiction. Take for example his second motive, where living traditions are textualized according to generic conventions, which resonates with Coppa's definition of fan fiction from the Introduction;[22] or his fourth motive, 'apocryphal works which no longer have their basis directly in New Testament writings, but are simply interested in individual

16. Elaine Tveit, 'General Hux's Cat Millicent Is Fan Fiction At Its Finest', *Dork Side of the Force*, 2 December 2016, https://dorksideoftheforce.com/2016/02/12/general-huxs-cat-millicent-is-fan-fiction-at-its-finest/.

17. Jerry White, 'Jeanne Dielmann Was My Star Wars', *The Dalhousie Review* 96, no. 1 (2016): 129.

18. See, for example, Aja Romano, 'Star Wars Has Always Been Political. Here's Why the Alt-Right Is Claiming Otherwise', *Vox*, 31 December 2016, https://www.vox.com/culture/2016/12/31/14024262/star-wars-political-alt-right-backlash; Marlow Stern, '"Alt-Right" Trumpsters Discover True Meaning of "Star Wars," Wage #DumpStarWars Campaign', *The Daily Beast*, 9 December 2016, sec. entertainment, https://www.thedailybeast.com/articles/2016/12/08/alt-right-neo-nazis-discover-true-meaning-of-star-wars-wage-dumpstarwars-campaign.

19. Viveca S. Greene, '"Deplorable" Satire: Alt-Right Memes, White Genocide Tweets, and Redpilling Normies', *Studies in American Humor* 5, no. 1 (2019): 31–69, doi:10.5325/studamerhumor.5.1.0031.

20. Nicole Veneto, '"That Lightsaber. It Belongs to Me.": Patriarchal Anxiety and the Fragility of White Men's Masculinity in The Force Awakens', *FilmMatters* 8, no. 3 (2017): 32, doi:10.1386/fm.8.3.30_1.

21. Wilhelm Schneemelcher, *New Testament Apocrypha. Volume I, Gospels and Related Writings*, trans. R. McL. Wilson, rev. ed. (Cambridge: James Clarke, 2003), 55–56.

22. See pp. 20–21.

persons who are mentioned in the New Testament'.[23] This appears to be extremely similar to what Jenkins calls 'refocalization', as discussed in relation to Mary Magdalene's role in the endings of Mark.[24] His mention of gap-filling and allowance that entertainment plays a role also appear similar to the fannish forces discussed previously. Henry Jenkins's two forces of fascination and frustration about texts, as discussed in Chapter 1, and Paul Booth's concept of fan play, as discussed in Chapter 2, resonate strongly with this suggestion by Schneemelcher. Many of the forces hypothesized by Schneemelcher for the creation of the Apocrypha are also present in fan studies.

Schneemelcher's final reason why Apocrypha were written down resonates strongly with the concepts of headcanon just described. He addresses the situation where apocryphal texts are being created amongst a variety of already existing traditions. 'There were' he writes, 'churches which ascribed authority to the traditions still living among them, and which hence for their part ... created works in which these traditions were brought together in writing'.[25] In his view, certain ancient communities had living traditions which they brought together in writings. In some cases, this might well be what happened, communities set in writing a commonly held piece of oral fan fiction that fundamentally influenced their own interpretation of the Christian storyworld. At the same time, there is no need for a community to accept an interpretation before it comes into writing. An apocryphon could just as easily be someone's headcanon which gained traction. Key here is to note how the expanded universe of Christianity could affect the experience of reading the oldest narratives. Even if a piece of the universe was not seen to be canonical, or generally accepted as authoritative for any group or community, that piece still affects the reading of other, more generally accepted texts. It is hard to imagine anyone who truly believes that Millicent the Cat is canonical to the *Star Wars* universe, yet the ginger cat is present in thousands of works of art, and for many the cat-loving General Hux is not quite as evil as the canonical *Star Wars* films would suggest.

The reimagining of General Hux demonstrates the role that fan products play in the interpretation of canonical sources. 'No authoritative definition', argues Brandon Hawk, 'however official, will ever stop individuals from creating their own personal sense of what is considered canonical'.[26] Fan products and non-canonical sources have a fundamental influence on the canon. Similarly in Christianity, Apocrypha and other derivative media become incorporated into existing traditions: the Christmas stable has an ox, an ass, and often even a little drummer boy, none of which are canonical. In fact, the stable is not even in the canonical accounts. Admittedly few contemporary people would imagine the drummer boy to have been present in first-century Palestine, but this is not

---

23. Schneemelcher, *New Testament Apocrypha Vol. I*, 55.
24. See pp. 42–47.
25. Schneemelcher, *New Testament Apocrypha Vol. I*, 55.
26. Hawk, 'Canonizing Star Wars'.

the case for the ox and ass. I will examine this example in detail below. For now, General Hux and Millicent demonstrate the political aspects at play in worldbuilding.

In this chapter I will examine these political aspects in more detail. In the previous two chapters I looked at the political aspects of how early Christians policed the canon and gatekept interpretations and members. Here, I will look at the political implications of living in the ancient Christian transmedia storyworld. Dan Hassler-Forest argues that worldbuilding has 'inherently political aspects'.[27] For Hassler-Forest, creating, inhabiting and studying storyworlds is not an innocent process for two main reasons. The first is fundamental and relates to the powerplay that is inherent to creating storyworlds. The second builds on the first and the example given above of General Hux: the storyworld obliquely influences interpretations. I will explore both in turn.

World Building is Political

Above I briefly introduced the term storyworld, which is the key focus of this chapter. The concept of a storyworld has been part of the literary landscape for decades, but only recently have rigorous attempts been made to define the concept. At its most basic level, a storyworld is the world that a story evokes in the mind of the reader or listener. It seems that it is extremely intuitive to presume that a narrative can (and should) conjure up a new world for the narrative to take place in.[28] As a person consumes a text, they create a mental world for the text to take place in. When they consume another text, another world is created. This process is so intuitive, that it often seems unnecessary to spend much time on fleshing out this basic assumption. David Herman, in his *Basic Elements of Narrative*, deals with this preconception in his introduction to storyworlds:

> Storyworlds can be defined as the worlds evoked by narratives; reciprocally, narratives can be defined as blueprints for a specific mode of world-creation. Mapping words (or other kinds of semiotic cues) onto worlds is a fundamental – perhaps the fundamental – requirement for narrative sense-making; yet this mapping operation may seem so natural and normal that no 'theory', no specialized nomenclature or framework of concepts, is necessary to describe and explain the specific procedures involved.[29]

---

27. Dan Hassler-Forest, 'The Politics of World Building: Heteroglossia in Janelle Monáe's Afrofuturist WondaLand', in *World Building. Transmedia, Fans, Industries*, ed. Marta Boni, Transmedia: Participatory Culture and Media Convergence (Amsterdam University Press, 2017), 378, doi:10.5117/9789089647566/ch21.

28. Marie-Laure Ryan, 'Transmedial Storytelling and Transfictionality', *Poetics Today* 34 (2013): 364, doi:10.1215/03335372-2325250.

29. David Herman, *Basic Elements of Narrative* (Chichester: Wiley-Blackwell, 2009), 105.

Until rather recently, very little research has examined the way a narrative or narratives create storyworlds. The last decades have seen a rising interest in storyworlds among narrative scholars.[30] Partially this is due to the waning influence of structuralism and a greater emphasis on subjectivity as inherent to interpretation, but also potentially related to the rise in contemporary narratives that span multiple texts (transfictional narratives) or multiple media (transmedia narratives).[31] As mentioned above, when a person consumes a text, they create a storyworld for that text. Often, a new text would evoke a new storyworld. This is not the case for transmedia or transfictional narratives, where multiple texts – dozens or even hundreds – evoke the same, single storyworld.[32] Contemporary storytelling is full of examples of this transmedia phenomenon. Take for example the *Marvel Cinematic Universe*[33] or *Star Wars*.

To introduce us to the political aspects of world building, allow me to step aside to the world of Greek myths, which is closer to ancient Christianity both temporally and culturally than contemporary fan works. Sarah Iles Johnston's *The Story of Myth* examines the storyworld of the Greek myths. She makes some significant claims about the Greek mythic storyworld which I would like to bring into conversation with early Christianity and contemporary media and fan studies:

> It was precisely myths' representation of the gods and heroes as existing in a world that looked much like the Primary World that helped to make it possible for the Greeks to believe that those gods and heroes still existed at the time the myths were being told (even if they no longer manifested themselves so grandly and so frequently as they once had).
>
> Greek myths provided templates against which such manifestations of gods and heroes could be shaped, measured, and confirmed. The myths also … provided a story world that bound their protagonists – divine, heroic, and human – into a larger network. Each bond of this network was tight enough to secure the others; each story could thereby accredit, and be accredited by, the others. Yet the bonds were supple, as well, allowing the sort of revision that kept Greek myths in step with changing beliefs about the gods and changing practices

---

30. Herman, *Basic Elements of Narrative*, 106.

31. Though of course, as is demonstrated in this chapter, these 'trans' storyworlds are nothing new.

32. The reality is more complex: worlds can overlap or converge, similar stories can invoke multiple, different instances of the same world, etc. See Jan-Noël Thon, 'Converging Worlds: From Transmedial Storyworlds to Transmedial Universes', *Storyworlds: A Journal of Narrative Studies* 7 (2015): 21–53, doi:10.5250/storyworlds.7.2.0021; Ryan, 'Transmedial Storytelling and Transfictionality'.

33. The *Marvel Cinematic Universe*, usually called MCU, is a media franchise and shared universe evoked by superhero films made by Marvel Studios, based on Marvel comics. The MCU is taken to have begun with *Iron Man* (2008) and now – 15 years later – consists of around 30 films and 20 TV series.

in their honor. They were supple enough, too, that interesting new details and episodes could emerge, keeping the stories and their characters vigorously alive.[34]

Johnston, here, makes a few key claims about the Greek storyworld, that I would like to evaluate in the context of ancient Christianity. She claims that 1) the storyworld of Greek myth takes place in our world, not a separate fantastical realm and thus 2) the storyworld is a template to measure manifestations of the divine.

Johnston's first argument is that the storyworld of myth is not a fantastical place, but the real world the audience inhabits. Thus, mythology reinforced belief in mythological gods and heroes, and these 'were presumed to still exist and intervene in the lives of mortals at the time that the myths were being narrated'.[35] Johnston's argument is based on the common assumption that narratives either take place in a Primary world (the world of the audience) or a Secondary world (a new, imaginary world).[36] For example a narrative such as *Saving Private Ryan* (1998), which tells a story of the Second World War, would take place in the Primary world, whereas a narrative like *The Hobbit* (1937) should be situated in a Secondary World. This simplistic dichotomy has been nuanced in recent years by film and media scholars, as I will discuss below. For now, it suits our purposes well enough.

Johnston's argument that the storyworld is the real world – not a fantastical place – holds true for the narratives about Jesus and other early Christ-followers as well. Realism seems to be clearly the intention of many of the Christian texts. Take for example the opening to the Gospel of Luke. Luke explains in the prologue to their gospel that they attempt to elucidate 'the truth' on the events that 'have been fulfilled among us', including accounts of 'eyewitnesses' (Luke 1:1–4). Or take the introduction to the Infancy Gospel of Thomas: 'I, Thomas the Israelite, announce and make known to you all, brothers from among the Gentiles, the mighty childhood deeds of our Lord Jesus Christ, which he did when he was born in our land' (Infancy Gospel of Thomas 1). These texts are presented as taking place in the real world. It is key here to notice that there is no indication that some Christian texts take place in the real world, and some in a fictional one. Luke and Thomas present their works as equally factual. There is similarly no textual reason to

---

34. Johnston, *The Story of Myth*, 144, 146.
35. Johnston, *The Story of Myth*, 26.
36. This distinction and terminology were first formulated as such by J. R. R. Tolkien in a lecture in 1939: 'What really happens is that the story-maker proves a successful "sub-creator". He makes a Secondary World which your mind can enter. Inside it, what he relates is 'true': it accords with the laws of that world. You therefore believe it, while you are, as it were, inside. The moment disbelief arises, the spell is broken; the magic, or rather art, has failed. You are then out in the Primary World again, looking at the little abortive Secondary World from outside'. J. R. R. Tolkien, 'On Fairy-Stories', in *Essays Presented to Charles Williams*, reprint (Grand Rapids: Eerdmans, 1966), 60.

assume that the prefect Agrippa from the Acts of Paul is meant to be less historical than the governor Pontius Pilate in the canonical Gospels (yet this is often assumed[37]). These ancient Christian texts about Jesus and other early Christ-followers take place in the real world, irrespective of whether the text ended up being considered canonical or apocryphal.

Now, some may feel the miraculous nature of some of the early Christian literature might not fit in a realistic account, and is rather part of ancient fabulous narratives of *non-existent* wondrous places, animals and people. But research into ancient narratives shows that this is not the case. Johnston spends significant time demonstrating how the 'fabulous' Greek myths were in fact seen by ancient audiences to take place in the reality of the ancient world, and Janet Spittler has done similar work on the apocryphal acts. Arguing against some who see these as 'fabulous literature', Spittler convincingly argues that 'the miracles reported in the apocryphal acts ... are very much understood to take place in the "real world".[38] Surely the fabulous events and locales of the apocryphal acts are meant to astonish audiences – just as those from Greek mythology *and* history[39] – but this astonishment is because the narratives are understood to be realistic and taking place in the real world.[40] It was exactly this presentation of myths as taking place in the world of the audience 'that helped to make it possible for the Greeks to believe that those gods and heroes still existed at the time the myths were being told'.[41] Thus, the Christian storyworld of apostles, demons, miracles, conversions and preaching simultaneously reinforced the believability of the earliest Christian narratives, bolstered contemporary belief in divine manifestations and miracles, *and* built continuity between the first-century setting of Jesus and Christ-followers and the later reception and production contexts.[42]

Allow me to put this theory in conversation with comments of a couple of Apocrypha scholars. Jens Schröter has argued that non-canonical texts cannot be adequately studied by simply looking at how they relate to canonical ones. Rather, we should look at the 'contribution of the non-canonical gospels to the perspectives

---

37. This phenomenon is discussed in detail in Chapter 3.

38. Janet Spittler, 'The Development of Miracle Traditions in the Apocryphal Acts of the Apostles', in *Between Canonical and Apocryphal Texts: Processes of Reception, Rewriting and Interpretation in Early Judaism and Early Christianity*, ed. Jörg Frey, Tobias Nicklas, and Claire Clivaz (Mohr Siebeck, 2019), 363, doi:10.1628/978-3-16-155232-8. See also the articles co-collected by Spittler: Tobias Nicklas and Janet E. Spittler, eds., *Credible, Incredible: The Miraculous in the Ancient Mediterranean*, Wissenschaftliche Untersuchungen zum Neuen Testament 321 (Tübingen: Mohr Siebeck, 2013).

39. Spittler notes that fabulous lands, animals and peoples are found 'above all in historiography (e.g. Tacitus, Livy, Polybius), biography (e.g. Suetonius and Plutarch) and natural history (e.g. Pliny and Aelian)'. Spittler, 'Development of Miracle Traditions', 379.

40. Spittler, 'Development of Miracle Traditions', 378–79.

41. Johnston, *The Story of Myth*, 144, 146.

42. See also pp. 47–51.

on Jesus's meaning emerging in the second and third centuries more seriously'.[43] Schröter sees these texts as closely related to the canonical gospels, but this is 'not the most important aspect'.[44] Rather, they are '"reinventions" or "creative interpretations"' that are 'aimed at making the figure of Jesus and his teaching meaningful for their own time'.[45] Julia Snyder makes a similar point about the relationship between apocryphal acts and the canonical book of Acts.[46] Both scholars emphasise that these apocryphal texts should not be read backwards in light of the canon, but in their own production and reception contexts as attempts to keep the Christian storyworld alive and up-to-date.

Take Schröter's example of the Akhmîm fragment that is part of the Gospel of Peter, who was one of Jesus's twelve disciples. This text retells the narratives of the death and resurrection of Jesus, and does so with an extreme emphasis on the 'hostility of the Jews towards Jesus' and includes strong 'anti-Jewish polemic'.[47] Schröter suggests that these themes are the result of a specific historical situation, and in this context the narratives from the gospels 'gain a new meaning'.[48] To borrow Jenkins's term,[49] the Akhmîm fragment 'personalizes' the canonical gospels: it 'effaces the gap between the realm of their own experience and the fictional space of their favorite programs'.[50] But this is not an innocent process. Adapting the narratives in this way impacts the interpretation of the canonical gospel narratives, strengthening and extending any potential hostility between Jesus and other Jewish people of his time. Ultimately, this example of recontextualization demonstrates two major outcomes. First, it causes the canonical gospels to be more Judeophobic,[51] a process we will look at in the next section. Second, it allows it to

---

43. Jens Schröter, 'Apocryphal and Canonical Gospels within the Development of the New Testament Canon', *Early Christianity* 7, no. 1 (2016): 31, doi:10.1628/186870316X14555506071137.

44. Schröter, 'Apocryphal and Canonical Gospels', 32.

45. Schröter, 'Apocryphal and Canonical Gospels', 32.

46. She argues that 'when producing their own narratives [the producers of the apocryphal acts] were simply not thinking about' Acts. They 'chose to tell stories in their own way, apparently unconstrained by a text that would in some circles be seen as "canonical"'. Julia Snyder, 'Relationships between the Acts of the Apostles and Other Apostle Narratives', in *Between Canonical and Apocryphal Texts: Processes of Reception, Rewriting and Interpretation in Early Judaism and Early Christianity*, ed. Jörg Frey, Tobias Nicklas, and Claire Clivaz (Tübingen: Mohr Siebeck, 2019), 340–41, doi:10.1628/978-3-16-155232-8.

47. Schröter, 'Apocryphal and Canonical Gospels', 40.

48. Schröter, 'Apocryphal and Canonical Gospels', 41.

49. See my application of Jenkins's concept to the Gospel of Mark on p. 47–51.

50. Henry Jenkins, *Textual Poachers: Television Fans & Participatory Culture* (London: Routledge, 1992), 176.

51. On the term 'Judeophobic' as a preferred term for discrimination against people who identify as Jewish (i.e. replacing antisemitism, anti-Semitism, or anti-Judaism), see Sarah E. Rollens, Eric Vanden Eykel, and Meredith Warren, 'Confronting Judeophobia in the Classroom', *Journal for Interdisciplinary Biblical Studies* 2, no. 1 (2020): 81–82.

more seamlessly fit into the contemporary context. This means it enforces continuity between the first-century setting of Jesus and his disciples, and much later production and reception context of the Akhmîm fragment. The transmedia storyworld of ancient Christianity – just as the Greek mythic storyworld – allowed for the fleshing out of characters and the rewriting of characters' narratives. In this way the age-old story of Christ was kept, to borrow Johnston's terminology, 'vigorously alive'.

These living narratives, argues Johnston, would have been templates to measure manifestations of the divine. Here we return to Johnston's first point, that the world of myth and the world of the audience are the same place. Though for many the divine would not manifest in the same way as in the mythological storyworld, the expectation of an active involvement would be present. Johnston, explains 'although it might not be reasonable to expect to encounter more nine-headed snakes in Lerna or three-bodied giants in Spain . . . or to expect gods to transmogrify people into new animals and plants . . . it would be reasonable to expect the heroes and the gods to remain an active part of the contemporary world'.[52] The gods now work behind the scenes, but the miraculous – rain to the thirsty, healing to the sick, the yearly harvest – could still be evaluated and imagined in this storyworld of Greek myth. In the Christian context, even though not nearly as many people are raised from the dead as in the time of the apostles, the less miraculous current events – daily bread, good luck, healing to the sick – are still part of that miraculous first century and interpreted in that worldview. The two mutually reinforce one another: current events are read to be miraculous, thanks to the storyworld of miracles; and the storyworld of miracles must be real, as even now we still have miraculous events. This is the politics of world building that Hassler-Forest alerts us to. Johnston's argument about how ancient people perceived the Greek storyworld as Primary changes the perception of reality: by insisting that the mythological characters are real, reality itself is subtly changed to reinforce belief in the gods and the myths. The same is true for the Christian storyworld.

Mark Wolf's *Building Imaginary Worlds* is one of the first major academic engagements with world creation.[53] He significantly nuances the status quo, contesting that there are Primary and Secondary worlds. In his view, worlds exist on a continuum from extreme 'secondariness' (such as sci-fi and fantasy worlds) to extreme closeness to reality (e.g. autobiography and historical drama). This means that some realities are more fictional than others, and some fictional worlds are more real than others. No longer is it a simple binary, but each world is more or less secondary. 'A world's "secondariness" depends on the extent to which a place is detached from the Primary World and different from it, and the degree to which its fictional aspects have been developed and built'.[54] Thus two aspects play a role

---

52. Johnston, *The Story of Myth*, 146.
53. Mark J. P. Wolf, *Building Imaginary Worlds: The Theory and History of Subcreation* (New York: Routledge, 2013), doi:10.4324/9780203096994.
54. Wolf, *Building Imaginary Worlds*, 26.

in how secondary a world is seen to be: its fictional development and its difference to reality.

More recently, Wolf's extension of the Primary/Secondary dichotomy has been further nuanced, based primarily on problematizing the modernist roots of the concept Primary World. Here we return again to Hassler-Forest, who points out that 'Wolf's definition of world building clearly relies on the assumption of an unambiguous distinction between what constitutes a "realistic" representation of a diegetic world and a fictional environment that defamiliarizes its audience from realistic defaults by altering a number of these coordinates'.[55] In other words, the entire dichotomy Primary/Secondary world relies on complete agreement of the audience on what constitutes reality and what is realistic, otherwise no judgement can be made on the secondariness of a world. Making these judgements is usually an unconscious phenomenon. A person analyses the storyworld based on their own experiences of the world, but also their prejudices, assumptions, ideologies and agendas. Thus, experiencing any world becomes, first, an 'epistemological endeavor',[56] and as audiences have different worldviews, experiences and beliefs, judgements on secondariness will differ wildly.

Take for example the miracles of canonical New Testament: Jesus heals the sick, walks on water, expels demons, and raises the dead. Depending on an audience's assumptions and beliefs, these events can indicate that the New Testament storyworld is more or less primary. Many Christians may feel these are real, historical events, whereas others may assume they are fiction. The existence of the entire field of Christian apologetics, where defences are formulated against objections to parts of Christian storyworlds, demonstrates the political aspects at work here. Not to mention places like the Creation Museum or Ark Encounter in Kentucky, built specifically to reinforce beliefs that the world is only several thousand years old. This issue of historicity of the New Testament storyworld becomes more contentious when we consider the way many contemporary academic and religious audiences view the miracles of the Apocrypha as clearly secondary, even when they assume those of the canon are primary. Consider, for example, J. K. Elliott's use of the words 'crudely sensational', 'imaginative reconstructions', 'fanciful', 'legendary', and 'a large collection of fantasies' to describe the contents of the Apocrypha he himself edits; words he does not use for the canonical texts.[57] Or take the many similar examples Janet Spittler mentions, where Apocrypha are assumed to the secondary based on their status, not their contents.[58] Or, indeed, the way Dan Brown's *The Da Vinci Code* (2003) ignited belief in the Apocrypha as historical fact, and the many evangelical responses championing the

---

55. Hassler-Forest, 'Politics of World Building', 380.
56. Hassler-Forest, 'Politics of World Building', 380.
57. J. K. Elliott, *The Apocryphal New Testament: A Collection of Apocryphal Christian Literature in an English Translation* (Oxford: Clarendon Press, 1993), 69, 165, 100.
58. Spittler, 'Development of Miracle Traditions', 357–59.

New Testament as the only source of fact about Jesus and the apostles.[59] These examples highlight an extremely important point that even Wolf's more nuanced portrayal of worldbuilding hides: the political implications of where a world is placed on the primary–secondary continuum.[60] As worlds are considered to be more primary or more secondary, they are automatically judged to be more realistic or fantastical. These worlds, when they are judged or defended as primary, influence how audiences view the world around them. But, as evidenced by these few examples, judgements on secondariness are often by their very nature political. Furthermore, as I will discuss in the following section, judging and theorizing worlds purely on their secondariness obscures the power of storyworlds – both realist and fantastical – to destabilize and deconstruct social and historical structures and conventions.

Inhabiting the Early Christian Storyworld

Leaving aside the point that any judgement of how a storyworld's realism is political, let me move on to Hassler-Forest's second point: that inhabiting a storyworld is political as well. In doing this I will also take a step further into the early Christian storyworld. So far, I have focussed on written texts, but now we will step into the wider transmedia storyworld. This storyworld is engendered by the vast collection of texts – art, liturgies, hymns, pilgrimages – that early Christianity produced.

Before we jump into this discussion, a short exploration of the term 'text' is needed. In this chapter, as is usual in critical theory, I will use the term 'text' in the broad sense best illustrated by Alan McKee's definition:

> whenever we produce an interpretation of something's meaning – a book, television programme, film, magazine, T-shirt or kilt, piece of furniture or ornament – we treat it as a text. A text is something that we make meaning from.[61]

This definition takes texts beyond the written word, which is a vital step for analysing contemporary transmedia, where texts can include toys, videogames, posters, and theme park rides, to name a few.[62] It is also vital for analysing the ancient Christian media landscape, which includes art, material culture, relics,

---

59. Tony Burke, *Secret Scriptures Revealed: A New Introduction to the Christian Apocrypha* (London: SPCK, 2013), 1–2.

60. Hassler-Forest, 'Politics of World Building', 380.

61. Alan McKee, *Textual Analysis: A Beginner's Guide* (London: Sage, 2003), 4.

62. Consider also Jonathan Gray's warning that texts are incomplete without their mediation through paratexts: 'A film or program is but one part of the text, the text always being a contingent entity, either in the process of forming and transforming or vulnerable to further formation or transformation.' The entirety of our engagement with a text is more than just the text itself. Jonathan Gray, *Show Sold Separately: Promos, Spoilers, and Other Media Paratexts* (New York: New York University Press, 2010), 7.

liturgies, pilgrimage sites, and the like. All of these are texts that we make meaning from. I will use 'written texts' or 'writings' to help differentiate between the specific and broader uses of the term in the chapter.

Early Christians lived in a vast storyworld of parabiblical texts, from writings to liturgies, from hymns to art. The Christian Apocrypha outnumber the writings that became canonical by more than ten to one.[63] To this collection we can add the hundreds of writings and sermons of early Christian leaders, the thousands of works of art, and the many prayers, hymns and liturgies, and the innumerable relics, pilgrimage sites and religious spaces. Each of these are a text and these thousands of texts are connected to one another, making what contemporary literary scholarship would term a transmedia storyworld: a storyworld that spans multiple media. Roberta Pearson, in introducing such storyworlds in a media studies context, immediately gives the example of the Christian storyworld. 'Jesus Christ', she writes 'had his textual origins in the four gospels of the New Testament but the character almost immediately spans out across successive periods' available media, from painting to sculptures to illuminated manuscripts to stained glass windows and eventually to analogue and digital screens'.[64] While it is probably not entirely historically correct to claim that Jesus's textual origins were in the four gospels – oral and other written sources predate these – it is important to note that the massive storyworld of Christianity grows around the central figure of Jesus. Pearson points out that 'vast and expansive fictional storyworlds' surrounding a central character or group of characters 'built upon an accumulation of multiple texts have existed for millennia: the Greek gods, the Christian God, Robin Hood, and King Arthur are but a few instantiations'.[65]

These transmedia storyworlds have existed for millennia, and the early Christian media landscape is an excellent example of such a storyworld. Denzell Richards, when historicizing the existence of transmedia, elucidates a major difference between contemporary and older forms of this phenomenon, which applies to the ancient Christian storyworld as well.[66] The core of this difference, like many in this

---

63. Tony Burke, 'Introduction', in *New Testament Apocrypha: More Noncanonical Scriptures Volume Two*, ed. Tony Burke (Grand Rapids: Eerdmans, 2020), xiii. To give an indication of the contents of this collection of writings, The North American Society for the Study of Christian Apocryphal Literature maintains a bibliography of Christian Apocrypha, the *e-Clavis: Christian Apocrypha*. As of February 2023, there are 358 texts in the list. North American Society for the Study of Christian Apocryphal Literature, 'E-Clavis: Christian Apocrypha', https://www.nasscal.com/e-clavis-christian-apocrypha/.

64. Roberta Pearson, 'Transmedia Characters', in *The Routledge Companion to Transmedia Studies*, ed. Matthew Freeman and Renira Rampazzo Gambarato (New York: Routledge, 2018), 148, doi:10.4324/9781351054904-17.

65. Pearson, 'Transmedia Characters', 148.

66. Denzell Richards, 'Historicizing Transtexts and Transmedia', in *The Rise of Transtexts: Challenges and Opportunities*, ed. Benjamin W. L. Derhy Kurtz and Mélanie Bourdaa, Routledge Research in Cultural and Media Studies (Abingdon: Routledge, 2017), doi:10.4324/9781315671741-9.

book, can be attributed to differences in the media landscape. Contemporary transmedia, firmly grounded in Romantic authorship, late capitalism, mass media, and copyrightable texts, takes a top-down approach of 'closely directed ... narrative seriality' in order to create a 'unified and coordinated entertainment experience';[67] historical forms, however, are more 'bottom-up, open, flexible and participatory'.[68] Key to note here is that while contemporary transmedia are *owned* by an individual or a corporation, historical ones were communally owned. Bringing fans into this discussion, then, means that 'regardless of how creative or influential particular fanworks may be, contemporary "grass-roots" audiences never have the same cultural influence or power over the construction, presentation and dissemination of texts, as those who own the commercial rights and/or are invested with the cultural authority to determine, delimit, and exploit these'.[69]

Contemporary fans, while certainly influential to a transmedia enterprise, do not have the same power as the rights owners who produce the storyworld. But this is not true for ancient audiences, where 'original authors are either unknown mythic figures ... or the earliest textual source is by an identified author but already an adaptation or an existing spoken-word story'.[70] This resonates strongly with the early Christian media landscape, where the texts are often attributed to mythic figures (Matthew, Enoch, Mark, Jeremiah, Paul) and based on oral traditions (Q, Gospel of Thomas). Thus, historical transmedia themselves should be seen as unfixed, 'repeatedly appropriated, adapted and varied', a negotiation between storyteller and audience.[71] This fits nicely with how Eva Mroczek has attempted to decentre the concept of a fixed text as a book in ancient Judaism and Christianity. Her example of the prophet Jeremiah is useful here. There is a canonical writing bearing his name, which has 'two major forms of the text', yet neither is 'the central player in the ancient literary imagination'; the central player can rather be found in the collection of – oral and written – 'tropes and traditions that circulated in connection with Jeremiah'.[72] As a transmedia entity existing in at least two large written 'books of Jeremiah' and hundreds of other traditions, Jeremiah was the product of centuries-long negotiations between storytellers and audiences.[73] This means that when ancient Jews and Christians refer to Jeremiah, they are referring

---

67. Though this may be the intention, the outcome is often one that is much more emergent and ad hoc. Karin Fast and Henrik Örnebring, 'Transmedia World-Building: *The Shadow* (1931–Present) and *Transformers* (1984–Present)', *International Journal of Cultural Studies* 20, no. 6 (2017): 636–52, doi:10.1177/1367877915605887.
68. Richards, 'Historicizing Transtexts and Transmedia', 18.
69. Richards, 'Historicizing Transtexts and Transmedia', 19.
70. Richards, 'Historicizing Transtexts and Transmedia', 17.
71. Richards, 'Historicizing Transtexts and Transmedia', 17.
72. Eva Mroczek, *The Literary Imagination in Jewish Antiquity* (New York: Oxford University Press, 2016), 45–50.
73. See Chapter 4 for an examination of how this negotiation also influences canon formation.

to the transmedial character Jeremiah, based on the many traditions about Jeremiah, including the canonical text.[74] And this character inhabits a transmedia storyworld that is constantly in negotiation as new texts come into being.

When we look at the Christian storyworld, then, it is important to emphasize its transmedia nature. Written texts have played a dominant role in Christianity, yet it is the other media that most Christians would have encountered. For instance, David Cartlidge and J. K. Elliott, in their work on Apocrypha and art, make the point that 'until the invention of the printing press, most of the faithful learned about the Nativity of Christ, the Crucifixion, the life of the Virgin Mary, and the lives of Christian heroes, saints and apostles from liturgies, sermons and church and funerary decorations, and not from books'.[75] The parts of the Christian storyworld, be that characters, places, objects, folklore or rules and values, were predominantly communicated through media other than the written word.

Sometimes people feel that artworks are little more than an adaption of a written text, yet the reality is far more complex. All texts contribute to the transmedia storyworld. Robin Margaret Jensen, in her introduction to early Christian art, discusses this complexity:

> We may discover that some images preceded texts and the texts then provided commentary on the visual symbols. However, at the very least visual imagery never merely retold or condensed a text into corresponding pictorial language, but rather made meaning in its own right – by using symbols and allegories already present in written expression (narratives, commentaries, etc.) in such a way as to become a communication mode in itself – one that paralleled, commented upon, and expanded the text, rather than simply amplifying or serving the text.[76]

Visual media are texts in their own right. They create storyworlds in the same way the ancient written texts do. Utilizing key aspects of the storyworld – from characters to symbols and allegories – the art overlaps with the writings, expanding them, modifying them, and even preceding them. Jensen gives the example of an image where Jesus is figured in the New Eden giving the law to either the apostle Peter or the apostle Paul. Such a narrative does not exist in any written text as such, rather it is a 'dogmatic' event that stitches together multiple variables from other stories.[77] There are many more examples like this.

A common Roman image of the apostle Peter is the so-called water miracle, where the jailed Peter strikes a rock, receives water, and baptizes his jailers. This

---

74. Mroczek, *Literary Imagination*, 47.

75. David R. Cartlidge and J. K. Elliott, *Art and the Christian Apocrypha* (London: Routledge, 2001), 15.

76. Robin M. Jensen, *Understanding Early Christian Art* (London: Routledge, 2000), 5, doi:10.4324/9780203407639.

77. Jensen, *Understanding Early Christian Art*, 100.

narrative is surely inspired by the narrative of Moses striking the rock to receive water in the desert in Exodus 17:1–6.[78] This is probably also associated with the famous narrative where Jesus gives Peter his name (meaning 'rock'), and promises to build his church on that rock (Matthew 16:18–19). Jutta Dresken-Weiland gives numerous examples of non-written media that include this narrative, from sarcophagi, to lamps and glasses.[79] She concludes that these stories about Peter 'were so well-known that they were not written down and left only faint traces in later texts'.[80] Indeed there is only one writing that contains a reference to this narrative, and an incomplete one at that. In Chapter 5 of the Martyrdom of Blessed Peter the Apostle by Pseudo-Linus, the jailers recall that they 'were baptized in the name of the Holy Trinity in a spring brought forth from stone by prayers and the glorious sign of the cross'.[81] Thus, there is one written text that alludes to Peter baptizing his Roman jailers, and no writing where Peter strikes the rock as Moses did. Yet, other media show that this narrative was anchored 'deeply in the minds and memory of fourth-century Christians'.[82] Indeed, the Roman location of Peter's miracle remained fixed in the minds of Christians as a site for pilgrimages all the way into the medieval era, and even now the Mamertine Prison in Rome is often claimed to be the same place.[83] Up to this day, experiences of this site remain interpreted and seen through the lens of this ancient transmedia narrative. And these narratives recorded on sarcophagi, lamps, glasses and other artifacts are – in some way – authoritative, even to the Roman tourism department.[84]

78. Robin M. Jensen, 'Introduction', in *The Routledge Handbook of Early Christian Art*, ed. Robin M. Jensen and Mark D. Ellison (New York: Routledge, 2018), 11, doi:10.4324/9781315718835-1.

79. Jutta Dresken-Weiland, 'The Role of Peter in Early Christian Art: Images from the 4th to the 6th Century', in *The Early Reception and Appropriation of the Apostle Peter (60-800 CE): The Anchors of the Fisherman*, ed. Roald Dijkstra, Euhormos: Greco-Roman Studies in Anchoring Innovation 1 (Leiden: Brill, 2020), 118–19, doi:10.1163/9789004425682_008.

80. Dresken-Weiland, 'Role of Peter in Early Christian Art', 119.

81. Translation taken from David L. Eastman, *The Ancient Martyrdom Accounts of Peter and Paul*, Writings from the Greco-Roman World 39 (Atlanta: SBL Press, 2015), doi:10.2307/j.ctt15zc51m. Eastman's book also contains the Latin text.

82. Dresken-Weiland, 'Role of Peter in Early Christian Art', 119.

83. See, for example, a 2010 news report in *The Telegraph* which even refers to the miraculous spring: Nick Squires, 'Archeologists Find Evidence of St Peter's Prison', *The Telegraph*, 25 June 2010, https://www.telegraph.co.uk/news/worldnews/7852507/Archeologists-find-evidence-of-St-Peters-prison.html. Many such references can be found, see for example, 'In the floor ... is a well, which, according to the legend, miraculously came into existence while St. Peter was imprisoned here, enabling the Apostle to baptize his jailers, Sts. Processus and Martinianus', Maurice M. Hassett, 'Mamertine Prison', in *Catholic Encyclopedia* (New York: Encyclopedia Press, 1910), 579.

84. See, https://www.turismoroma.it/en/places/mamertine-prison-carcer-tullianum [accessed 15 September 2023].

As noted above, media and fan scholars often mention ancient Christianity as an example of transmedial storyworlds.[85] This point is rarely developed by biblical scholars.[86] To my knowledge, the one exception is Monika Amsler, who has written an article on transmedia storytelling in late antiquity.[87] She focusses not on visual media, but on sports fandom and athletes. Her highly innovative argument is that the Christian transmedia storyworld was created and kept alive through the real-life experiences of the Christian martyrs, the so-called 'athletes of Christ',[88] and the shrines and basilicas where these saints were venerated. Pilgrimages to veneration sites provided 'a full and even physical immersion' in the transmedia storyworld of Christianity.[89] Amsler's argument thus demonstrates another way the early Christian storyworld was fully immersive and transcended texts and media.

Returning to Roberta Pearson's claim above, the storyworld of Christianity, as these examples show, is indeed 'vast and expansive ... built upon an accumulation of multiple texts'[90] – written, non-written, canonical and non-canonical. In this sense, being part of early Christianity was to consume a vast transmedia enterprise. Each piece of media contributed to the wider storyworld, extending and developing key aspects, modifying and expanding the Christian universe. And thus, each piece of media, each text remains authoritative. In this enormous world, the Christian Apocrypha remain a valuable witness to aspects of an expanded universe.

Storyworld Influences Readings

Earlier I gave the example of evil General Hux's cat Millicent. Here we saw that an unauthorized and – to be honest – silly tweet had potentially far-reaching consequences for the *Star Wars* transmedia storyworld; a terrible villain has turned into a lovable rogue. Mark Wolf gives another simple example from *Star Wars* of how a contemporary non-canonical text can influence the interpretation of canon. 'Encountering [the original villainous antagonist] Darth Vader first as a LEGO minifigure or as bobble-head toy will reduce the air of menace that he had in his

---

85. See, for example, Ryan, 'Transmedial Storytelling and Transfictionality', 362; Richards, 'Historicizing Transtexts and Transmedia', 20–23; Pearson, 'Transmedia Characters', 148.

86. There has been some interest in how characters migrate between texts (and thus storyworlds), but these approaches – to my knowledge – do engage with the storyworld itself. See, e.g. Jan Rüggemeier and Elizabeth E. Shively, 'Introduction: Towards a Cognitive Theory of New Testament Characters: Methodology, Problems, and Desiderata', *Biblical Interpretation* 29, no. 4–5 (2021): 403–29, doi:10.1163/15685152-29040001.

87. Monika Amsler, 'Martyrs, Athletes, and Transmedia Storytelling in Late Antiquity', *Transformative Works and Cultures* 31 (2019), doi:10.3983/twc.2019.1645.

88. Amsler, 'Martyrs, Athletes, and Transmedia Storytelling', para. 4.8.

89. Amsler, 'Martyrs, Athletes, and Transmedia Storytelling', para. 6.4.

90. Pearson, 'Transmedia Characters', 148.

original appearance in Star Wars in 1977'.[91] There is no one who would argue that the Darth Vader toys give canonical interpretations of his characterization, yet as, children enter the *Star Wars* storyworld through (video)games, for example, they experience it as a 'bright, cheery world where everything is comedic and no one dies',[92] not a dark world inspired in part by the Vietnam War. These non-canonical and even non-serious texts are influential on interpretation and thus – in some way – authoritative.

The expanding storyworld of Christianity would have impacted the reading of the oldest Christian narratives. The most obvious way to examine how ancient readers were influenced by parabiblical texts is to look whether scribes included parabiblical information in their copying of canonical writings. Elliott, in looking at this exact issue, argues that 'despite the apparent popularity of many of the apocrypha, their texts seem not to have significantly influenced New Testament scribes'.[93] After examining several examples, he concludes that though there is overlap between parabiblical texts and variant readings of canonical texts, the variants 'can be explained within the context of the New Testament manuscript tradition without any reference to deviations in the apocryphal sources'.[94]

Nevertheless, Elliott gives two concrete examples where exactly this happens. He found two copies of 2 Timothy where the canonical text is adapted to match parabiblical sources. Two manuscripts, dating from the tenth and thirteenth century, include references to the Acts of Paul and Thecla. This apocryphal text starts with the apostle Paul arriving in Iconium, where he is met by Onesiphorus, his wife Lectra and his sons Simmia and Zeno. Paul preaches in Onesiphorus's house and a young woman, Thecla, hears him. She is completely enraptured by Paul's preaching and does not move for three days. Her mother and fiancé become concerned and incite the town. Paul is thrown in jail. The story continues wonderfully, but this is all the narrative we need to understand the additions to 2 Timothy. In the usual text of 2 Timothy 3:11 reference is made to Paul's suffering in Antioch, Iconium, and Lystra. A reader of this short reference might remember the apocryphal story of Paul's imprisonment in Iconium due to Thecla and her family. This might be why one of the manuscripts of 2 Timothy adds to the sentence on Paul's suffering the phrase 'which were suffered on account of Thecla'. A similar thing happens at the end of 2 Timothy, where a number of greetings are given to various people. Usually the text reads 'Greet Prisca and Aquila, and the household of Onesiphorus' (2 Tim 4:19). Onesiphorus is the name of Paul's host in Iconium in the Acts of Paul and Thecla, and both of these manuscripts adapt this sentence to say 'Greet Prisca and Aquila, Lectra his wife, and Simmia and Zeno his sons, and the household of Onesiphorus'. This second addition is slightly peculiar as it makes it appear that Aquila is the person mentioned in the Acts of Paul and Thecla, not

91. Wolf, *Building Imaginary Worlds*, 278.
92. Wolf, *Building Imaginary Worlds*, 247.
93. J. K. Elliott, 'The Influence of the Apocrypha on Manuscripts of the New Testament', *Apocrypha* 8 (1997): 266, doi:10.1484/J.APOCRA.2.300956.
94. Elliott, 'Influence of the Apocrypha', 270.

Onesiphorus. Nevertheless, the influence of parabiblical texts on the canonical texts is evident.

Besides these two concrete examples, Elliott cannot find evidence of any other New Testament manuscript being influenced by apocryphal texts. As the number of New Testament manuscripts is exceedingly large, Elliott may simply not have discovered other examples, so he concludes his article with a call for responses. 'If any reader knows or discovers any examples of New Testament manuscripts betraying an influence from an apocryphal source.... I would be grateful for such information. In the absence of such additional evidence I think we must accept my general conclusion that the apocryphal texts have not influenced scribes of the New Testament.'[95] Since Elliott's publication in 1997, I have found no evidence that more have been discovered.[96] Yet, more recent studies in New Testament manuscripts show that the way Elliott frames his question might well be too narrow. When Elliott looks for 'influence on the scribes of the New Testament', he limits his search to the text itself, casting aside the paratextual evidence. Scribes create both text and paratext (headings, titles, illustrations, etc.) and if we broaden our search to scribal paratext, this influence is everywhere. Kelsie Rodenbiker's examination of the book of 2 Peter in manuscripts illustrates the influence well. She notes that 'a variety of inscriptions and subscriptions from a broad span of time preserve two key details associated with Peter: an honorific title of "chief of the apostles," and his association with Rome, where he is said to have been martyred'.[97] These characteristics of Peter, not to be found in any canonical text, certainly influence the scribes as they add them above and below the text to 2 Peter. Rodenbiker's conclusion, that 'the cumulative amassing of tradition around the figure of Peter contributes to the "canonical" reception',[98] demonstrates clearly how the early Christian storyworld influences the reading of earliest texts.

Though there are few examples of the transmedia storyworld of Christianity directly changing the texts of the earliest writings, there is much more evidence of how it affected the reading of those writings. Let me take, as an example, the birth of Jesus Christ as found in Luke 2 and Matthew 1–2. In artistic portrayals of this event, and indeed in nativity scenes worldwide, it is usual to 'depict the ox and the ass ... with their heads leaning over the crib in which the Christ Child lies'.[99] In

---

95. Elliott, 'Influence of the Apocrypha', 271.

96. But, see this forthcoming article which I understand will include some examples, Elizabeth Schrader Polczer, 'Apocryphal within the Canonical: Unorthodox Influence on the New Testament Text Transmission', in *Pen, Print, and Pixels: Advances in Textual Criticism in the Digital Era*, ed. Daniel B. Wallace, David Flood, and Elijah Hixson (Peabody, MA: Hendrickson, forthcoming).

97. Kelsie G. Rodenbiker, 'The Second Peter: Pseudepigraphy as Exemplarity in the Second Canonical Petrine Epistle', *Novum Testamentum* 65, no. 1 (2023): 127, doi:10.1163/15685365-bja10038.

98. Rodenbiker, 'The Second Peter', 129.

99. Cartlidge and Elliott, *Art and the Christian Apocrypha*, 18.

hymns, the ox and ass often bow to the new-born Jesus. These two animals are not in the canonical accounts of the birth of Christ, yet they are often found in receptions of the Christmas stable. How the animals first came to be so omnipresent is not entirely clear. The oldest text we have that mentions the ox and ass comes from the beginning of the third century. The influential Christian theologian Origen of Alexandria mentions both animals in his Homily on Luke 2.[100] He introduces both animals into the stable by quoting a seemingly unrelated passage from the prophet Isaiah 'the ox knows his owner and the ass his master's manger'.[101] Origen, in his preaching on the Christian stable, introduces animals based on other texts from the Christian storyworld.

Though Origen is the oldest text we have with an ox and ass, the most complete and famous written mention of the ox and ass comes from the apocryphal Gospel of Pseudo-Matthew, from around the seventh century:

> Now, on the third day after the birth of the Lord, Mary went out of the cave and into a stable, and she placed the boy in a manger, and an ox and an ass bent their knees and worshipped him. Then was fulfilled what was spoken by the prophet Isaiah, who said, 'The ox knows his owner and the ass the manger of his Lord.' And these animals, staying by his side, were constantly worshipping him. Then was fulfilled what was spoken by the prophet Habakkuk, who said, 'Between the two animals you will make yourself known.' (*Gospel of Pseudo-Matthew* 14.1–4)[102]

Pseudo-Matthew does the same thing Origen does; he introduces animals into the stable by referring to other texts from the Christian storyworld. Besides Isaiah, Pseudo-Matthew references a second passage from the Septuagint (the Greek translation of the Hebrew Bible/Old Testament): Habakkuk 3:2.[103] This may be their own invention, or bear witness to additional details of existing traditions. The

---

100. Tobias Nicklas, 'The Influence of Jewish Scriptures on Early Christian Apocrypha', in *The Oxford Handbook of Early Christian Apocrypha*, ed. Andrew F. Gregory and C. M. Tuckett, Oxford Handbooks (Oxford: Oxford University Press, 2015), 144, doi:10.1093/oxfordhb/9780199644117.013.8.

101. Origen, *Homilies on Luke*, trans. Joseph T. Lienhard, The Fathers of the Church 94 (Washington D.C.: Catholic University of America Press, 1996), 55, doi:10.2307/j.ctt32b0dn.

102. Translation from Brandon W. Hawk, *The Gospel of Pseudo-Matthew and the Nativity of Mary*, Early Christian Apocrypha 8 (Eugene, OR: Cascade Books, 2020). The Latin critical edition is Jan Gijsel, trans., *Libri de nativitate Mariae: Pseudo-Matthaei Evangelium, textus et commentarius, Libellus de nativitate sanctae Mariae, textus et commentarius*, Corpus Christianorum: Series Apocryphorum 9 (Turnhout: Brepols, 1997).

103. The reference is almost certainly to the Septuagint, as no known Hebrew version has 'animals' in that verse. See Bogdan Gabriel Bucur, *Scripture Re-Envisioned: Christophanic Exegesis and the Making of a Christian Bible* (Leiden: Brill, 2018), 191–207, doi:10.1163/9789004386112.

second is slightly less likely as there is no evidence of a Christmas interpretation to Habakkuk 3 before this text.[104] Thus both Origen and Pseudo-Matthew cite their Scriptures as a source for the two animals to supplement the accounts in Luke and Matthew.

Hugo Lundhaug has discussed a possible mental process that underlies this supplementation of narratives.[105] The process revolves around making sense of the Christmas narratives found in Luke and Matthew, which do not easily fit together. Lundhaug uses the so-called theory of Conceptual Blending to suggest how the 'historical process of interpretation may be conceptualized'.[106] A precise discussion of his method is not useful here, but the idea is that after a new narrative is created through the blending of Matthew and Luke, there is a phase of 'completion' and then 'elaboration'. In the completion phase, details from long-term memory are used to 'flesh out the already composed picture'.[107] Pregnant people do not walk long distances, so Mary rode a ... donkey. The child is lain in a feeding trough (a manger), so the birth must be in a stable. Now that there is a complete blended narrative, it is 'simulated mentally'; it is elaborated on with missing details. For example, the shepherds are seen to have gifts, because the magi have them. The number of magi is also imagined: three gifts must mean three magi. And importantly for our discussion, 'since there is a manger and the birth takes place in a stable, it follows that there must be animals present'.[108] Finally, knowing that there must be animals (though we do not know which ones) activates intertexts, and the storyworld becomes highly important. 'Animals that can be found within the canon', which for Origen and Pseudo-Matthew surely included Isaiah and Habakkuk, 'would thus be especially prone to be recruited'.[109] And the passage in Isaiah 1:3, which even refers to a feeding trough, fits rather well with the Christmas nativity.

This process that Lundhaug outlines resonates strongly with how Goodman conceptualizes the way fans attempt to keep universes consistent and coherent. In Chapter 1, I outlined three authoritative discourses – the universe, canon, and fandom. There, I discussed how, when two pieces of canon are contradictory, fandom can step in to create an authoritative fantext that fixes the issue: fix-it fic. Here we see a different process, building on the same basic principles. Two pieces

---

104. Cécile Dogniez, '"Au milieu de deux vivants, tu seras connu": lectures juive et chrétienne d'Habacuc 3, 2ᶜ', in *Judaïsme et christianisme chez les Pères*, ed. Marie-Anne Vannier, Judaïsme antique et origines du christianisme 8 (Turnhout: Brepols, 2016), 165–85, doi:10.1484/M.JAOC-EB.5.110703.

105. Hugo Lundhaug, 'Canon and Interpretation: A Cognitive Perspective', in *Canon and Canonicity: The Formation and Use of Scripture*, ed. Einar Thomassen (Copenhagen: Museum Tusculanum Press, University of Copenhagen, 2010), 67–90.

106. Lundhaug, 'Canon and Interpretation', 78.
107. Lundhaug, 'Canon and Interpretation', 79.
108. Lundhaug, 'Canon and Interpretation', 80.
109. Lundhaug, 'Canon and Interpretation', 82.

of canon (Matthew and Luke) tell the same story and thus reflect a single event in the universe. Fanworks – homilies of Origen, retellings of Matthew by Pseudo-Matthew, or art on sarcophagi and church walls – have stepped in to create a complete universe, incorporating Matthew and Luke, and also other parts of canon, such as Isaiah or Habakkuk. But fandom is not a unified discourse: 'fanworks (not only fan fiction, but fan art, fan vids, and so on) do not only attempt to complete the textual universe; they offer a huge variety of different and often mutually exclusive textual representations of the fiction'.[110] I already discussed antagonism and mutual exclusivity of fan engagement in the previous two chapters, here we can simply note that Origen and Pseudo-Matthew's interpretations of the birth of Christ differ. They both have the ox and ass present, but in Pseudo-Matthew Jesus is born in a cave and lain in a manger in a stable *after* the shepherds visit, whereas Origen's homily has the shepherds visit Jesus in the manger. Elsewhere, Origen places the manger in a cave, not a stable at all (Contra Celsum 1.51). Thus, ultimately, though a storyworld requires a certain amount of coherence, there is also space for diversity of opinion and narrative.

Regardless of how the ox and the ass made it into the Christmas nativity, it is clear that they are there to stay. Though the oldest gospels make no mention of ox and ass, audiences – both ancient and contemporary – perceive their presence. The ox and the ass are similar to what fans call 'fanon': a 'process whereby material that is created as an addition or supplement to the canon becomes accepted and used by other fanfiction writers'.[111] Fanon can also be a widespread interpretation of an event that canon leaves vague, for example the common assumption that there were three magi from the east.[112] For a fannish innovation to become fanon, it needs to become pervasive among a group of fans, and eventually though most fans are aware of the interpretation, very few fans are aware of its origins. The ox and ass were innovations at some point, and have become extremely common, yet few are aware of their origins. There is a communal process happening that elevates a fannish reading to fanon: a large group of fans need to come to see the fan fiction as useful.

But not every narrative becomes or remains fanon: the nativity cave, present in both Pseudo-Matthew and Origen, is far less omnipresent.[113] Some fan innovations are picked up by communities, whereas others fall by the wayside. Fan author

---

110. Lesley Goodman, 'Disappointing Fans: Fandom, Fictional Theory, and the Death of the Author', *The Journal of Popular Culture* 48, no. 4 (August 2015): 666, doi:10.1111/jpcu.12223.

111. Bronwen Thomas, 'Canons and Fanons: Literary Fanfiction Online', *Dichtung Digital* 37 (2007), doi: 10.25969/mediarep/17701.

112. Lundhaug, 'Canon and Interpretation', 81.

113. The Christmas cave is still seen in Christmas 'stables' worldwide. The pilgrimage site, as Jody Vaccaro Lewis notes, for the birth of Christ is a cave: 'the Emperor Constantine commissioned the building of the Basilica of the Nativity over the designated cave in Bethlehem, which was completed in the 330s and remains a popular pilgrimage site today';

Melusina reflects that 'fan inventions become fanon because they resonate with readers and writers'.[114] This is an affective process, and not only the result of critical reading and writing. As Alasdair Stuart explains, 'fanon is critical interpretation combined with emotional attachment',[115] and it is specifically the emotional attachment that appears to influence whether a piece of fanon endures. Additionally, as fanon is a communal product, there are differences between fan communities; what is fanon for the one is not fanon for another. Take the magi: in the West usually seen as three, but in the Eastern tradition there are usually twelve.[116] Different communities have accepted different fan innovations as fanon. And finally, fanon is constantly shifting: 'fanon is something that is collaboratively achieved and subject to constant revision and updating'.[117] An example of this could be the addition of the little drummer boy, nowadays often found in Christmas stables, who finds his origins in the 1951 carol of the same name.[118] After almost two millennia, a single piece of fan art became so influential that for many it required an update to the Christmas fanon.

Moving from fanon to the entire world of fan production, fandom itself functions as an expanding transmedia enterprise of sorts. Taken together, the combined production of fans creates storyworlds encompassing (parts of) those of the canonical texts. 'The entirety of stories and critical commentary written in a fandom', Busse and Hellekson explain, 'offers an ever-growing, ever-expanding version of the characters. These multitudes of interpretations of characters and canon scenes are often contradictory yet complementary to one another and the

---

Jody Vaccaro Lewis, 'The Inn, the Manger, the Swaddling Cloths, the Shepherds, and the Animals', in *The Oxford Handbook of Christmas*, ed. Timothy Larsen, Oxford Handbooks (Oxford University Press, 2020), 227, doi:10.1093/oxfordhb/9780198831464.013.19. Similarly there is artistic evidence of the cave, especially in Eastern Orthodox iconography, which usually takes the following form: 'the Christ Child lies in a manger within the cave of apocryphal tradition, flanked by an ox and an ass, while Mary reclines beside him'. Mary B. Cunningham, 'Eastern Orthodoxy', in *The Oxford Handbook of Christmas*, ed. Timothy Larsen, Oxford Handbooks (Oxford University Press, 2020), 132, doi:10.1093/oxfordhb/9780198831464.013.11.

114. Melusina, 'More Than You Ever Wanted to Know About Canon and Fanon', *Cultural Infidelities Meta* (blog), 2004, https://web.archive.org/web/20210419031505/https://www.culturalinfidelities.com/Meta/more-than-you-ever-wanted-to-know.htm [accessed 19 April 2021].

115. Stuart Alasdair, 'Dean Winchester and Commander Shepard Walk Into A Bar: Why Fanon Matters', *Uncanny Magazine* 17 (July–August 2017).

116. Lundhaug, 'Canon and Interpretation', 81. Or, for another example, see the enduring role of the Christmas cave in the Eastern Orthodox tradition, see footnote 112.

117. Thomas, 'Canons and Fanons'.

118. Todd Decker, 'Carols and Music Since 1900', in *The Oxford Handbook of Christmas*, ed. Timothy Larsen, Oxford Handbooks (Oxford University Press, 2020), 334, doi:10.1093/oxfordhb/9780198831464.013.28.

source text'.[119] Fans, communally, create different versions of the world engendered by original texts. They create new worlds, which are larger, different, and even contradictory. This 'fantext' is in essence a fannish storyworld, created by fans from their canons. And, the relationship between fantext and canon is reciprocal. Busse and Hellekson continue, pointing out that it is obvious 'how fans' understanding of the sources is always already filtered through the interpretations and characterizations existing in the fantext'.[120]

While fanon is the product of cooperation between fans, it also influences authors and producers. Fanon can 'ascend' to become canon.[121] There are examples of fan-created characters being included in later instalments of a series, such as the *My Little Pony: Friendship is Magic*[122] pony 'Derpy Hooves'.[123] Here fans named and developed a personality and backstory for a character who appeared once in the background of a scene. Producers began to put that character into the show more often, and after a while 'featured prominently in a story of her own'.[124] Something similar can be seen in *Lord of the Rings*[125] fandom, where a background character in the Council of Elrond from *The Fellowship of the Ring* (2001) came to be known to fans as Figwit.[126] Figwit's fame grew, even sparking a documentary film released in 2004.[127] In the later filming of *Return of the King* (2003), Figwit became an

---

119. Kristina Busse and Karen Hellekson, 'Introduction: Work in Progress', in *Fan Fiction and Fan Communities in the Age of the Internet: New Essays*, ed. Karen Hellekson and Kristina Busse (Jefferson, NC: McFarland, 2006), 7.

120. Busse and Hellekson, 'Introduction: Work in Progress', 7.

121. Stijn Reijnders et al., 'Fandom and Fan Fiction', in *The International Encyclopedia of Media Effects*, ed. Patrick Rössler, Cynthia A. Hoffner, and Liesbet Zoonen (Hoboken, NJ: Wiley, 2017), 6, doi:10.1002/9781118783764.wbieme0176.

122. *My Little Pony: Friendship is Magic* was an animated TV show producing 221 episodes between 2010 and 2019, and film in 2017. The series was created by Lauren Faust, at the behest of toy manufacturer Hasbro. The show included many transmedia products, including toys, comics, card games, and video games.

123. Derek Johnson, 'Participation Is Magic: Collaboration, Authorial Legitimacy, and the Audience Function', in *A Companion to Media Authorship*, ed. Jonathan Gray and Derek Johnson (Oxford: Wiley-Blackwell, 2013), 143–52, doi:10.1002/9781118505526.ch7.

124. Johnson, 'Participation Is Magic', 143.

125. In this instance, the fandom refers to the trilogy of films – *The Fellowship of the Ring* (2001), *The Two Towers* (2002) and *The Return of the King* (2003) – directed by Peter Jackson. Jackson's films are based on the *Lord of the Rings* books written by J. R. R. Tolkien in the mid-twentieth century.

126. In typical fannish style, Figwit's name is an acronym for 'Frodo is great ... who is THAT?!?', because when the protagonist Frodo 'says 'I will take it!', we are so impressed we start to think 'Frodo is great!' But before we finish, the camera pans and we see Figwit, smoldering enigmatically in the background. All other thoughts are whisked away by that elf – who is THAT?! He's gorgeous!' *Figwit Lives!*, http://figwitlives.net/.

127. *Frodo Is Great ... Who Is That?!!*, directed by Hannah Clarke, Stan Alley, and Nick Booth (Midnight Film, 2004).

established character in the trilogy, and credit is given to fans in the DVD commentary on the film.[128] Other times, unnamed characters adopt their fan name in later instalments, such as the beast in Disney's *Beauty and the Beast* (1991) coming to be known as Adam.[129] There are hundreds of examples of ascended canon.[130]

Meredith Warren, in one of the earliest biblical studies articles on fan fiction, demonstrates similar occurrences in biblical texts. After giving some examples of how fan fiction influenced later books in the fandom: fanon inventions became canon,[131] she argues that similar processes can be found in the Old Testament Pseudepigrapha, 'where the Torah has been interpolated with later traditions from the outside sources'.[132] In other words, derivative fantexts sometimes have the power to alter their sources. More often, however, as evidenced by how derivative texts influence rabbinical and patristic biblical interpretation, fantexts influence the reading and interpretation of canon. To borrow Warren's conclusion 'the apocrypha and pseudepigrapha pervade our reading of the canon … even if subconsciously'.[133] Thus, though neither Luke nor Matthew make explicit mention of an ox or an ass in the stable, readers assume they are there and illuminated manuscripts include them – right next to text that does not.

All texts, whether they are serious or silly, canonical or non-canonical, end up being authoritative or influential to those who engage with them, though of course some are more widely authoritative than others. From Lego Darth Vader to Hux's cat, from Thecla causing Paul's suffering to the ox and the ass, all these fannish innovations influence the reading and interpretation of texts. Sometimes this influence is clear, but most often narratives from the expanded storyworld affect the reading of other narratives in ways that are not always obvious. It may not be obvious to all that the creation of Millicent the Cat is more than just a simple joke,

---

128. Dimitra Fimi, 'Filming Folklore: Adapting Fantasy for the Big Screen through Peter Jackson's Lord of the Rings', in *Picturing Tolkien: Essays on Peter Jackson's The Lord of the Rings Film Trilogy*, ed. Janice M. Bogstad and Philip E. Kaveny (Jefferson, NC: McFarland, 2011), 95–97.

129. Tok Thompson, 'The Beauty, the Beast, and the Fanon: The Vernacularization of the Literary Canon and an Epilogue to Modernity', in *Folklore and Social Media*, ed. Trevor J. Blank and Andrew Peck (Louisville, CO: University Press of Colorado, 2020), 161, doi:10.7330/9781646420599.c008. For more examples see, 'Ascended Fan Nickname', *TV Tropes*, https://tvtropes.org/pmwiki/pmwiki.php/Main/AscendedFanNickname.

130. Community edited website *TV Tropes* lists scores of examples on its page: 'Ascended Fanon', *TV Tropes*, https://tvtropes.org/pmwiki/pmwiki.php/Main/AscendedFanon.

131. Meredith Warren, 'My OTP: Harry Potter Fanfiction and the Old Testament Pseudepigrapha', *Scriptura* 8 (2006): 53–66.

132. Warren, 'My OTP', 64. See also, Hindy Najman, 'The Vitality of Scripture Within and Beyond the "Canon"', *Journal for the Study of Judaism* 43, no. 4–5 (2012): 497–518, doi:10.1163/15700631-12341237.

133. Warren, 'My OTP', 66.

causing the Hilterian Hux to be recast as a cat-loving rogue. Similarly, it is not immediately obvious that the addition of an ox and ass to the Christmas stable is Judeophobic.[134] Earlier, I discussed how Origen originally introduced the ox and ass to the stable, but didn't give the complete context of his homily. Here is a longer citation:

> That was the manger of which the inspired prophet said, 'The ox knows his owner and the ass his master's manger' [Isaiah 1:3]. The ox is a clean animal, the ass an unclean animal. 'The ass knows his master's manger'. The people of Israel did not know their Lord's manger, but an unclean animal from among the Gentiles did. Scripture says, 'Israel, indeed, did not know me, and my people did not understand me' [Isaiah 1:3]. Let us understand this manger. (*Homilies on Luke* 13.7)[135]

Origen's ox and ass go hand in hand with strong Judeophobic imagery. The ox, quite simply, symbolizes that the people of Israel rejected Jesus Christ and that God has rejected them because of this. Though for many the placement of an ox and ass in the stable may not reference anti-Jewish thinking, for many it does. Take for example, Léonide Ouspensky and Vladimir Lossky in their reference work on Eastern Orthodox icons. They explain the importance of the presence of the animals:

> In the cave, close by the manger, stand an ox and an ass. The Gospels do not speak of them. Yet in all the pictures of the Nativity of Christ, they are immediately beside the Divine Child. Their place in the very centre of the icon points to the importance given by the Church to this detail. It is nothing less than the fulfilment of the prophecy of Isaiah (1:3) which has the deepest instructive significance: 'The ox knows his owner, and the ass his master's crib: but Israel does not know Me, and the people has not regarded Me'. By the presence of the animals, the icon reminds us of Isaiah's prophecy and calls us to the knowledge and understanding of the mystery of the Divine Dispensation.[136]

Though much may be obscured by the theological language here, the meaning is rather simple. The central place of the animals in the stable shows how central they are to the Christian church. For the church they symbolize the fulfilment of prophecy that Israel will not accept Jesus as the Messiah and salvation will pass on

---

134. A useful discussion of the ox and ass in ancient images, albeit one that admits how these images are potentially 'disparaging toward the Jews' yet avoids the issue of Judeophobia completely, can be found in Ronald V. Huggins, 'The Ox and the Donkey', *Midwestern Journal of Theology* 9, no. 2 (2010): 179–93. I critically discuss this article below.

135. Origen, *Homilies on Luke*, 55.

136. Léonide Ouspensky and Vladimir Lossky, *The Meaning of Icons*, trans. G. E. H. Palmer and E. Kadloubovsky, 2nd ed. (Crestwood, NY: St. Vladimir's Seminary Press, 1999), 159.

to Christians. This theological thinking, often called 'supersessionism' as Christianity is seen to supersede Judaism, has increasingly come under fire.[137] The Judeophobic interpretation of the ox and ass can be found in Christian interpretations throughout history, including the common blaming of Jewish people for the death of Jesus,[138] and it is extremely easy to find contemporary sources that maintain this interpretation of the ox and ass, without any critical engagement.[139]

Ronald Huggins, in his extensive discussion of images of the ox and the ass, also shortly discusses if this Judeophobic interpretation also influenced the portrayal of the animals in art. He mentions, by way of an autobiographical example, one altarpiece where the ass is inside the stable and the ox stands outside looking, and another painting where the ass is looking at Mary in adoration and the ox is staring at a grate in the ground, presumably for the removal of feces.[140] In other words, in the first painting the ox is excluded from the stable, in the second the ox does not partake in the religious veneration. Regarding the second he readily agrees that this is 'disparaging towards Judaism', for the first he feels that the image contains 'nothing that could be read as in any way disparaging towards the Jews', especially as 'one is hard pressed to find an example of a more charmingly and affectionately rendered ox'.[141] Huggins concludes his article with a long citation of important fifth-century theologian Augustine of Hippo's Sermon 204, including the sentence 'from the Jews came the horned ox, since among them the horns of the cross were prepared for Christ'. Horrifically, Huggins calls this 'one of the most moving expositions of the role of the ox'.[142] For me, the way Huggins discusses the two animals is highly reminiscent of how Gloria Wekker describes 'white innocence'.[143] His circumvention of and apologetic attitude towards these Judeophobic images, resonates strongly with the way white Dutch people defend the traditional

---

137. A good place to look into this topic in a bit more detail would be Sarah E. Rollens, Eric Vanden Eykel, and Meredith Warren, eds., *Judeophobia in the New Testament: Texts, Contexts, and Pedagogy* (Grand Rapids, MI: Eerdmans, 2024).

138. Huggins, 'The Ox and the Donkey', 193.

139. A short search on Google provides thousands of sermons and bible studies repeating this interpretation, including http://ldolphin.org/isaiah64.html [accessed 15 September 2023]; https://www.biblestudytools.com/gnt/isaiah/1-3.html [accessed 15 September 2023]; https://www.studylight.org/commentary/isaiah/1-3.html [accessed 15 September 2023]; https://biblehub.com/commentaries/isaiah/1-3.htm [accessed 15 September 2023].

140. Huggins, 'The Ox and the Donkey', 187–90. The images Huggins describes are available in colour and higher quality online: https://www.museum-joanneum.at/blog/die-vision-der-schmerzlosen-geburt-christi/ [accessed 15 September 2023]; https://www.museum-joanneum.at/en/alte-galerie/exhibitions/exhibitions/eternity-and-its-effigy/the-godly-child-nativity [accessed 15 September 2023].

141. Huggins, 'The Ox and the Donkey', 188, 191.

142. Huggins, 'The Ox and the Donkey', 193.

143. Gloria Wekker, *White Innocence: Paradoxes of Colonialism and Race* (Durham, NC: Duke University Press, 2016).

Sinterklaas festivities: specifically people dressing up as the enslaved *Zwarte Piet* (Black Pete) – blackface and all. '*Zwarte Piet*', Wekker summarizes, 'is considered by many white Dutch people to be . . . an innocent and thoroughly pleasant traditional festivity', the figure is 'harmless and innocent' and certainly not racist.[144] These same white Dutch people insist that 'the Netherlands is and always has been color-blind and antiracist.'[145] White innocence is evident in the Dutch psyche as 'a society that has managed to convince itself that nearly four hundred years of colonialism have, miraculously, not left any traces of racism, either in culture, history, language, representations of the self and the other, or in institutions'.[146] Indeed, many Dutch wholeheartedly insist that there is nothing racist about *Zwarte Piet*. Examining this, Wekker concludes 'I am led to suspect bad faith',[147] and I suspect the same amongst some Christian interpreters. Huggins is able to innocently discuss Judeophobic texts and images, and even decide on behalf of marginalized groups whether images are actually 'disparaging' or not. He's also able to innocently cite extremely Judeophobic texts, and selectively cite them to allow him to end his article invoking a Christian call to recognize Jesus, including a final 'Amen'.[148] Now surely the example of *Zwarte Piet* is more obviously problematic, yet the political implications are the same. Every time white people wear blackface to embody *Zwarte Piet*, a racist narrative is reinforced and reinscribed, whether or not they are intending to be racist. Similarly, every time the Christmas stable includes an ox and ass, a supersessionist and Judeophobic narrative is reinforced and reinscribed.[149]

Conclusions and Significance

In this chapter I tackled the conceptual question why derivative texts matter. Drawing on critical theory on storyworlds and world building, I examined the political implications of living in the Christian storyworld. Though, as I discussed in Chapters 3 and 4, the canon of this storyworld was strongly policed, the heteroglossic reality remained. And those many voices were, though maybe not equally authorized, influential, and authoritative. In contemporary fandoms non-canonical, non-authorized, and even downright silly texts become influential to both the way individual fans view their fandom and fandom itself. In (early) Christianity the same is true.

As the Christian storyworld is built and reinforced this influences the way people view both the real world and the texts that are part of the storyworld. The

---

144. Wekker, *White Innocence*, 142, 147.
145. Wekker, *White Innocence*, 31.
146. Wekker, *White Innocence*, 166.
147. Wekker, *White Innocence*, 18.
148. Huggins, 'The Ox and the Donkey', 193.
149. Other examples of this same process abound, see, e.g. John F. A. Sawyer, 'Combating Prejudices about the Bible and Judaism', *Theology* 94, no. 760 (July 1991): 271, doi:10.1177/0040571X9109400405.

Christian storyworld which is strongly grounded in the so-called Primary World, reinforces certain assumptions about the real world: the existence of miracles, healings and God. This means that the many texts that make up the storyworld influence interpretations of the world the audiences inhabits, and naturally of the (canonical) texts. In this way, all texts are authoritative. The influence of the storyworld on the interpretation of texts – and indeed on the way fans see the world – is never innocent and always political. Examples of non-canonical influence from *Star Wars* illuminated potentially problematic, Judeophobic aspects in early Christianity. Ultimately, it should be clear that derivative texts matter. They influence interpretations of texts, they influence texts, and they even influence the way we imagine real world itself.

Bringing the discussion of the last three chapters together, allow me a few final words on the role authority plays in policing storyworlds. For every transmedia storyworld, there will always be a diversity of voices. The storyworld coheres, but cannot be completely consistent and univocal. Thus, there is a natural 'tension between the authoritative desire to unify on the one hand and the hybrid, constructed nature of "heteroglot" utterances on the other'.[150] In other words, there is a tension between the desire for a coherent singular storyworld and the diverse nature of the transmedial and transfictional universe. Hassler-Forest argues that this authoritative desire for coherence is present among storyworld creators, and also academics studying these worlds. Here lies the danger: 'this exclusive focus on narrative and aesthetic coherence has far-reaching political implications. The desire to create, navigate, or otherwise engage with an imaginary world that is stable and coherent expresses a desire to understand what Wolf describes as the Primary World in similar terms'.[151] The authoritative desire to build a single coherent narrative for our storyworlds shows an underlying desire to structure the actual world in the same way. The desire to police a vast collection of narratives in diverse media and cultures, and to canonize a single interpretation and instantiation of the storyworld, shows the same desire to police and canonize the world we inhabit. In this way my discussion of early Christian reactions to derivative works – canonization, heresiology and world building and policing – demonstrates a fundamental view of how the world should be: univocal, coherent, consistent, logical and orthodox.

---

150. Hassler-Forest, 'Politics of World Building', 381.
151. Hassler-Forest, 'Politics of World Building', 382.

Epilogue

'I COULDN'T GET THESE LEGENDS OUT OF MY MIND'

As more and more biblical scholars become aware of fan communities and practices, there is an increasing amount of people who see these fields as an obvious heuristic. The overlapping – yet different! – usage of the term 'canon' is often pointed out. There are many popular and scholarly writings which note strong similarities between ancient Jewish and Christian texts, and contemporary fan fiction.[1] There is certainly evidence that contemporary fan studies can enrich the study of ancient texts, and the opposite is also true.[2] In this book I have examined the interplay between the objects and theories of fan studies and biblical studies, and its implications for early Christian texts in a sustained way that hasn't been published before. Throughout this book I have traced commonalities between ancient Christian products and contemporary fan products. I have explored how contemporary research and theory on fan communities and fan cultures can elucidate ancient texts and communities. It was never my aim to argue that ancient Christians were fans or that Christian writings were fan fiction, rather the argument was one of similarities and dissimilarities. I remind the reader of my allusion to my own fandom, *The Hitch Hiker's Guide to the Galaxy*, from the Introduction. Like the Guide, I am sure this book 'has many omissions and contains much that is apocryphal, or at least wildly inaccurate'.[3]

Throughout this book, I have highlighted commonalities and analogies from fan cultures that elucidate the study of early Christian communities and texts. I will not repeat those arguments here. This interdisciplinary project broke the ground for a fuller exploration of the interplay between the fields of biblical studies and fan studies. It is my hope that this work is productive for the study of ancient parabiblical texts, and that it can serve as a starting point for much further research in this field. Hopefully this work functions as a gateway to engagement with fan studies methods for other scholars of ancient Christian and Jewish texts. Many

---

1. See, for examples, pp. 11–13.

2. See, for example, Ika Willis, 'The Classical Canon and/as Transformative Work', *Transformative Works and Cultures* 21 (2016), doi:10.3983/twc.2016.0807.

3. Douglas Adams, *The Hitch Hiker's Guide to the Galaxy*, Pan Original (London: Pan Books, 1979), 4.

topics in fandom remain unexplored in this book, for example material culture and material fan practices (e.g. cosplay and replica building), religious and fan pilgrimage, mimetic fan practices and martyrdom, and the concept of superfandom, fan auteurs and church organization and authority.[4]

Returning to Anne Rice for the final time in this exploration of fan fiction and early Christian literature, I wish to offer a meta-reflection on the issues tackled in this book and on the field of biblical studies in general. If biblical studies is going to borrow from fan studies, it also needs to learn from the meta-considerations of that field. We would be silly to keep repeating mistakes made by others.

Rice's Author's Note has been a rich seam for this work, touching on fannish desires to extend narratives, the difficulties in separating fact and fiction, the enduring influence of derivative texts, and the politics inherent in authorizing some texts above others. As Rice reflects on her love and use of the non-canonical narratives – the 'legends' as she calls them – she concludes 'I couldn't get these legends out of my mind'.[5] As I have discussed throughout this book, these narratives endure and remain influential. Whether they are legends, myths, tall tales, historical fact, or alternative traditions, they exist, they influence readers and readings, and they polarize.

The final aspect of Rice's author's note to consider in our discussion is her final wishes for her work. After she explains what her intentions were and justifies her choices, she dedicates her book as follows:

> This is a book I offer to all Christians—to the fundamentalists, to the Roman Catholics, to the most liberal Christians in the hope that my embrace of more conservative doctrines will have some coherence for them in the here and now of the book. I offer it to scholars in the hope that they will perhaps enjoy seeing the evidence of the research that's gone into it, and of course I offer it to those whom I so greatly admire who have been my teachers though I've never met them and probably never will.
>
> I offer this book to those who know nothing of Jesus Christ in the hope that you will see him in these pages in some form. I offer this novel with love to my readers who've followed me through one strange turn after another in the hope that Jesus will be as real to you as any other character I've ever launched into the world we share.
>
> After all, is Christ Our Lord not the ultimate supernatural hero, the ultimate outsider, the ultimate immortal of them all?[6]

---

4. Matt Hills, '"Proper Distance" in the Ethical Positioning of Scholar-Fandoms: Between Academics' and Fans' Moral Economies?', in *Fan Culture: Theory/Practice*, ed. Katherine Larsen and Lynn S. Zubernis (Newcastle upon Tyne: Cambridge Scholars, 2012), 20; Anastasia Salter and Mel Stanfill, *A Portrait of the Auteur as Fanboy: The Construction of Authorship in Transmedia Franchises* (Jackson, MS: University Press of Mississippi, 2020), doi:10.14325/mississippi/9781496830463.001.0001.

5. Anne Rice, *Christ the Lord: Out of Egypt: A Novel* (New York: Knopf, 2005), 451.

6. Rice, *Christ the Lord*, 2005, 452–53.

Rice's dedication highlights the subjectivity of her work. Though she sets out to narrate the 'Jesus of the gospels', here she explains that she embraces 'conservative doctrines'. She allowed her faith to influence her research. The goal of her book is similarly subjective: she writes in the hope that non-Christians come to 'see' Jesus. Her final words link the Jesus of her book to herself and her work through the usual characters in her previous books (and thus the characters that her fans are used to reading about). Jesus, like vampires, is an immortal, heroic outsider.

This note illustrates how fandom, like any other area of research, is an inherently subjective phenomenon. It is also deeply embodied. Consider the definitions of fans that I discussed in the Introduction to this book: fans are 'obsessed',[7] 'emotionally involved',[8] and have 'deep, positive emotional conviction'.[9] Anne Rice claims multiple times that she has an 'obsession' with the figure of Jesus Christ.[10] From this passion she writes her book. Her fandom lies at the heart of her work as an author. In this epilogue, I'd like to move on to another level of and final reflection on the discussion of fandom. What does it mean to be – similar to Rice – both a fan *and* a scholar of one's fandom? Discussions of this topic in fan studies can illuminate a similar issue in the field of biblical studies. How is a scholar's research affected by the intertwining of their embodiment and identity with their object of research? Many fan scholars are themselves fans, and this dual identity has formed some aspects of the field. Take, for example, Henry Jenkins's much-cited 1992 work *Textual Poachers*. Immediately in his acknowledgements he identifies as a fan.[11] Jenkins uses his dual identity as fan *and* academic to 'serve and speak for fan communities'.[12] Duffett discusses this dual nature in depth.[13] He gives some examples of how fan scholars discuss their hybrid identity as 'aca-fan'. He quotes Jenkins saying 'I come to both *Star Trek* and fan fiction as a fan first and a scholar second. My participation as a fan long precedes my academic interest in it', and cites another aca-fan saying 'this entire book is an example of a childhood passion channelled into an academic career'.[14] Duffett highlights how this could be problematic:

> They are ... ready to use the space of academia to their advantage *as fans*. Such scholars have not only dropped the old concern to maintain a critical distance from their object of study. They have also reduced the distance between fandom and the academy by proclaiming their dual identities. Aca-fandom has therefore questioned the norms of academic subjectivity.

---

7. Matt Hills, *Fan Cultures* (London: Routledge, 2002), ix.
8. Cornel Sandvoss, *Fans: The Mirror of Consumption* (Cambridge: Polity Press, 2005), 8.
9. Mark Duffett, *Understanding Fandom: An Introduction to the Study of Media Fan Culture* (London: Bloomsbury, 2013), 18.
10. Rice, *Christ the Lord*, 429, 430.
11. Henry Jenkins, *Textual Poachers: Television Fans & Participatory Culture* (London: Routledge, 1992), vii.
12. Duffett, *Understanding Fandom*, 267.
13. Duffett, *Understanding Fandom*, 262–69.
14. Duffett, *Understanding Fandom*, 267.

Aca-fans highlight a troubling issue at the heart of academic scholarship: the assumption of objectivity. The issue they highlight is *not* that aca-fandom is subjective while the rest of scholarship is objective. Rather, the existence of self-proclaimed aca-fans remind scholarship that objectivity is a 'rhetorical claim', 'an adopted strategy'.[15] These claims at objectivity are dangerous because all knowledge is political; the aca-fans foreground the dangers inherent to claiming unembodied objectivity. Aca-fans highlight other issues as well. Consider Matt Hills's discussion of the ethics of being both a fan and a scholar. He highlights the 'the need for those of us writing academically about fandom, but also drawing on fan identities, to carefully consider just who we are speaking for, and what scholar/fan exclusions might structure this engagement'.[16] The difficulty is twofold. First, there is the issue of normativity: as a fan, you are more likely to foreground your own experiences in your analyses. These experiences easily become normative for academic discussions of fandom. At the same time there is the issue of identity, as both a fan and a scholar, there are multiple bids for your identity. Hills argues that these identities 'continue to act as differential interpretive communities with divergent norms and discursive practices … the identities cannot be united without losing sight of these contexts'.[17] While some fan scholars feel that scholarship and fandom can – and *should* – co-exist,[18] Hills argues the opposite: that academia and fandom represent vastly differing contexts, and that there is an inherent loss associated with uniting them.

All of these issues (subjectivity/objectivity, normativity, identity) are of course not new claims, but these kinds of issues are not always sufficiently explored in the field of biblical studies, where many scholars see or saw the texts they study as authoritative Scripture. Their identity as Christian is so normative and taken for granted, that the issues highlighted by aca-fans are hardly considered. Scholars often speak with dual identities as both Christians and academics. Countless academic monographs in biblical studies include a dedication to God, and major academic conferences of biblical scholars include Christian worship, in some cases mandatory. Let me be clear that I am also talking about myself here. I come from a Christian tradition, I have taught at Christian seminaries, and I regularly lead Christians in worship. These aspects of me, of my history, of my embodiment influence my scholarship – of this I am all too aware. But, I am also fully aware (and I hope that my scholarship reflects this) that my scholarship cannot be absolutely objective, and that my experiences are not normative. Indeed, it is the subjectivity of my research that makes it *mine*.

15. Duffett, *Understanding Fandom*, 268.
16. Hills, 'Proper Distance', 14.
17. Hills, 'Proper Distance', 16–17.
18. See, for example, Kristina Busse and Karen Hellekson, 'Introduction: Work in Progress', in *Fan Fiction and Fan Communities in the Age of the Internet: New Essays*, ed. Karen Hellekson and Kristina Busse (Jefferson, NC: McFarland, 2006), 24–25.

These issues of subjectivity, normativity, and identity recently came to a head in New Testament studies, when Stephen Young accused New Testament scholarship of being protectionist, that is 'the privileging of a source's own claims to such an extent that interpreters let them dictate academic analysis.'[19] He argued that New Testament scholars were so invested in those texts as Scripture, that they did little more than attempt to describe the thinking of the authors of the texts. Young's accusation is hardly surprising, as describing what the author is trying to say is exactly what 'exegesis' – the standard method of biblical studies – attempts to do. Kavin Rowe's response did (at least in the eyes of many scholars) little to counteract Young's fundamental claims.[20] Indeed, the last sentence of his first paragraph demonstrates exactly the double agenda that Christian scholars of the Bible – aca-fans in a sense – have: 'we should study the New Testament because it might tell the truth about God'.[21] Young has continued making similar points about New Testament scholars and scholarship, more recently by demonstrating that extremely popular New Testament scholar N. T. Wright uses his position as an academic to legitimize evangelical, patriarchal, Judeophobic theological stances.[22] 'Wright', argues Young, 'can then leverage *his* version of a Jewish Paul to legitimate *his* conservative Protestant project as historical. The effect is to authorize *his* interpretations.'[23] Of course, Wright never portrays these interpretations as *his*. They are objective, unembodied facts.

The question that aca-fandom raises in this context is how much Wright's fandom, or investment in his type of Christianity, influences the conclusions he reaches. Take for example, Katherine Larsen and Lynn S. Zubernis's warning that 'much of the academic work on fandom is influenced by aca-fans' pre-theoretical investments in specific fan practices'.[24] The influence of a lifetime of fandom cannot help but influence the outcomes of one's scholarship. This means that Wright's

---

19. Stephen L. Young, '"Let's Take the Text Seriously": The Protectionist Doxa of Mainstream New Testament Studies', *Method & Theory in the Study of Religion* 32, nos. 4–5 (2019): 328, doi:10.1163/15700682-12341469.

20. C. Kavin Rowe, 'What If It Were True? Why Study the New Testament', *New Testament Studies* 68, no. 2 (2022): 144–55, doi:10.1017/S002868852100031X.

21. Rowe, 'What If It Were True?', 144.

22. See also the vital points that Blossom Stefaniw makes about the academic and the intellectual being gendered male. Blossom Stefaniw, 'Feminist Historiography and Uses of the Past', *Studies in Late Antiquity* 4, no. 3 (2020): 260–83, doi:10.1525/sla.2020.4.3.260; Blossom Stefaniw, 'Masculinity, Historiography, and Uses of the Past: An Introduction', *Journal of Early Christian History* 11, no. 1 (2021): 1–14, doi:10.1080/2222582X.2021.1931903.

23. Stephen L. Young, 'So Radically Jewish That He's an Evangelical Christian: N.T. Wright's Judeophobic and Privileged Paul', *Interpretation: A Journal of Bible and Theology* 76, no. 4 (2022): 347, doi:10.1177/00209643221107910, emphasis mine.

24. Katherine Larsen and Lynn S. Zubernis, 'Introduction', in *Fan Culture: Theory/Practice*, ed. Katherine Larsen and Lynn S. Zubernis (Newcastle upon Tyne: Cambridge Scholars, 2012), 4.

scholarship, and his own experiences as a conservative, evangelical Christian, causes an 'annihilation or exnomination of fan practices beyond the scope of the scholar's pre-theoretical affective relationships'.[25] A lifetime of a certain type of Christian engagement with the New Testament is hard to put aside, and thus a Christian aca-fan can easily see their experience as objective or normative. The same holds for Rowe, seen rather clearly in his dismissal of other reactions to the New Testament: 'the response to the truth of the New Testament can never be other than a lived response'.[26] The same holds for me, if in a different way, for I too have a lifetime of engagement with Christian texts.

Though I have chosen to critique Wright and Rowe, the same criticism can be made of any scholar with a passion for their field, including myself. It is my hope that as biblical studies engages more with fan studies, we can develop more awareness of our own situatedness as fans, whether of Christianity, parabiblical texts, or ancient history. Following Hills's advice, we might be less likely to try to collapse the identities of fan *and* scholar into one; or we might be less likely to see our experiences and our embodiment as normative. Maybe we can learn from the mistakes being made in fan (studies) circles, just as fan studies can learn from our long tradition of 'aca-fans' in biblical studies. Writing on fan studies and race, Rukmini Pande hopes that her (excellent) book offers 'one step toward crafting newer, more self-reflexive, and more critical approaches toward media fandom'.[27] It is my hope that biblical studies can take similar steps. And, if nothing else, we can hopefully nurture an acceptance of our own subjectivity, and a deeper understanding of the passion and emotion that drove those who created and preserved the texts we study. They, like Anne Rice (and like myself), just 'couldn't get those legends out of their minds'.

---

25. Hills, 'Proper Distance', 21.
26. Rowe, 'What If It Were True?', 154.
27. Rukmini Pande, *Squee from the Margins: Fandom and Race*, Fandom & Culture (Iowa City, IA: University of Iowa Press, 2018), 196.

BIBLIOGRAPHY

Adams, Douglas. *The Hitch Hiker's Guide to the Galaxy*. Pan Original. London: Pan Books, 1979.
Alasdair, Stuart. 'Dean Winchester and Commander Shepard Walk Into A Bar: Why Fanon Matters'. *Uncanny Magazine* 17 (July–August 2017).
Alexander, Philip S. 'What Happened To The Jewish Priesthood After 70?' In *A Wandering Galilean: Essays in Honour of Seán Freyne*, edited by Zuleika Rodgers, Margaret Daly-Denton, and Anne Fitzpatrick-McKinley, 3–33. Supplements to the Journal for the Study of Judaism 132. Leiden: Brill, 2009. doi:10.1163/ej.9789004173552.i-622.9.
Amsler, Monika. 'Martyrs, Athletes, and Transmedia Storytelling in Late Antiquity'. *Transformative Works and Cultures* 31 (2019). doi:10.3983/twc.2019.1645.
Amsler, Monkia. 'The Making of Ḥanina Ben Dosa: Fan Fiction in the Babylonian Talmud'. *Transformative Works and Cultures* 31 (15 December 2019). doi:10.3983/twc.2019.1647.
Apocrypals. 'Biblerella (The Acts of Paul and Thecla)'. 21. https://apocrypals.libsyn.com/21-biblerella-the-acts-of-paul-and-thecla.
Apostolic Fathers. *The Apostolic Fathers I*. Translated by Bart D. Ehrman. Loeb Classical Library 24. Cambridge, MA: Harvard University Press, 2003.
Aspree. 'The Young "Messiah": Christians Delight in Really Bad Fanfiction'. *The Aquila Report*, 14 March 2016. https://theaquilareport.com/the-young-messiah-christians-delight-in-really-bad-fanfiction/.
Aune, David E. 'The Problem of the Messianic Secret'. *Novum Testamentum* 11, nos. 1–2 (1969): 1–31. doi:10.1163/156853669X00010.
Baarda, Tjitze. 'The Shechem Episode in the Testament of Levi: A Comparison with Other Traditions'. In *Sacred History and Sacred Texts in Early Judaism: A Symposium in Honour of A. S. van Der Woude*, edited by J. N. Bremmer and F. García Martínez, 11–74. Kampen: Kok Pharos, 1992.
Bacon-Smith, Camille. *Enterprising Women: Television Fandom and the Creation of Popular Myth*. Philadelphia, PA: University of Pennsylvania Press, 1992.
Bader, Mary Anna. *Tracing the Evidence: Dinah in Post-Hebrew Bible Literature*. Studies in Biblical Literature 102. New York: Lang, 2008.
Barclay, John M. G. 'There Is Neither Old Nor Young? Early Christianity and Ancient Ideologies of Age'. *New Testament Studies* 53, no. 2 (2007): 225–41. doi:10.1017/S0028688507000136.
Barenblat, Rachel. 'Fan Fiction and Midrash: Making Meaning'. *Transformative Works and Cultures* 17 (2014). doi:10.3983/twc.2014.0596.
Barenblat, Rachel. 'Gender, Voice, and Canon'. *Transformative Works and Cultures* 31 (15 December 2019). doi:10.3983/twc.2019.1589.
Barenblat, Rachel. 'Transformative Work: Midrash and Fanfiction'. *Religion & Literature* 43 (2011): 171–77.
Bauckham, Richard. 'The Brothers and Sisters of Jesus: An Epiphanian Response to John P. Meier'. *Catholic Biblical Quarterly* 56, no. 4 (1994): 686–700.

Bauer, Walter. *Orthodoxy and Heresy in Earliest Christianity*. Edited by Robert A. Kraft and Gerhard Krodel. 2nd ed. Philadelphia, PA: Fortress, 1971.

Bauer, Walter. *Rechtgläubigkeit und Ketzerei im ältesten Christentum*. Beiträge zur historische Theologie 10. Tübingen: Mohr, 1933.

Becker, Jürgen. *Untersuchungen zur Entstehungsgeschichte der Testamente der zwölf Patriarchen*. Arbeiten zur Geschichte des antiken Judentums und des Urchristentums 8. Leiden: Brill, 1970.

Bergren, Theodore A. *1 Clement: A Reader's Edition*. Washington, D.C.: Catholic University of America Press, 2020. doi:10.2307/j.ctv104tb3c.

Birkhold, Matthew H. *Characters before Copyright: The Rise and Regulation of Fan Fiction in Eighteenth-Century Germany*. Law and Literature. Oxford: Oxford University Press, 2019.

Block, Alex Ben. '5 Questions With George Lucas: Controversial "Star Wars" Changes, SOPA and "Indiana Jones 5"'. *Hollywood Reporter*, 9 February 2012. https://www.hollywoodreporter.com/movies/movie-news/george-lucas-star-wars-interview-288523/.

Bode, Lisa. 'Transitional Tastes: Teen Girls and Genre in the Critical Reception of Twilight'. *Continuum* 24, no. 5 (2010): 707–19. doi:10.1080/10304312.2010.505327.

Bonnstetter, Beth E., and Brian L. Ott. '(Re)Writing Mary Sue: *Écriture Féminine* and the Performance of Subjectivity'. *Text and Performance Quarterly* 31 (2011): 342–67. doi:10.1080/10462937.2011.602706.

Booth, Paul. *Digital Fandom 2.0: New Media Studies*. 2nd ed. Digital Formations 114. New York: Peter Lang, 2017.

Booth, Paul. *Playing Fans: Negotiating Fandom in the Digital Age*. Iowa City, IA: University of Iowa Press, 2015.

Borchardt, Francis. 'Influence and Power: The Types of Authority in the Process of Scripturalization'. *Scandinavian Journal of the Old Testament* 29 (2015): 182–96.

Bovon, François. 'Beyond the Canonical and the Apocryphal Books, the Presence of a Third Category: The Books Useful for the Soul'. *Harvard Theological Review* 105, no. 2 (2012): 125–37. doi:10.1017/S0017816012000466.

Bovon, François. 'Canonical and Apocryphal Acts of Apostles'. *Journal of Early Christian Studies* 11 (2003): 165–94.

Bovon, François. '"Useful for the Soul": Christian Apocrypha and Christian Spirituality'. In *The Oxford Handbook of Early Christian Apocrypha*, edited by Andrew Gregory, Tobias Nicklas, Christopher M. Tuckett, and Joseph Verheyden, 185–95. Oxford Handbooks. Oxford: Oxford University Press, 2015. doi:10.1093/oxfordhb/9780199644117.013.33.

Brakke, David. *The Gnostics: Myth, Ritual, and Diversity in Early Christianity*. Cambridge, MA: Harvard University Press, 2010.

Brakke, David. 'A New Fragment of Athanasius's Thirty-Ninth *Festal Letter*: Heresy, Apocrypha, and the Canon'. *Harvard Theological Review* 103, no. 1 (2010): 47–66. doi:10.1017/S0017816009990307.

Braudy, Leo. *The Frenzy of Renown: Fame & Its History*. Oxford: Oxford University Press, 1986.

Brock, Ann Graham. 'Mary Magdalene'. In *The Oxford Handbook of New Testament, Gender, and Sexuality*, edited by Benjamin H. Dunning, 429–48. Oxford Handbooks. Oxford: Oxford University Press, 2019.

Bruin, Tom de. 'A Bad Taste in My Mouth: Spirits as Embodied Senses in the Testaments of the Twelve Patriarchs'. *Journal for Interdisciplinary Biblical Studies* 4, no. 1 (2022): 17–38. doi:10.17613/tv6x-xw92.

Bruin, Tom de. 'In Defence of New Testament Satanologies: A Response to Farrar and Williams'. *Journal for the Study of the New Testament* 44, no. 3 (2022): 435–51. doi:10.1177/0142064X211045311.

Bruin, Tom de. *The Great Controversy: The Individual's Struggle between Good and Evil in the* Testaments of the Twelve Patriarchs *and in Their Jewish and Christian Contexts*. Novum Testamentum et Orbis Antiquus 106. Göttingen: Vandenhoeck & Ruprecht, 2015.

Bruin, Tom de. 'Joseph the Good and Delicate Man: Masculinity in the *Testaments of the Twelve Patriarchs*'. *Lectio Difficilior*, no. 1 (2020).

Bruin, Tom de. 'Nostalgia, Novelty, and the Subversion of Authority in "The Testaments of the Twelve Patriarchs"'. *Transformative Works and Cultures* 31 (2019). doi:10.3983/twc.2019.1553.

Bruin, Tom de. 'Testaments of the Twelve Patriarchs'. In *Critical Dictionary of Apocalyptic and Millenarian Movements*, edited by James G. Crossley and Alastair Lockhart, 14 October 2022. https://www.cdamm.org/articles/testaments-of-the-twelve-patriarchs.

Buchinger, Harald. 'Liturgy and Early Christian Apocrypha'. In *The Oxford Handbook of Early Christian Apocrypha*, edited by Andrew Gregory, Tobias Nicklas, Christopher M. Tuckett, and Joseph Verheyden, 361–77. Oxford Handbooks. Oxford: Oxford University Press, 2015. doi:10.1093/oxfordhb/9780199644117.013.40.

Bucur, Bogdan Gabriel. *Scripture Re-Envisioned: Christophanic Exegesis and the Making of a Christian Bible*. Leiden: Brill, 2018. doi:10.1163/9789004386112.

Burke, Tony. 'Early Christian Apocrypha in Contemporary Theological Discourse'. In *The Oxford Handbook of Early Christian Apocrypha*, edited by Andrew F. Gregory, Tobias Nicklas, C. M. Tuckett, and Joseph Verheyden, 441–58. Oxford Handbooks. Oxford: Oxford University Press, 2015. doi:10.1093/oxfordhb/9780199644117.013.30.

Burke, Tony. 'Early Christian Apocrypha in Popular Culture'. In *The Oxford Handbook of Early Christian Apocrypha*, edited by Andrew F. Gregory, Tobias Nicklas, C. M. Tuckett, and Joseph Verheyden, 424–40. Oxford Handbooks. Oxford: Oxford University Press, 2015. doi:10.1093/oxfordhb/9780199644117.013.29.

Burke, Tony, ed. *Fakes, Forgeries, and Fictions: Writing Ancient and Modern Christian Apocrypha: Proceedings from the 2015 York University Christian Apocrypha Symposium*. Eugene, Oregon: Cascade Books, 2017.

Burke, Tony. 'Heresy Hunting in the New Millennium'. *Studies in Religion/Sciences Religieuses* 39, no. 3 (2010): 405–20. doi:10.1177/0008429810373319.

Burke, Tony. 'Introduction'. In *Fakes, Forgeries, and Fictions: Writing Ancient and Modern Christian Apocrypha: Proceedings from the 2015 York University Christian Apocrypha Symposium*, edited by Tony Burke, 1–32. Eugene, OR: Cascade Books, 2017.

Burke, Tony. 'Introduction'. In *New Testament Apocrypha: More Noncanonical Scriptures Volume Two*, edited by Tony Burke, xiii–xx. Grand Rapids: Eerdmans, 2020.

Burke, Tony. *Secret Scriptures Revealed: A New Introduction to the Christian Apocrypha*. London: SPCK, 2013.

Burrus, Virginia. 'The Heretical Woman as Symbol in Alexander, Athanasius, Epiphanius, and Jerome'. *Harvard Theological Review* 84, no. 3 (July 1991): 229–48. doi:10.1017/S0017816000024007.

Busse, Kristina. 'Beyond Mary Sue: Fan Representation and the Complex Negotiation of Gendered Identity'. In *Seeing Fans: Representations of Fandom in Media and Popular Culture*, edited by Lucy Kathryn Bennett and Paul Booth, 159–68. London: Bloomsbury Academic, 2016.

Busse, Kristina. *Framing Fan Fiction: Literary and Social Practices in Fan Fiction Communities*. Iowa City, IA: University of Iowa Press, 2017.
Busse, Kristina. 'Geek Hierarchies, Boundary Policing, and the Gendering of the Good Fan'. *Participations: Journal of Audience and Reception Studies* 10, no. 1 (2013): 73–91.
Busse, Kristina. 'The Return of the Author: Ethos and Identity Politics'. In *A Companion to Media Authorship*, edited by Jonathan Gray and Derek Johnson, 48–68. Malden, MA: Wiley Blackwell, 2013.
Busse, Kristina, and Karen Hellekson. 'Introduction: Work in Progress'. In *Fan Fiction and Fan Communities in the Age of the Internet: New Essays*, edited by Karen Hellekson and Kristina Busse, 5–32. Jefferson, NC: McFarland, 2006.
Cartlidge, David R., and J. K. Elliott. *Art and the Christian Apocrypha*. London: Routledge, 2001.
Catholic Encyclopedia. New York: Encyclopedia Press, 1910.
Clark, Elizabeth A. 'Women, Gender, and the Study of Christian History'. *Church History* 70, no. 3 (2001): 395–426. doi:10.2307/3654496.
Clement. *Clemens Alexandrinus II: Stromata, Buch I–IV*. Edited by Ludwig Früchtel and Otto Stählin. Die Griechischen Christlichen Schriftsteller Der Ersten Drei Jahrhunderte 52. Berlin: Akademie, 1960.
Clement. *Stromateis. Books One to Three*. Translated by John Ferguson. The Fathers of the Church 85. Washington, D.C.: Catholic University of America Press, 1991.
Click, Melissa A., Jennifer Stevens Aubrey, and Elizabeth Behm-Morawitz. 'Introduction'. In *Bitten by Twilight: Youth Culture, Media and the Vampire Franchise*, edited by Melissa A. Click, Jennifer Stevens Aubrey, and Elizabeth Behm-Morawitz, 1–19. Mediated Youth 14. New York: Peter Lang, 2010.
Clogston, Centi. '21 Authors Who Write Fanfiction'. *Lawrence Public Library*, 17 May 2019. https://lplks.org/blogs/post/21-published-authors-who-write-fanfiction/.
Collins, Adela Yarbro. *Mark: A Commentary*. Hermeneia: A Critical and Historical Commentary on the Bible. Minneapolis, MN: Fortress, 2007.
Collins, Billie Jean, ed. *The SBL Handbook of Style: For Biblical Studies and Related Disciplines*. 2nd ed. Atlanta, GA: SBL Press, 2014.
Conway, Colleen M. *Behold the Man: Jesus and Greco-Roman Masculinity*. Oxford: Oxford University Press, 2008.
Coogan, Jeremiah. 'Reading (in) a Quadriform Cosmos: Gospel Books in the Early Christian Bibliographic Imagination'. *Journal of Early Christian Studies* 31, no. 1 (2023). doi:10.1353/earl.2023.0004.
Cook, Roy T. 'Canonicity and Normativity in Massive, Serialized, Collaborative Fiction'. *The Journal of Aesthetics and Art Criticism* 71, no. 3 (2013): 271–76. doi:10.1111/jaac.12021.
Coppa, Francesca. 'Introduction: Five Things That Fanfiction Is, and One Thing It Isn't'. In *The Fanfiction Reader: Folk Tales for the Digital Age*, edited by Francesca Coppa, 1–17. Ann Arbor: University of Michigan Press, 2017.
Cunningham, Mary B. 'Eastern Orthodoxy'. In *The Oxford Handbook of Christmas*, edited by Timothy Larsen, 125–40. Oxford Handbooks. Oxford University Press, 2020. doi:10.1093/oxfordhb/9780198831464.013.11.
Davidsen, Markus Altena. 'Fiction-Based Religion: Conceptualising a New Category against History-Based Religion and Fandom'. *Culture and Religion* 14 (2013): 378–95.
Decker, Todd. 'Carols and Music Since 1900'. In *The Oxford Handbook of Christmas*, edited by Timothy Larsen, 328–45. Oxford Handbooks. Oxford University Press, 2020. doi:10.1093/oxfordhb/9780198831464.013.28.

Derecho, Abigail. 'Archontic Literature: A Definition, a History, and Several Theories of Fan Fiction'. In *Fan Fiction and Fan Communities in the Age of the Internet: New Essays*, edited by Karen Hellekson and Kristina Busse, 61–78. Jefferson, NC: McFarland, 2006.

Derrida, Jacques. *Archive Fever: A Freudian Impression*. Religion and Postmodernism. Chicago, IL: University of Chicago Press, 1996.

deSilva, David A. 'Apocrypha and Pseudepigrapha'. In *Oxford Bibliographies in Biblical Studies*. Oxford: Oxford University Press, 2020. doi:10.1093/OBO/9780195393361-0007.

deSilva, David A. 'The *Testaments of the Twelve Patriarchs* as Witnesses to Pre-Christian Judaism: A Re-Assessment'. *Journal for the Study of the Pseudepigrapha* 23 (2013): 21–68. doi:10.1177/0951820713502411.

Desjardins, Michel. 'Bauer and Beyond: On Recent Scholarly Discussions of Αἵρεσις in the Early Christian Era'. *Second Century: A Journal of Early Christian Studies* 8, no. 2 (1991): 65–82.

Diehl, Judith A. 'What Is a "Gospel"? Recent Studies in the Gospel Genre'. *Currents in Research* 9 (2011): 171–99. doi:10.1177/1476993X10361307.

Diski, Jenny. 'God Almighty'. *The Guardian*, 12 March 2005. https://www.theguardian.com/books/2005/dec/03/fiction.annerice.

Dobschütz, Ernst von. *Das Decretum Gelasianum de libris recipiendis et non recipiendis*. Texte und Untersuchungen zur Geschichte der altchristlichen Literatur, 38.4. Leipzig: J. C. Hinrichs, 1912.

Dogniez, Cécile. '"Au milieu de deux vivants, tu seras connu": lectures juive et chrétienne d'Habacuc 3, 2ᶜ'. In *Judaïsme et christianisme chez les Pères*, edited by Marie-Anne Vannier, 165–85. Judaïsme antique et origines du christianisme 8. Turnhout: Brepols Publishers, 2016. doi:10.1484/M.JAOC-EB.5.110703.

Dresken-Weiland, Jutta. 'The Role of Peter in Early Christian Art: Images from the 4th to the 6th Century'. In *The Early Reception and Appropriation of the Apostle Peter (60–800 CE): The Anchors of the Fisherman*, edited by Roald Dijkstra, 115–34. Euhormos: Greco-Roman Studies in Anchoring Innovation 1. Leiden: Brill, 2020. doi:10.1163/9789004425682_008.

Duffett, Mark. *Understanding Fandom: An Introduction to the Study of Media Fan Culture*. London: Bloomsbury, 2013.

Dulk, Matthijs den. *Between Jews and Heretics: Refiguring Justin Martyr's Dialogue with Trypho*. Routledge Studies in the Early Christian World. Abingdon: Routledge, 2018. doi:10.4324/9781351243490.

Dunc. 'The Continuing Adventures of Millicent the Cat (on Tumblr)'. *Club Jade*, 2 June 2017. https://clubjade.net/the-continuing-adventures-of-millicent-the-cat-on-tumblr/.

Dunc. 'Pablo Made a Funny and Now General Hux Has a Cat Named Millicent (at Least on Tumblr)'. *Club Jade*, 2 August 2016. https://clubjade.net/pablo-made-a-funny-and-now-general-hux-has-a-cat-named-millicent-at-least-on-tumblr/.

Dunlop, Kathryn, and Carissa Wolf. 'Fans Behaving Badly: Anime Metafandom, Brutal Criticism, and the Intellectual Fan'. *Mechademia* 5 (2010): 267–83.

Dunn, James D. G. 'The Messianic Secret in Mark'. *Tyndale Bulletin* 21 (1970): 92–117.

Eastman, David L. *The Ancient Martyrdom Accounts of Peter and Paul*. Writings from the Greco-Roman World 39. Atlanta: SBL Press, 2015. doi:10.2307/j.ctt15zc51m.

Ehrman, Bart D. *The Orthodox Corruption of Scripture: The Effect of Early Christological Controversies on the Text of the New Testament*. Oxford: Oxford University Press, 1996.

Elder, Nicholas A. 'Joseph and Aseneth: An Entertaining Tale'. *Journal for the Study of Judaism* 51 (2020): 19–42. doi:10.1163/15700631-12511267.

Elliott, J. K. *The Apocryphal New Testament: A Collection of Apocryphal Christian Literature in an English Translation*. Oxford: Clarendon Press, 1993.

Elliott, J. K. 'The Influence of the Apocrypha on Manuscripts of the New Testament'. *Apocrypha* 8 (1997): 265–72. doi:10.1484/J.APOCRA.2.300956.

Elliott, J. K. 'The Non-Canonical Gospels and the New Testament Apocrypha: Currents in Early Christian Thought and Beyond'. In *The Non-Canonical Gospels*, edited by Paul Foster, 1–12. London: T & T Clark, 2008.

Eron, Lewis John. '"That Women Have Mastery Over Both King and Beggar" (TJud. 15.5) – The Relationship of the Fear of Sexuality to the Status of Women in Apocrypha and Pseudepigrapha: 1 Esdras (3 Ezra) 3–4, Ben Sira and the Testament of Judah'. *Journal for the Study of the Pseudepigrapha* 9 (1991): 43–66. doi:10.1177/095182079100000904.

Eusebius. *Ecclesiastical History, Books 6–10*. Translated by Deferrari Roy J. The Fathers of the Church 29. Washington D.C.: Catholic University of America Press, 1969.

Eusebius. *Ecclesiastical History, Volume 1: Books 1–5*. Translated by Kirsopp Lake. Loeb Classical Library 153. Cambridge, MA: Harvard University Press, 1926.

Eusebius. *Ecclesiastical History, Volume II: Books 6–10*. Translated by J. E. L. Oulton. Loeb Classical Library 265. Cambridge, MA: Harvard University Press, 1932.

Evans, Ernest. *Tertullian's Homily on Baptism: The Text Edited with an Introduction, Translation, and Commentary*. Eugene, OR: Wipf & Stock, 2016.

Eyl, Jennifer. 'Apocryphal Acts of the Apostles'. In *The Oxford Handbook of New Testament, Gender, and Sexuality*, edited by Benjamin H. Dunning, 386–404. Oxford Handbooks. Oxford University Press, 2019. doi:10.1093/oxfordhb/9780190213398.013.18.

Fanlore. 'Anne Rice'. https://fanlore.org/wiki/Anne_Rice.

Fanlore. 'Fanfiction'. https://fanlore.org/wiki/Fanfiction.

Fantalkin, Alexander, and Oren Tal. 'The Canonization of the Pentateuch: When and Why? (Part I)'. *Zeitschrift Für Die Alttestamentliche Wissenschaft* 124, no. 1 (2012): 1–18. doi:10.1515/zaw-2012-0001.

Fantalkin, Alexander, and Oren Tal. 'The Canonization of the Pentateuch: When and Why? (Continued, Part II)'. *Zeitschrift Für Die Alttestamentliche Wissenschaft* 124, no. 2 (2012): 201–12. doi:10.1515/zaw-2012-0015.

Fast, Karin, and Henrik Örnebring. 'Transmedia World-Building: *The Shadow* (1931–Present) and *Transformers* (1984–Present)'. *International Journal of Cultural Studies* 20, no. 6 (2017): 636–52. doi:10.1177/1367877915605887.

Fathallah, Judith. '"BEING A FANGIRL OF A SERIAL KILLER IS NOT OK": Gatekeeping Reddit's True Crime Community'. *New Media & Society*, 2022, 1–20. doi:10.1177/14614448221138768.

Fathallah, Judith. *Fanfiction and the Author: How Fanfic Changes Popular Cultural Texts*. Transmedia: Participatory Culture and Media Convergence. Amsterdam: Amsterdam University Press, 2017.

Fathallah, Judith. 'Statements and Silence: Fanfic Paratexts for *ASOIAF/Game of Thrones*'. *Continuum* 30, no. 1 (2016): 75–88. doi:10.1080/10304312.2015.1099150.

Ferguson, Everett. 'Factors Leading to the Selection and Closure of the New Testament Canon: A Survey of Some Recent Studies'. In *The Canon Debate: On the Origins and Formation of the Bible*, edited by Lee Martin McDonald and James A Sanders, 295–320. Peabody, MA: Hendrickson, 2002.

Figwit Lives! http://figwitlives.net/.

Fimi, Dimitra. 'Filming Folklore: Adapting Fantasy for the Big Screen through Peter Jackson's Lord of the Rings'. In *Picturing Tolkien: Essays on Peter Jackson's The Lord of the Rings Film Trilogy*, edited by Janice M. Bogstad and Philip E. Kaveny, 84–101. Jefferson, NC: McFarland, 2011.

Fish, Stanley. *Is There a Text in This Class? The Authority of Interpretive Communities*. Cambridge, MA: Harvard University Press, 1980.

Fisk, Bruce N. 'One Good Story Deserves Another: The Hermeneutics of Invoking Secondary Biblical Episodes in the Narratives of Pseudo-Philo and the Testaments of the Twelve Patriarchs'. In *The Interpretation of Scripture in Early Judaism and Christianity: Studies in Language and Tradition*, edited by Craig A. Evans, 217–39. Journal for the Study of the Pseudepigrapha Supplement Series 33. Sheffield: Sheffield Academic Press, 2000.

France, R. T. *The Gospel of Mark: A Commentary on the Greek Text*. New International Greek Testament Commentary. Grand Rapids, MI: Eerdmans, 2002.

Frilingos, Christopher A. 'Parents Just Don't Understand: Ambiguity in Stories about the Childhood of Jesus'. *Harvard Theological Review* 109, no. 1 (2016): 33–55. doi:10.1017/S0017816015000474.

Frodo Is Great . . . Who Is That?!! Directed by Hannah Clarke, Stan Alley, and Nick Booth. Midnight Film, 2004.

Frow, John. 'Is Elvis a God?: Cult, Culture, Questions of Method'. *International Journal of Cultural Studies* 1 (1998): 197–210.

Gagné, André, trans. *The Gospel According to Thomas: Introduction, Translation and Commentary*. Apocryphes 16. Turnhout: Brepols, 2019. doi:10.1484/M.APOCR-EB.5.117535.

Gallagher, Edmon L. *Hebrew Scripture in Patristic Biblical Theory: Canon, Language, Text*. Supplements to Vigiliae Christianae 114. Leiden: Brill, 2012.

Gallagher, Edmon L., and John D. Meade. *The Biblical Canon Lists from Early Christianity: Texts and Analysis*. Oxford: Oxford University Press, 2017.

Gathercole, Simon J. 'Other Apocryphal Gospels and the Historical Jesus'. In *The Oxford Handbook of Early Christian Apocrypha*, edited by Andrew Gregory, Tobias Nicklas, Christopher M. Tuckett, and Joseph Verheyden, 250–68. Oxford Handbooks. Oxford: Oxford University Press, 2015. doi:10.1093/oxfordhb/9780199644117.013.37.

Genette, Gerard. *Palimpsests: Literature in the Second Degree*. Translated by C. Newman and C. Doubinsky. Lincoln, NE: University of Nebraska Press, 1997.

Genette, Gerard. *Paratexts: Thresholds of Interpretation*. Cambridge: Cambridge University Press, 1997.

Gijsel, Jan, trans. *Libri de nativitate Mariae: Pseudo-Matthaei Evangelium, textus et commentarius, Libellus de nativitate sanctae Mariae, textus et commentarius*. Corpus Christianorum Series Apocryphorum 9. Turnhout: Brepols, 1997.

Gilfillan Upton, Bridget. *Hearing Mark's Endings: Listening to Ancient Popular Texts through Speech Act Theory*. Biblical Interpretation Series 79. Leiden: Brill, 2006.

Goodman, Lesley. 'Disappointing Fans: Fandom, Fictional Theory, and the Death of the Author'. *The Journal of Popular Culture* 48, no. 4 (August 2015): 662–76. doi:10.1111/jpcu.12223.

Gray, Jonathan. *Show Sold Separately: Promos, Spoilers, and Other Media Paratexts*. New York: New York University Press, 2010.

Greene, Viveca S. '"Deplorable" Satire: Alt-Right Memes, White Genocide Tweets, and Redpilling Normies'. *Studies in American Humor* 5, no. 1 (2019): 31–69. doi:10.5325/studamerhumor.5.1.0031.

Haines-Eitzen, Kim. *The Gendered Palimpsest: Women, Writing, and Representation in Early Christianity*. Oxford: Oxford University Press, 2012.

Harmon, Lee. 'Book Review: Christ the Lord: Out of Egypt'. *Dubious Disciple*, 20 December 2010. https://www.dubiousdisciple.com/2010/12/book-review-christ-the-lord-out-of-egypt.html.

Harrington, Daniel J. 'The Reception of Walter Bauer's *Orthodoxy and Heresy in Earliest Christianity* during the Last Decade'. *Harvard Theological Review* 73, no. 1–2 (1980): 289–98. doi:10.1017/S0017816000002170.

Harrison, R. K. 'Old Testament and New Testament Apocrypha'. In *The Origin of the Bible*, edited by Philip Wesley Comfort, 79–94. Wheaton, IL: Tyndale House, 2020.

Hartog, Paul A. 'Introduction'. In *Orthodoxy and Heresy in Early Christian Contexts: Reconsidering the Bauer Thesis*, edited by Paul A. Hartog, 1–5. Cambridge: James Clarke, 2015.

Hartog, Paul A., ed. *Orthodoxy and Heresy in Early Christian Contexts: Reconsidering the Bauer Thesis*. Cambridge: James Clarke, 2015. doi:10.2307/j.ctt1cgf14m.

Hassler-Forest, Dan. 'The Politics of World Building: Heteroglossia in Janelle Monáe's Afrofuturist WondaLand'. In *World Building. Transmedia, Fans, Industries*, edited by Marta Boni, 377–91. Transmedia: Participatory Culture and Media Convergence. Amsterdam University Press, 2017. doi:10.5117/9789089647566/ch21.

Hawk, Brandon W. 'Canonizing Star Wars'. *Brandon W. Hawk* (blog), 1 May 2022. https://brandonwhawk.net/2022/01/05/canonizing-star-wars/.

Hawk, Brandon W. *The Gospel of Pseudo-Matthew and the Nativity of Mary*. Early Christian Apocrypha 8. Eugene, OR: Cascade Books, 2020.

Hellekson, Karen. 'A Fannish Field of Value: Online Fan Gift Culture'. *Cinema Journal* 48 (2009): 113–18. doi:10.1353/cj.0.0140.

Hellekson, Karen, and Kristina Busse, eds. *The Fan Fiction Studies Reader*. Iowa City, IA: University of Iowa Press, 2014.

Hellekson, Karen, and Kristina Busse. 'Fan Identity and Feminism'. In *The Fan Fiction Studies Reader*, edited by Karen Hellekson and Kristina Busse, 75–81. Iowa City, IA: University of Iowa Press, 2014.

Hellekson, Karen, and Kristina Busse. 'Introduction: Why a Fan Fiction Studies Reader Now?' In *The Fan Fiction Studies Reader*, edited by Karen Hellekson and Kristina Busse, 1–18. Iowa City, IA: University of Iowa Press, 2014.

Herman, David. *Basic Elements of Narrative*. Chichester: Wiley-Blackwell, 2009.

Herzog, Alexandra Elisabeth. '"But This Is My Story and This Is How I Wanted to Write It": Author's Notes as a Fannish Claim to Power in Fan Fiction Writing'. *Transformative Works and Cultures* 11 (2012). doi:10.3983/twc.2012.0406.

Hillel, Vered. 'Patriarchs, Testaments of the Twelve;. In *T&T Clark Encyclopedia of Second Temple Judaism*, edited by Loren T. Stuckenbruck and Daniel M. Gurtner, 411–15. London: T&T Clark, 2019.

Hills, Matt. *Fan Cultures*. London: Routledge, 2002.

Hills, Matt. '"Proper Distance" in the Ethical Positioning of Scholar-Fandoms: Between Academics' and Fans' Moral Economies?' In *Fan Culture: Theory/Practice*, edited by Katherine Larsen and Lynn S. Zubernis, 14–37. Newcastle upon Tyne: Cambridge Scholars, 2012.

Hills, Matt. 'Sacralising Fandom? From the "loss Hypothesis" to Fan's Media Rituals'. *Kinephanos* 4 (2013): 8–16.

Hills, Matt. '"Twilight" Fans Represented in Commercial Paratexts and Inter-Fandoms: Resisting and Repurposing Negative Fan Stereotypes'. In *Genre, Reception, and Adaptation in the 'Twilight' Series*, edited by Anne Morey, 113–30. Ashgate Studies in Childhood, 1700 to the Present. London: Routledge, 2016. doi:10.4324/9781315584331-8.

Hollander, Harm W. 'Israel and God's Eschatological Agent in the Testaments of the Twelve Patriarchs'. In *Aspects of Religious Contact and Conflict in the Ancient World*, edited by Pieter W. van der Horst, 91–104. Utrechtse Theologische Reeks 31. Utrecht: Faculteit der Godgeleerdheid, Universiteit Utrecht, 1995.

Hollander, Harm W., and Marinus de Jonge. *The Testaments of the Twelve Patriarchs: A Commentary*. Studia in Veteris Testamenti Pseudepigrapha 8. Leiden: Brill, 1985.

Horrell, David G. *The Social Ethos of the Corinthian Correspondence: Interests and Ideology from 1 Corinthians to 1 Clement*. Studies of the New Testament and Its World. Edinburgh: T & T Clark, 1996.

Huggins, Ronald V. 'The Ox and the Donkey'. *Midwestern Journal of Theology* 9, no. 2 (2010): 179–93.

Hultgård, Anders. *L'eschatologie des Testaments des Douze Patriarches: I. Interprétation des textes*. Acta Universitatis Upsaliensis Historia Religionum 6. Stockholm: Almqvist & Wiksell, 1977.

Hultgård, Anders. *L'eschatologie des Testaments des Douze Patriarches: II. Composition de l'ouvrage, textes et traductions*. Acta Universitatis Upsaliensis Historia Religionum 7. Stockholm: Almqvist & Wiksell, 1981.

Hurtado, Larry W. 'Who Read Early Christian Apocrypha?' In *The Oxford Handbook of Early Christian Apocrypha*, edited by Andrew Gregory, Tobias Nicklas, Christopher M. Tuckett, and Joseph Verheyden, 153–66. Oxford Handbooks. Oxford: Oxford University Press, 2015. doi:10.1093/oxfordhb/9780199644117.013.1.

Jacobi, Christine. 'Jesus' Body: Christology and Soteriology in the Body-Metaphors of the *Gospel of Philip*'. In *Connecting Gospels: Beyond the Canonical/Non-Canonical Divide*, edited by Sarah Parkhouse and Francis Watson, 77–96. Oxford: Oxford University Press, 2018.

James, Montague R. *The Apocryphal New Testament Being the Apocryphal Gospels, Acts, Epistles and Apocalypses*. Oxford: Clarendon, 1924.

Jenkins, Henry. *Convergence Culture: Where Old and New Media Collide*. New York: New York University Press, 2006.

Jenkins, Henry. 'The Cultural Logic of Media Convergence'. *International Journal of Cultural Studies* 7, no. 1 (March 2004). doi:10.1177/1367877904040603.

Jenkins, Henry. *Fans, Bloggers, and Gamers: Exploring Participatory Culture*. New York: New York University Press, 2006.

Jenkins, Henry. 'Reception Theory and Audience Research: The Mystery of the Vampire's Kiss'. In *Reinventing Film Studies*, edited by Christine Gledhill and Linda Williams, 165–82. London: Arnold, 2000.

Jenkins, Henry. *Textual Poachers: Television Fans & Participatory Culture*. London: Routledge, 1992.

Jensen, Robin M. 'Introduction'. In *The Routledge Handbook of Early Christian Art*, edited by Robin M. Jensen and Mark D. Ellison, 1–17. New York: Routledge, 2018. doi:10.4324/9781315718835-1.

Jensen, Robin M. *Understanding Early Christian Art*. London: Routledge, 2000. doi:10.4324/9780203407639.

Jindra, Michael. 'It's about Faith in Our Future: *Star Trek* Fandom as Cultural Religion'. In *Religion and Popular Culture in America*, edited by Bruce David Forbes and Jeffrey H. Mahan, 165–80. Berkeley, CA: University of California Press, 2000.

Jindra, Michael. '*Star Trek* Fandom as Religious Phenomenon'. *Sociology of Religion* 55 (1994): 27–51.

Johnson, Derek. 'Fantagonism: Factions, Institutions, and Constitutive Hegemonies of Fandom'. In *Fandom: Identities and Communities in a Mediated World*, edited by Jonathan Gray, Cornel Sandvoss, and C. Lee Harrington, 2nd ed., 369–86. New York: New York University Press, 2017. doi:10.18574/nyu/9781479845453.003.0025.

Johnson, Derek. 'Fantagonism, Franchising, and Industry Management of Fan Privilege'. In *The Routledge Companion to Media Fandom*, edited by Suzanne Scott and Melissa A. Click, 395–405. New York: Routledge, 2018. doi:10.4324/9781315637518-47.

Johnson, Derek. 'Participation Is Magic: Collaboration, Authorial Legitimacy, and the Audience Function'. In *A Companion to Media Authorship*, edited by Jonathan Gray and Derek Johnson, 133–57. Oxford: Wiley-Blackwell, 2013. doi:10.1002/9781118505526.ch7.

Johnston, Sarah Iles. *The Story of Myth*. Cambridge, MA: Harvard University Press, 2018.

Jones, Sara Gwenllian. 'The Sex Lives of Cult Television Characters'. In *The Fan Fiction Studies Reader*, edited by Karen Hellekson and Kristina Busse, 116–29. Iowa City, IA: University of Iowa Press, 2014.

Jonge, Marinus de. 'The Future of Israel in the Testaments of the Twelve Patriarchs'. *Journal for the Study of Judaism in the Persian, Hellenistic and Roman Period* 17 (1986): 196–211.

Jonge, Marinus de. 'The Pre-Mosaic Servants of God in the Testaments of the Twelve Patriarchs and in the Writings of Justin and Irenaeus'. *Vigiliae Christianae* 39 (1985): 157–70.

Jonge, Marinus de. 'The Testaments of the Twelve Patriarchs'. In *The Apocryphal Old Testament*, edited by Hedley F. D. Sparks, 505–601. Oxford: Clarendon Press, 1984.

Jonge, Marinus de, Harm W. Hollander, Henk Jan de Jonge, and Theo Korteweg. *The Testaments of the Twelve Patriarchs: A Critical Edition of the Greek Text*. Pseudepigrapha Veteris Testamenti Graece 1. Leiden: Brill, 1978.

Jorgensen, David W. 'Approaches to Orthodoxy and Heresy in the Study of Early Christianity'. *Religion Compass* 11, no. 7–8 (2017): 1–14. doi:10.1111/rec3.12227.

Kahane, Ahuvia. 'Fan Fiction, Early Greece, and the Historicity of Canon'. *Transformative Works and Cultures* 21 (2016). doi:10.3983/twc.2016.0681.

Kee, Howard C. 'The Ethical Dimensions of the Testaments of the XII as a Clue to Provenance'. *New Testament Studies* 24 (1978): 259–70. doi:10.1017/S002868850000789X.

Keith, Chris. *The Gospel as Manuscript: An Early History of the Jesus Tradition as Material Artifact*. Oxford: Oxford University Press, 2020.

Kelhoffer, James A. *Miracle and Mission: The Authentication of Missionaries and Their Message in the Longer Ending of Mark*. Wissenschaftliche Untersuchungen zum Neuen Testament 2. Reihe 112. Tübingen: Mohr Siebeck, 2000.

Kevin, Robert Oliver. 'The Lost Ending of the Gospel According to Mark: A Criticism and a Reconstruction'. *Journal of Biblical Literature* 45, no. 1/2 (1926): 81. doi:10.2307/3260167.

Kjos, Berit. 'Anne Rice Re-Imagines Jesus and Christian Leaders Applaud'. *Kjos Ministries*, January 2006. http://www.crossroad.to/articles2/006/anne-rice.htm.

Kolenkow, Anitra B. 'Testaments: The Literary Genre "Testament"'. In *Early Judaism and Its Modern Interpreters*, edited by Robert A. Kraft and George W. E. Nickelsburg, 259–67. The Bible and Its Modern Interpreters. Atlanta, GA: Scholars Press, 1986.

Kugel, James L. *How to Read the Bible: A Guide to Scripture, Then and Now*. New York: Free Press, 2007.

Kugel, James L. 'Levi's Elevation to the Priesthood in Second Temple Writings'. *Harvard Theological Review* 86 (1993): 1–64.
Kugel, James L. *In Potiphar's House: The Interpretive Life of Biblical Texts*. New York: HarperCollins, 1990.
Kugel, James L. 'Reuben's Sin with Bilhah in the Testament of Reuben'. In *Pomegranates and Golden Bells: Studies in Biblical, Jewish, and Near Eastern Ritual, Law, and Literature in Honor of Jacob Milgrom*, edited by David P. Wright, David N. Freedman, and Avi Hurvitz, 525–54. Winona Lake, IN: Eisenbrauns, 1995.
Kugel, James L. 'Some Translation and Copying Mistakes from the Original Hebrew of the Testaments of the Twelve Patriarchs'. In *The Dead Sea Scrolls: Transmission of Traditions and Production of Texts*, edited by Sarianna Metso, Hindy Najman, and Eileen Schuller, 45–56. Studies on the Texts of the Desert of Judah 92. Leiden: Brill, 2010.
Kugel, James L. 'The Story of Dinah in the Testament of Levi'. *Harvard Theological Review* 85 (1992): 1–34.
Kugel, James L. *Traditions of the Bible: A Guide to the Bible As It Was at the Start of the Common Era*. Cambridge, MA: Harvard University Press, 1998.
Kugler, Robert A. 'The *Testaments of the Twelve Patriarchs*: A Not-So-Ambiguous Witness to Early Interpretive Practices'. In *A Companion to Biblical Interpretation in Early Judaism*, edited by Matthias Henze, 337–60. Grand Rapids, MI: Eerdmans, 2012.
Kugler, Robert A. *The Testaments of the Twelve Patriarchs*. Guides to Apocrypha and Pseudepigrapha. Sheffield: Sheffield Academic Press, 2001.
Larsen, Kasper Bro. 'Fan Fiction and Early Christian Apocrypha: Comparing Hypertextual Practices'. *Studia Theologica – Nordic Journal of Theology* 73 (2019): 43–59. doi:10.1080/0039338X.2018.1552894.
Larsen, Katherine, and Lynn S. Zubernis. 'Introduction'. In *Fan Culture: Theory/Practice*, edited by Katherine Larsen and Lynn S. Zubernis, 1–13. Newcastle upon Tyne: Cambridge Scholars, 2012.
Lassley Knight, Jennifer. 'Herodias, Salomé, and John the Baptist's Beheading: A Case Study of the Topos of the Heretical Woman'. *International Social Science Review* 93, no. 1 (2017): 1–15.
Lewis, Jody Vaccaro. 'The Inn, the Manger, the Swaddling Cloths, the Shepherds, and the Animals'. In *The Oxford Handbook of Christmas*, edited by Timothy Larsen, 223–36. Oxford Handbooks. Oxford University Press, 2020. doi:10.1093/oxfordhb/9780198831464.013.19.
Lindgren Leavenworth, Maria. 'The Paratext of Fan Fiction'. *Narrative* 23 (2015): 40–60.
Lindgren Leavenworth, Maria, and Malin Isaksson. *Fanged Fan Fiction: Variations on Twilight, True Blood and The Vampire Diaries*. Jefferson, NC: McFarland, 2013.
Loader, William. *Philo, Josephus, and the Testaments on Sexuality: Attitudes towards Sexuality in the Writings of Philo and Josephus and in the Testaments of the Twelve Patriarchs*. Grand Rapids, MI: Eerdmans, 2011.
Long, Geoffrey A. 'Transmedia Storytelling Business, Aesthetics and Production at the Jim Henson Company'. MA thesis, Massachusetts Institute of Technology, 2007.
Lostpedia. 'About Lostpedia', 24 April 2010. https://lostpedia.fandom.com/wiki/Lostpedia:About.
Lundhaug, Hugo. 'Canon and Interpretation: A Cognitive Perspective'. In *Canon and Canonicity: The Formation and Use of Scripture*, edited by Einar Thomassen, 67–90. Copenhagen: Museum Tusculanum Press, University of Copenhagen, 2010.
Lundhaug, Hugo. 'Textual Fluidity and Monastic Fanfiction: The Case of the *Investiture of the Archangel Michael* in Coptic Egypt'. In *The Archangel Michael in Africa: History,*

Cult, and Persona, edited by Ingvild Sælid Gilhus, Alexandros Tsakos, and Marta Camilla Wright, 59–74. London: Bloomsbury Academic, 2019. doi:10.5040/9781350084742.

Luz, Ulrich. *Matthew 8–20: A Commentary on Matthew 8–20*. Hermeneia: A Critical and Historical Commentary on the Bible. Minneapolis, MN: Fortress Press, 2001.

Lyden, John C. 'Whose Film Is It, Anyway? Canonicity and Authority in Star Wars Fandom'. *Journal of the American Academy of Religion* 80, no. 3 (2012): 775–86. doi:10.1093/jaarel/lfs037.

Lyons-Pardue, Kara. *Gospel Women and the Long Ending of Mark*. The Library of New Testament Studies 614. London: T&T Clark, 2020.

Magness, J. Lee. *Marking the End: Sense and Absence in the Gospel of Mark: Sense and Absence in the Gospel of Mark*. Wipf and Stock Publishers, 2002.

Marshall, John W. 'Trophy Wives of Christ: Tropes of Seduction and Conquest in the Aprocryphal Acts'. In *Reading and Teaching Ancient Fiction Jewish, Christian, and Greco-Roman Narratives*, edited by Sara Raup Johnson, Rubén R Dupertuis, and Christine Rita Shea, 43–70. Writings from the Greco-Roman World Supplement Series 11. Atlanta, GA: SBL Press, 2018.

Martin, G. R. R. 'Someone Is Angry On the Internet'. *LiveJournal*, 7 May 2010. https://grrm.livejournal.com/151914.html.

Mason, Eric. *'You Are a Priest Forever': Second Temple Jewish Messianism and the Priestly Christology of the Epistle to the Hebrews*. Leiden: Brill, 2008. doi:10.1163/ej.9789004149878.i-228.

Matthews, Shelly. 'Thinking of Thecla: Issues in Feminist Historiography'. *Journal of Feminist Studies in Religion* 17 (2001): 39–55.

McCracken, Allison. 'Fic: Why Fanfiction Is Taking Over the World by Anne Jamison'. *Cinema Journal* 54 (2015): 170–75. doi:10.1353/cj.2015.0023.

McDonald, Lee Martin. *The Biblical Canon: Its Origin, Transmission, and Authority*. Grand Rapids, MI: Baker Books, 2006.

McDonald, Lee Martin. *The Formation of the Biblical Canon: Volume I: The Old Testament: Its Authority and Canonicity*. 4th ed. London: Bloomsbury T&T Clark, 2017.

McDonald, Lee Martin. *The Formation of the Biblical Canon: Volume II: The New Testament: Its Authority and Canonicity*. 4th ed. London: Bloomsbury T&T Clark, 2017.

McKee, Alan. *Textual Analysis: A Beginner's Guide*. London: Sage, 2003.

Melusina. 'More Than You Ever Wanted to Know About Canon and Fanon'. *Cultural Infidelities | Meta* (blog), 2004. https://www.culturalinfidelities.com/Meta/more-than-you-ever-wanted-to-know.htm.

Menn, Esther Marie. *Judah and Tamar (Genesis 38) in Ancient Jewish Exegesis: Studies in Literary Form and Hermeneutics*. Supplements to the Journal for the Study of Judaism 51. Leiden: Brill, 1997. doi:10.1163/9789004497764.

Metzger, Bruce M. *The Canon of the New Testament: Its Origin, Development, and Significance*. Oxford: Clarendon Press, 1987.

Metzger, Bruce M. *A Textual Commentary on the Greek New Testament, Second Edition*. 4th ed. London: United Bible Societies, 1994.

Metzger, Bruce M., and Bart D. Ehrman. *The Text of the New Testament: Its Transmission, Corruption, and Restoration*. 4th ed. Oxford: Oxford University Press, 2005.

Meyer, Marvin W. *The Gospels of the Marginalized: The Redemption of Doubting Thomas, Mary Magdalene, and Judas Iscariot in Early Christian Literature*. Eugene, OR: Cascade Books, 2012.

Middleton, Francesca. 'Abusing Text in the Roman and Contemporary Worlds'. *Transformative Works and Cultures* 21 (2016). doi:10.3983/twc.2016.0672.

Mittell, Jason. 'Sites of Participation: Wiki Fandom and the Case of Lostpedia'. *Transformative Works and Cultures* 3 (2009). doi:10.3983/twc.2009.0118.

Moss, Candida R. 'Between the Lines'. *Studies in Late Antiquity* 5, no. 3 (2021): 432–52. doi:10.1525/sla.2021.5.3.432.

Moss, Candida R. *God's Ghostwriters: Enslaved Christians and the Making of the Bible*. Boston: Little, Brown and Company, 2024.

Moss, Candida R. 'The Secretary: Enslaved Workers, Stenography, and the Production of Early Christian Literature'. *The Journal of Theological Studies* 74, no. 1 (2023): 20–56. doi:10.1093/jts/flad001.

Mroczek, Eva. *The Literary Imagination in Jewish Antiquity*. New York: Oxford University Press, 2016.

Najman, Hindy. 'The Vitality of Scripture Within and Beyond the "Canon"'. *Journal for the Study of Judaism* 43, no. 4–5 (2012): 497–518. doi:10.1163/15700631-12341237.

Najman, Hindy, and Irene Peiran Garrison. 'Pseudepigraphy as an Interpretative Construct'. In *The Old Testament Pseudepigrapha: Fifty Years of the Pseudepigrapha Section at the SBL*, edited by Matthias Henze and Liv Ingeborg Lied, 331–58. Early Judaism and Its Literature 50. Atlanta, GA: SBL Press, 2019.

Nasrallah, Laura Salah. '"Out of Love for Paul": History and Fiction and the Afterlife of the Apostle Paul'. In *Early Christian and Jewish Narrative: The Role of Religion in Shaping Narrative Forms*, edited by Ilaria Ramelli and Judith Perkins, 73–96. Wissenschaftliche Untersuchungen Zum Neuen Testament 348. Tübingen: Mohr Siebeck, 2015.

Nestle, Eberhard, and Barbara Aland. *Novum Testamentum Graece*. 28th ed. Stuttgart: Deutsche Bibelgesellschaft, 2012.

Nicklas, Tobias. 'The Influence of Jewish Scriptures on Early Christian Apocrypha'. In *The Oxford Handbook of Early Christian Apocrypha*, edited by Andrew F. Gregory and C. M. Tuckett, 141–52. Oxford Handbooks. Oxford: Oxford University Press, 2015. doi:10.1093/oxfordhb/9780199644117.013.8.

Nicklas, Tobias, and Janet E. Spittler, eds. *Credible, Incredible: The Miraculous in the Ancient Mediterranean*. Wissenschaftliche Untersuchungen Zum Neuen Testament 321. Tübingen: Mohr Siebeck, 2013.

North American Society for the Study of Christian Apocryphal Literature. 'E-Clavis: Christian Apocrypha'. https://www.nasscal.com/e-clavis-christian-apocrypha/.

Opferkuch, Stefan. 'Ein Rausch und seine Folgen. Parallelen zwischen der Erzählung von Noah als Weinbauer (Gen 9,20–27) und ihren Auslegungstraditionen und der Bilha-Episode in TestRub 3,11–15'. *Zeitschrift für die neutestamentliche Wissenschaft* 108 (2017): 281–305. doi:10.1515/znw-2017-0011.

Opoku-Gyamfi, Felix. 'Retelling the Story of Judah and Tamar in the Testament of Judah'. *Ilorin Journal of Religious Studies* 4, no. 2 (2014): 41–52.

Origen. *Homèlies Sur Saint Luc*. Translated by Henri Crouzel, François Fournier, and Pierre Périchon. Sources Chrétiennes 87. Paris: Cerf, 1962.

Origen. *Homilies on Luke*. Translated by Joseph T. Lienhard. The Fathers of the Church 94. Washington D.C.: Catholic University of America Press, 1996. doi:10.2307/j.ctt32b0dn.

Origen. *Origen: Contra Celsum*. Translated by Henry Chadwick. Cambridge: Cambridge University Press, 1980.

Os, Bas van. 'A Whore from Bethany? A Note on Mary Magdalene in Early Non-Christian Sources'. In *Mary Magdalene from the New Testament to the New Age and Beyond*, edited by Edmondo F. Lupieri, 128–32. Leiden: Brill, 2020. doi:10.1163/9789004411067_008.

Otto, Jennifer. *Philo of Alexandria and the Construction of Jewishness in Early Christian Writings*. Oxford: Oxford University Press, 2018.

Ouspensky, Léonide, and Vladimir Lossky. *The Meaning of Icons*. Translated by G. E. H. Palmer and E. Kadloubovsky. 2nd ed. Crestwood, NY: St. Vladimir's Seminary Press, 1999.

Pande, Rukmini. *Squee from the Margins: Fandom and Race*. Fandom & Culture. Iowa City, IA: University of Iowa Press, 2018.

Pappas, Nickolas. 'Authorship and Authority'. *Journal of Aesthetics & Art Criticism* 47 (1989): 325–32.

Parkhouse, Sarah. *Eschatology and the Saviour: The Gospel of Mary among Early Christian Dialogue Gospels*. Society for New Testament Studies Monograph Series 176. Cambridge: Cambridge University Press, 2019.

Parkhouse, Sarah. 'The Fetishization of Female *Exempla*: Mary, Thecla, Perpetua and Felicitas'. *New Testament Studies* 63, no. 4 (2017): 567–87. doi:10.1017/S0028688517000157.

Parkhouse, Sarah. '"Surely These Are Heterodox Teachings": The Gospel of Mary and Tertullian in Dialogue'. In *Telling the Christian Story Differently: Counter-Narratives from Nag Hammadi and Beyond*, edited by Sarah Parkhouse and Francis Watson, 77–94. The Reception of Jesus in the First Three Centuries 4. London: T&T Clark, 2020.

Parks, Sara. *Gender in the Rhetoric of Jesus: Women in Q*. Lanham, MD: Lexington Books, 2019.

Paulas, Rick. 'The Bible Is Nothing but Fan Fiction for Jesus'. *Vice*, 1 April 2014. https://www.vice.com/en/article/8gvpj5/the-bible-is-nothing-but-jesus-fan-fiction.

Pearson, Roberta. 'Transmedia Characters'. In *The Routledge Companion to Transmedia Studies*, edited by Matthew Freeman and Renira Rampazzo Gambarato, 148–56. New York: Routledge, 2018. doi:10.4324/9781351054904-17.

Peirano, Irene. *The Rhetoric of the Roman Fake: Latin* Pseudepigrapha *in Context*. Cambridge: Cambridge University Press, 2012.

Petersen, Anders Klostergaard. 'The Riverrun of Rewriting Scripture: From Textual Cannibalism to Scriptural Completion'. *Journal for the Study of Judaism* 43, no. 4–5 (2012): 475–96. doi:10.1163/15700631-12341236.

Petersen, Silke. '"Women" and "Heresy" in Patristic Discourses and Modern Studies'. In *Women and Knowledge in Early Christianity*, edited by Ulla Tervahauta, Ivan Miroshnikov, Outi Lehtipuu, and Ismo Dunderberg, 187–205. Vigiliae Christianae Supplements 144. Leiden: Brill, 2017. doi:10.1163/9789004344938_011.

Pflieger, Pat. '"Too Good to Be True": 150 Years of Mary Sue', 2002. http://www.merrycoz.org/papers/MARYSUE.xhtml.

Philonenko, Marc. 'Juda et Hérakles'. *Revue d'histoire et de philosophie religieuses* 50 (1970): 61–62.

Pinkowitz, Jacqueline Marie. '"The Rabid Fans That Take [Twilight] Much Too Seriously": The Construction and Rejection of Excess in Twilight Antifandom'. *Transformative Works and Cultures* 7 (2011). doi:10.3983/twc.2011.0247.

Plante, Courtney N., Stephen Reysen, Daniel Chadborn, Sharon E. Roberts, and Kathleen C. Gerbasi. '"Get out of My Fandom, Newbie": A Cross-Fandom Study of Elitism and Gatekeeping in Fans'. *Journal of Fandom Studies* 8, no. 2 (2020): 123–46. doi:10.1386/jfs_00013_1.

Pugh, Sheenagh. *The Democratic Genre: Fan Fiction in a Literary Context*. Bridgend: Seren, 2005.

Ramey, Margaret E. *The Quest for the Fictional Jesus: Gospel Rewrites, Gospel (Re)Interpretation, and Christological Portraits within Jesus Novels*. Cambridge: Lutterworth Press, 2017.

Raphael, Rebecca. 'Sacred Schematics, or Ships and Sanctuaries'. *Journal for Interdisciplinary Biblical Studies* 3, no. 2 (2021): 41–62. doi:10.17613/wnc7-8w05.

Reed, Annette Yoshiko. 'The Afterlives of New Testament Apocrypha'. *Journal of Biblical Literature* 134, no. 2 (2015): 401–25. doi:10.15699/jbl.1342.2015.2916.

Reed, Annette Yoshiko. 'The Modern Invention of "Old Testament Pseudepigrapha"'. *The Journal of Theological Studies* 60, no. 2 (2009): 403–36. doi:10.1093/jts/flp033.

Reed, Annette Yoshiko. 'Pseudepigraphy, Authorship, and the Reception of "the Bible" in Late Antiquity'. In *The Reception and Interpretation of the Bible in Late Antiquity*, edited by Lucian Turcescu and Lorenzo DiTommaso, 467–90. The Bible in Ancient Christianity 6. Leiden: Brill, 2008. doi:10.1163/ej.9789004167155.i-608.116.

Reijnders, Stijn, Abby Waysdorf, Koos Zwaan, and Linda Duits. 'Fandom and Fan Fiction'. In *The International Encyclopedia of Media Effects*, edited by Patrick Rössler, Cynthia A. Hoffner, and Liesbet Zoonen, 1–12. Hoboken, NJ: Wiley, 2017. doi:10.1002/9781118783764.wbieme0176.

Religion for Breakfast. 'Star Wars Fan Fiction Explains Early Christian Apocrypha'. *YouTube*, 22 August 2018. https://www.youtube.com/watch?v=rTTRIA_YWIA.

Rice, Anne. 'Anne's Profession of Faith'. *AnneRice.com: The Official Site*, 11 June 2008. http://annerice.com/ChristTheLord-Profession.html.

Rice, Anne. *Christ the Lord: Out of Egypt: A Novel*. New York: Knopf, 2005.

Rice, Anne. *Christ the Lord: Out of Egypt*. London: Arrow, 2007.

Richards, Denzell. 'Historicizing Transtexts and Transmedia'. In *The Rise of Transtexts: Challenges and Opportunities*, edited by Benjamin W. L. Derhy Kurtz and Mélanie Bourdaa, 15–32. Routledge Research in Cultural and Media Studies. Abingdon: Routledge, 2017. doi:10.4324/9781315671741-9.

Richlin, Amy. 'Sexuality in the Roman Empire'. In *A Companion to the Roman Empire*, edited by David S. Potter, 327–53. Blackwell Companions to the Ancient World. Malden, MA: Blackwell, 2006. doi:10.1002/9780470996942.ch18.

Roberts, Alexander, James Donaldson, and Cleveland A. Coxe, eds. *Ante-Nicene Fathers 3: Latin Christianity: Its Founder, Tertullian*. Ante-Nicene Fathers 3. Christian Literature Company, 1885.

Roberts, Alexander, James Donaldson, and Cleveland A. Coxe, eds. *Ante-Nicene Fathers 4: Fathers of the Third Century: Tertullian, Part Fourth; Minucius Felix; Commodian; Origen, Parts First and Second*. Ante-Nicene Fathers 4. Christian Literature Company, 1885.

Robinson, Maurice. 'Amid Perfect Contempt, a Place for the Genuine: The Long Ending of Mark as Canonical Verity'. In *Perspectives on the Ending of Mark: Four Views*, edited by David Adam Black, 40–79. Nashville, TN: Broadman & Holman, 2008.

Rodenbiker, Kelsie G. 'Disputing with the Devil: Jude, Michael the Archangel, and the Boundaries of Canon'. In *Antike Kanonisierungsprozesse und Identitätsbildung in Zeiten des Umbruchs: Tagungsband zur Internationalen Nachwuchstagung in Münster (26.-27. Mai 2017)*, edited by Marcel Friesen and Christoph Leonard Hesse, 267–82. Wissenschaftliche Schriften der WWU Münster Reihe 10 28. Münster: ULB Münster, 2019.

Rodenbiker, Kelsie G. 'The Second Peter: Pseudepigraphy as Exemplarity in the Second Canonical Petrine Epistle'. *Novum Testamentum* 65, no. 1 (2023): 109–31. doi:10.1163/15685365-bja10038.

Rollens, Sarah E., Eric Vanden Eykel, and Meredith Warren. 'Confronting Judeophobia in the Classroom'. *Journal for Interdisciplinary Biblical Studies* 2, no. 1 (2020): 81–106.

Rollens, Sarah E., Eric Vanden Eykel, and Meredith Warren, eds. *Judeophobia in the New Testament: Texts, Contexts, and Pedagogy*. Grand Rapids, MI: Eerdmans, 2024.

Romano, Aja. 'Star Wars Has Always Been Political. Here's Why the Alt-Right Is Claiming Otherwise'. *Vox*, 31 December 2016. https://www.vox.com/culture/2016/12/31/14024262/star-wars-political-alt-right-backlash.

Römer, Thomas. 'Moses Outside the Torah and the Construction of a Diaspora Identity'. *Journal of Hebrew Scriptures* 8 (2008). doi:10.5508/jhs.2008.v8.a15.

Rosen-Zvi, Ishay. 'Bilhah the Temptress: The *Testament of Reuben* and "The Birth of Sexuality"'. *Jewish Quarterly Review* 96 (2006): 65–94. doi:10.1353/jqr.2005.0098.

Rosland, Kristine Toft. 'Reading the "Apocryphon of John" as Genesis Fan Fiction'. *Transformative Works and Cultures* 31 (15 December 2019). doi:10.3983/twc.2019.1559.

Rothschild, Clare K. *The Muratorian Fragment: Text, Translation, Commentary*. Studies and Texts in Antiquity and Christianity 132. Tübingen: Mohr Siebeck, 2022.

Rowe, C. Kavin. 'What If It Were True? Why Study the New Testament'. *New Testament Studies* 68, no. 2 (2022): 144–55. doi:10.1017/S002868852100031X.

Rüggemeier, Jan, and Elizabeth E. Shively. 'Introduction: Towards a Cognitive Theory of New Testament Characters: Methodology, Problems, and Desiderata'. *Biblical Interpretation* 29, no. 4–5 (2021): 403–29. doi:10.1163/15685152-29040001.

Ruzer, Serge. *Early Jewish Messianism in the New Testament: Reflections in the Dim Mirror*. Jewish and Christian Perspectives Series 36. Leiden: Brill, 2020. doi:10.1163/9789004432932.

Ryan, Marie-Laure. 'Transmedial Storytelling and Transfictionality'. *Poetics Today* 34 (2013): 361–88. doi:10.1215/03335372-2325250.

Salter, Anastasia, and Mel Stanfill. *A Portrait of the Auteur as Fanboy: The Construction of Authorship in Transmedia Franchises*. Jackson, MS: University Press of Mississippi, 2020. doi:10.14325/mississippi/9781496830463.001.0001.

Salvage Editorial Collective. 'Salvage Perspectives #2: Awaiting the Furies'. *Salvage*, 9 November 2015. https://salvage.zone/in-print/salvage-perspectives-2-awaiting-the-furies/.

Sandvoss, Cornel. *Fans: The Mirror of Consumption*. Cambridge: Polity Press, 2005.

Sawyer, John F. A. 'Combating Prejudices about the Bible and Judaism'. *Theology* 94, no. 760 (July 1991): 269–78. doi:10.1177/0040571X9109400405.

Schneemelcher, Wilhelm. *New Testament Apocrypha. Volume I, Gospels and Related Writings*. Translated by R. McL. Wilson. Rev. ed. Cambridge: James Clarke, 2003.

Schrader Polczer, Elizabeth. 'Apocryphal within the Canonical: Unorthodox Influence on the New Testament Text Transmission'. In *Pen, Print, and Pixels: Advances in Textual Criticism in the Digital Era*, edited by Daniel B. Wallace, David Flood, and Elijah Hixson. Peabody, MA: Hendrickson, forthcoming.

Schröter, Jens. 'Apocryphal and Canonical Gospels within the Development of the New Testament Canon'. *Early Christianity* 7, no. 1 (2016): 24–46. doi:10.1628/186870316X14555506071137.

Schröter, Jens. 'Jesus and Early Christian Identity Formation: Reflections on the Significance of the Jesus Figure in Early Christian Gospels'. In *Connecting Gospels:*

Beyond the Canonical/Non-Canonical Divide, edited by Sarah Parkhouse and Francis Watson, 233–56. New York: Oxford University Press, 2018.

Scott, Suzanne. *Fake Geek Girls: Fandom, Gender, and the Convergence Culture Industry*. Critical Cultural Communication. New York: New York University Press, 2019.

Scott, Suzanne. 'Who's Steering the Mothership? The Role of the Fanboy Auteur in Transmedia Storytelling'. In *The Participatory Cultures Handbook*, edited by Aaron Alan Delwiche and Jennifer Jacobs Henderson, 43–52. New York: Routledge, 2013.

Sheffield, Jessica, and Elyse Merlo. 'Biting Back: Twilight Anti-Fandom and the Rhetoric of Superiority'. In *Bitten by Twilight: Youth Culture, Media and the Vampire Franchise*, edited by Melissa A. Click, Jennifer Stevens Aubrey, and Elizabeth Behm-Morawitz, 207–23. Mediated Youth 14. New York: Peter Lang, 2010.

Shively, Elizabeth E. 'Recognizing Penguins: Audience Expectation, Cognitive Genre Theory, and the Ending of Mark's Gospel'. *The Catholic Biblical Quarterly* 80 (2018): 273–92. doi:10.1353/cbq.2018.0051.

Shoemaker, Stephen J. 'Early Christian Apocryphal Literature'. In *The Oxford Handbook of Early Christian Studies*, edited by Susan Ashbrook Harvey and David G. Hunter, 521–48. Oxford Handbooks. Oxford: Oxford University Press, 2008. doi:10.1093/oxfordhb/9780199271566.003.0026.

Slingerland, H. Dixon. 'The Nature of Nomos (Law) Within the *Testaments of the Twelve Patriarchs*'. *Journal of Biblical Literature* 105 (1986): 39–48.

Smit, Peter-Ben. 'Masculinity and the Bible: Survey, Models, and Perspectives'. *Brill Research Perspectives in Biblical Interpretation* 2, no. 1 (2017): 1–97. doi:10.1163/24057657-12340007.

Smith, Geoffrey S. *Guilt by Association: Heresy Catalogues in Early Christianity*. Oxford: Oxford University Press, 2014. doi:10.1093/acprof:oso/9780199386789.001.0001.

Snyder, Julia. 'Relationships between the Acts of the Apostles and Other Apostle Narratives'. In *Between Canonical and Apocryphal Texts: Processes of Reception, Rewriting and Interpretation in Early Judaism and Early Christianity*, edited by Jörg Frey, Tobias Nicklas, and Claire Clivaz, 319–41. Tübingen: Mohr Siebeck, 2019. doi:10.1628/978-3-16-155232-8.

Sparks, Hedley F. D., ed. *The Apocryphal Old Testament*. Oxford: Clarendon Press, 1984.

Spittler, Janet. 'The Development of Miracle Traditions in the Apocryphal Acts of the Apostles'. In *Between Canonical and Apocryphal Texts: Processes of Reception, Rewriting and Interpretation in Early Judaism and Early Christianity*, edited by Jörg Frey, Tobias Nicklas, and Claire Clivaz, 357–80. Mohr Siebeck, 2019. doi:10.1628/978-3-16-155232-8.

Spurrill-Jones, Esther. 'Anne Rice's Out of Egypt Is Not About a Vampire Christ'. *The Book Cafe*, 21 January 2022. https://medium.com/the-book-cafe/anne-rices-out-of-egypt-is-not-about-a-vampire-christ-9cef0f602ea4.

Squires, Nick. 'Archeologists Find Evidence of St Peter's Prison'. *The Telegraph*, 25 June 2010. https://www.telegraph.co.uk/news/worldnews/7852507/Archeologists-find-evidence-of-St-Peters-prison.html.

Stanitzek, Georg. 'Texts and Paratexts in Media'. *Critical Inquiry* 32, no. 1 (September 2005): 27–42. doi:10.1086/498002.

Star Wars. 'The Legendary Star Wars Expanded Universe Turns a New Page', 25 April 2014. https://www.starwars.com/news/the-legendary-star-wars-expanded-universe-turns-a-new-page.

Stefaniw, Blossom. 'Feminist Historiography and Uses of the Past'. *Studies in Late Antiquity* 4, no. 3 (2020): 260–83. doi:10.1525/sla.2020.4.3.260.

Stefaniw, Blossom. 'Masculinity, Historiography, and Uses of the Past: An Introduction'. *Journal of Early Christian History* 11, no. 1 (2021): 1–14. doi:10.1080/222258 2X.2021.1931903.

Stein, Robert H. 'The Ending of Mark'. *Bulletin for Biblical Research* 18 (2008): 79–98.

Stern, Marlow. '"Alt-Right" Trumpsters Discover True Meaning of "Star Wars," Wage #DumpStarWars Campaign'. *The Daily Beast*, 9 December 2016, sec. entertainment. https://www.thedailybeast.com/articles/2016/12/08/alt-right-neo-nazis-discover-true-meaning-of-star-wars-wage-dumpstarwars-campaign.

Stone, Michael E. 'Ideal Figures and Social Context: Priest and Sage in the Early Second Temple Age'. In *Ancient Israelite Religion: Essays in Honor of Frank Moore Cross*, edited by P. D. Miller, Paul. D. Hanson, and D. McBride, 575–86. Philadelphia, PA: Fortress Press, 1987.

Stratton, Kimberly B. 'The Rhetoric of "Magic" in Early Christian Discourse: Gender, Power and the Construction of "Heresy"'. In *Mapping Gender in Ancient Religious Discourses*, edited by Todd Penner and Caroline Vander Stichele, 89–114. Biblical Interpretation Series 84. Leiden: Brill, 2006. doi:10.1163/ej.9789004154476.i-582.21.

Swist, Jeremy. '"Wolves of the Krypteia": Lycanthropy and Right-Wing Extremism in Metal's Reception of Ancient Greece and Rome'. *Metal Music Studies* 8, no. 3 (2022): 309–25. doi:10.1386/mms_00083_1.

T&T Clark Encyclopedia of Second Temple Judaism, edited by Loren T. Stuckenbruck and Daniel M. Gurtner. London: T&T Clark, 2019.

Tertullian. *Traité de la prescription contre les hérétiques*. Translated by R. F. Refoulé. Sources chrétiennes 46. 1957. Reprint, Paris: Cerf, 2006.

Thomas, Bronwen. 'Canons and Fanons: Literary Fanfiction Online'. *Dichtung Digital* 37 (2007). doi:10.25969/mediarep/17701.

Thomas, Paul. 'Canon Wars: A Semiotic and Ethnographic Study of a Wikipedia Talk Page Debate Concerning the Canon of *Star Wars*'. *The Journal of Fandom Studies* 6, no. 3 (2018): 279–300. doi:10.1386/jfs.6.3.279_1.

Thompson, Tok. 'The Beauty, the Beast, and the Fanon: The Vernacularization of the Literary Canon and an Epilogue to Modernity'. In *Folklore and Social Media*, edited by Trevor J. Blank and Andrew Peck, 161–78. Louisville, CO: University Press of Colorado, 2020. doi:10.7330/9781646420599.c008.

Thon, Jan-Noël. 'Converging Worlds: From Transmedial Storyworlds to Transmedial Universes'. *Storyworlds: A Journal of Narrative Studies* 7 (2015): 21–53. doi:10.5250/storyworlds.7.2.0021.

Tite, Philip L. 'It's Not So Secret Anymore: Shifts in the Study of Christian Apocrypha'. *Bulletin for the Study of Religion* 48, no. 3–4 (2020): 1–3. doi:10.1558/bsor.41168.

Tolkien, J. R. R. 'On Fairy-Stories'. In *Essays Presented to Charles Williams*, Reprint., 38–89. Grand Rapids: Eerdmans, 1966.

Tor.com. 'Anne Rice Admits to Writing Jesus Fan Fiction', 1 April 2009. https://www.tor.com/2009/04/01/april-fooanne-rice-admits-to-writing-jesus-fan-fiction/.

Tóth, Peter. 'Way Out of the Tunnel? Three Hundred Years of Research on the Apocrypha: A Preliminary Approach'. In *Retelling the Bible: Literary, Historical, and Social Contexts*, edited by Lucie Doležalová and Tamás Visi, 47–86. Frankfurt am Main: Lang, 2011.

Trevett, Christine. 'Spiritual Authority and the "heretical" Woman: Firmilian's Word to the Church in Carthage'. In *Portraits of Spiritual Authority*, edited by Jan Willem Drijvers and John Watt, 45–62. Religions in the Graeco-Roman World 137. Leiden: Brill, 1999. doi:10.1163/9789004295919_004.

Turk, Tisha. 'Fan Work: Labor, Worth, and Participation in Fandom's Gift Economy'. *Transformative Works and Cultures* 15 (2013). doi:10.3983/twc.2014.0518.
TV Tropes. 'Ascended Fan Nickname'. https://tvtropes.org/pmwiki/pmwiki.php/Main/AscendedFanNickname.
TV Tropes. 'Ascended Fanon'. https://tvtropes.org/pmwiki/pmwiki.php/Main/AscendedFanon.
Tveit, Elaine. 'General Hux's Cat Millicent Is Fan Fiction At Its Finest'. *Dork Side of the Force*, 2 December 2016. https://dorksideoftheforce.com/2016/02/12/general-huxs-cat-millicent-is-fan-fiction-at-its-finest/.
Uhlenbruch, Frauke, and Sonja Ammann. 'Fan Fiction and Ancient Scribal Cultures'. *Transformative Works and Cultures* 31 (2019). doi:10.3983/twc.2019.1887.
Ulrich, Eugene. 'The Notion and Definition of Canon'. In *The Canon Debate: On the Origins and Formation of the Bible*, edited by Lee Martin McDonald and James A Sanders, 21–35. Peabody, MA: Hendrickson, 2002.
Ulrichsen, Jarl H. *Die Grundschrift der Testamente der zwölf Patriarchen: Eine Untersuchung zu Umfang, Inhalt und Eigenart der ursprünglichen Schrift*. Uppsala: Almqvist & Wiksell, 1991.
Veneto, Nicole. '"That Lightsaber. It Belongs to Me": Patriarchal Anxiety and the Fragility of White Men's Masculinity in The Force Awakens'. *FilmMatters* 8, no. 3 (2017): 30–35. doi:10.1386/fm.8.3.30_1.
Walters, Lori J. 'Introduction'. In *Lancelot and Guinevere: A Casebook*, edited by Lori j Walters, xiii–lxxx. Arthurian Characters and Themes 4. New York: Routledge, 2000.
Warren, Meredith. 'My OTP: Harry Potter Fanfiction and the Old Testament Pseudepigrapha'. *Scriptura* 8 (2006): 53–66.
Wassén, Cecelia. 'The Story of Judah and Tamar in the Eyes of the Earliest Interpreters'. *Literature and Theology* 8 (1994): 354–66. doi:10.1093/litthe/8.4.354.
Wekker, Gloria. *White Innocence: Paradoxes of Colonialism and Race*. Durham, NC: Duke University Press, 2016.
Welborn, Larry L. 'Voluntary Exile as the Solution to Discord in 1 Clement'. *Zeitschrift Für Antikes Christentum / Journal of Ancient Christianity* 18, no. 1 (2014). doi:10.1515/zac-2014-0002.
White, Jerry. 'Jeanne Dielmann Was My Star Wars'. *The Dalhousie Review* 96, no. 1 (2016): 129–34.
Willis, Ika. 'The Classical Canon and/as Transformative Work'. *Transformative Works and Cultures* 21 (2016). doi:10.3983/twc.2016.0807.
Willis, Ika. '"Writers Who Put Themselves in the Story": Dante Alghieri, Roland Barthes, Lieutenant Mary-Sue and Me'. *Desiring the Text, Touching the Past: Towards an Erotics of Reception Conference*, Bristol, 2010.
Wilson, Allen, and Tom de Bruin. 'Teaching the New Testament as an Expanded Universe'. *Ancient Jew Review*, 16 August 2021. https://www.ancientjewreview.com/read/2021/8/16/teaching-the-new-testament-as-an-expanded-universe.
Wilson, Anna. 'Fan Fiction and Premodern Literature: Methods and Definitions'. *Transformative Works and Cultures* 36 (2021). doi:10.3983/twc.2021.2037.
Wilson, Anna. 'The Role of Affect in Fan Fiction'. *Transformative Works and Cultures* 21 (2016). doi:10.3983/twc.2016.0684.
Wilson, Brittany E. *Unmanly Men: Refigurations of Masculinity in Luke-Acts*. Oxford: Oxford University Press, 2015.
Windon, Brad. 'The Seduction of Weak Men: Tertullian's Rhetorical Construction of Gender and Ancient Christian "Heresy"'. In *Mapping Gender in Ancient Religious*

Discourses, edited by Todd Penner and Caroline Vander Stichele, 457–78. Biblical Interpretation Series 84. Leiden: Brill, 2006. doi:10.1163/ej.9789004154476.i-582.83.

Wisker, Gina. *Horror Fiction: An Introduction*. Continuum Studies in Literary Genre. New York: Continuum, 2005.

Wolf, Mark J. P. *Building Imaginary Worlds: The Theory and History of Subcreation*. New York: Routledge, 2013. doi:10.4324/9780203096994.

Wookieepedia. 'Canon', 24 October 2021. https://starwars.fandom.com/wiki/Canon#Canon_in_the_Holocron_continuity_database.

Young, Stephen L. '"Let's Take the Text Seriously": The Protectionist Doxa of Mainstream New Testament Studies'. *Method & Theory in the Study of Religion* 32, no. 4–5 (2019): 328–63. doi:10.1163/15700682-12341469.

Young, Stephen L. 'So Radically Jewish That He's an Evangelical Christian: N.T. Wright's Judeophobic and Privileged Paul'. *Interpretation: A Journal of Bible and Theology* 76, no. 4 (2022): 339–51. doi:10.1177/00209643221107910.

Zetterholm, Magnus. 'Introduction'. In *The Messiah: In Early Judaism and Christianity*, edited by Magnus Zetterholm, xxi–xxvii. Minneapolis, MN: Fortress Press, 2007.

Zubernis, Lynn, and Katherine Larsen. 'Make Space for Us! Fandom in the Real World'. In *A Companion to Media Fandom and Fan Studies*, edited by Paul Booth, 145–60. Wiley Blackwell Companions in Cultural Studies. Hoboken, NJ: Wiley Blackwell, 2018.

INDEX

aca-fan 171-4
Against Celsus (Origen) 50, 55, 160
Against Heresies (Irenaeus) 48
age politics. *see* elders; infantalization
Akhmîm fragment 147-8
Alexandrians, Letter to 106
amateurship (amateur status) 16, 64
Ammann, Sonja 40
Amsler, Monika 12, 155
Andrew (apostle) 46
'Anne's Profession of Faith' (Rice) 3
antisemitism. *see* Jewish people and Judeophobia
anonymous authors 18, 66, 70, 71
Apelles 134
Apocrypha 3-4, 14-15, 88-92, 138-9, 141-2, 146-7, 156-7
The Apocryphal New Testament (James & Elliott) 90-2
apostles 48, 49, 50, 133
archives 32-4
'Archontic Literature: A Definition, a History, and Several Theories of Fan Fiction' (Derecho) 32-3
Arthurian myths 17
Athanasius of Alexandria 100, 101
Augustine of Hippo 165
author's notes 67-8, 71, 87-8, 170-1

Bad Fans 123-6, 130, 131, 134, 135
Bader, Mary Anna 72-3
Barclay, John 126n79
Barenblat, Rachel 12
Basic Elements of Narrative (Herman) 143
Bauer, Walter 117-18, 119-20, 122
Beauty and the Beast 163
Bergren, Theodore 127
bias in academic study 171-4
Bode, Lisa 126, 130
Booth, Paul 62, 76, 85n125, 142
Borchardt, Francis 69n48
Bovon, François 21, 99-100

Brakke, David 119
Building Imaginary Worlds (Wolf) 148-9
Burke, Tony 4, 14, 29-30, 33-4, 90
Busse, Kristina 8, 24, 49, 51, 83, 101, 116-20, 125, 161-2

canon, a definition 22-5. *see also* hierarchy of texts; non-canon; received texts; useful canon; semi-canon
capitalism 16, 18-19
Cartlidge, David 153
Chee, Leland 107-8
Christian Apocrypha. *see* Apocrypha
Christ the Lord, Out of Egypt (Rice). *see* Rice, Anne
Clark, Elizabeth 132
classical texts 9, 10-11, 21, 82, 137, 144-6
Clement of Alexandria 64, 97, 98-9
Clement of Rome 126-7, 128-30
commercial control 152
community ownership 20-1, 31, 118-19, 135-6, 142, 152
Conceptual Blending 159
conventions 101, 127-8
Coogan, Jeremiah 111-12
Cook, Roy 95-6
Coppa, Francesca 15-18, 20-2
Coptic Orthodox Church 100
Corinthians 126-7, 128-30
corruption 55-6, 57
counter-narrative 46-7
Cyril of Jerusalem 99

The Da Vinci Code (Brown) 149
Darth Vader (*Star Wars*) 155-6
den Dulk, Matthijs 121-2, 125
Derecho, Abigail 32-3
derivative texts 5
Derrida, Jacques 32-3
deSilva, David 71-2
Dialogue with Trypho (Justin) 121-2, 125
Dinah 73-4

Diski, Jenny 87–8, 89
divine revelation 73–4, 77
Dresken-Weiland, Jutta 154
Duffett, Mark 7–8, 30, 171
Dunlap, Kathryn 124

Eastern Orthodox Church 161n113, 164
Ecclesiastical History (Eusebius) 99, 102, 105, 108, 110
Egyptian gospel 98
Ehrman, Bart 37, 55–6, 126
Elder, Nicholas 13, 33
elders 126n79, 128–9
Elliott, J.K. 90, 91–2, 149, 153, 156–7
emotional attachment 8, 9
enslaved scribes 65–6
Enterprising Women: Television Fandom and the Creation of Popular Myth (Bacon-Smith) 100–1
Eusebius 50, 80n101, 99, 102, 104–5, 108, 110
Eyl, Jennifer 16–17

Fake Geek Girl (Scott) 127–8
Fakes, Forgeries, Fictions: Writing Ancient and Modern Christian Apocrypha (Burke) 14
Fan Cultures (Hills) 123–4
fan fiction, a definition 2n6, 13–22, 32–3, 74, 141
fan play 62, 84
fan reference works 103–5, 107–8
fan strategies 52n145
fandom 8–10, 20–1, 66, 75, 100–1, 118–20
Fanlore (Coppa) 13, 15–18, 20–2
fanon 22, 95, 117, 139, 160–1, 162–3
fans, a definition 7–8, 9–10, 30–1, 126–31, 171
fanzines 101
fascination 31, 39, 62
Fathallah, Judith 31, 32–3, 76, 123, 125, 130–1
feminization 130–5, 136
Ferguson, Everett 111
Firmilian 131
Fish, Stanley 120
fix-it fiction 40–2, 43, 74–6
flame wars 120
forgeries 11, 14–15, 106, 109

Freer Logion 36, 51–4
frustration 29–31, 39, 62

gaps in narrative 61–2, 90, 142, 147–, 159–60
gatekeeping 27, 32–3, 122–6, 130–6, 166, 173
The Gendered Palimpsest (Haines-Eitzen) 45
gendering fandom 125, 127–8, 130–6
gender politics. *see* misogyny; women; women characters
Genesis 72
Genette, Gerard 66–7
gift economy
    in early Christian communities 119
    in fan communities 63–6
Gilfillan Upton, Bridget 38
Goodman, Lesley 41, 74–5, 159
The Gospel as Manuscript (Keith) 30
gospels 6, 21, 41–5, 51n137, 97, 97–103, 108, 111–12, 137–8
Graham Brock, Anne 44
Gray, Jonathan 150n62
Greek myths 10–11, 33, 137, 144–5, 146, 148

Habakkuk 158–9, 160
Haines-Eitzen, Kim 45
Harmon, Lee 88, 89
Hartog, Paul 118
Hassler-Forest. Dan 93, 99, 104, 107, 143, 149, 150, 167
Hawk, Brandon 139–40, 142
headcanon 27, 139–43
Hellekson, Karen 24, 49, 64, 83, 100, 161–2
heresy 98, 103, 116–18, 122–6, 131–6
Herman, David 143
Herzog, Alexandra 67, 69
Hidalgo, Pablo 140
hierarchy of texts 27, 33, 72, 99–106, 109–10, 113, 130, 138, 149–50
Hills, Matt 9, 123–4, 125, 126, 172
historical accuracy 2, 3, 88–92, 138, 146
The Hitch Hiker's Guide to the Galaxy 27, 95, 169
Homilies on Luke (Origen) 97–8, 158, 164
Horrell, David 129
Huggins, Ronald 165

Hurtado, Larry 20
Hux, General (*Star Wars*) 140–2, 155

identity 8, 30, 120, 130
infancy gospels 62
infantalization 126–30, 136
influence of texts 137, 138, 156, 163, 166–7, 170
interpretation 71–4, 76, 80–1, 85, 116–23, 147. *see also* headcanon
Investiture of the Archangel Michael 12
Irenaeus of Smyrna 48, 97, 111
Isaiah 158–9, 160, 164

Jacobi, Christine 21
James, M.R. 90–1, 97
Jenkins, Henry 30–1, 42, 46, 48, 52, 57, 62, 81, 82n109, 93, 123–4, 125, 171
Jensen, Robin Margaret 153
Jeremiah 152–3
Jerome, St 36, 52, 80n101, 109–10
Jewish people and Judeophobia 125, 147, 164–5, 167
Johnson, Derek 120–1, 122
Johnston, Sarah Iles 137, 144–6, 148
Jones, Sara Gwenllian 82, 83
Joseph and Aseneth 13, 33
Judas 43, 54
Judeophobia. *see* Jewish people and Judeophobia
Justin Martyr 48, 50, 97, 106, 121–2, 125

Keith, Chris 30, 105, 106
Kelhoffer, James 40, 47–8, 50, 52, 54–5
Kempe, Margery 49
Kolenkow, Anitra B 67n39
Kugel, James 52–3, 71–2, 84–5
Kugler, Robert 70n58, 84–5

Laodiceans, Letter to 106
Larsen, Kasper Bro 12
Larsen, Katherine 9, 173
Letter to Africanus (Origen) 109
The Literary Imagination in Jewish Antiquity (Mroczek) 34
'Longer Ending' of Mark 38–9, 41–2, 46, 47–8, 50–1
Lord of the Rings 24, 162–3
Lossky, Vladimir 164

Lost/Lostpedia 103–5
Lucas, George 107, 110–11, 139n9
Luke, Gospel of 54, 137–8, 145, 157–9, 160
Lundhaug, Hugo 12, 159
Luz, Ulrich 51n137
Lyden John 111
Lyons-Pardue, Kara 38–9, 44, 49, 55, 56–7

magi 161
Manasse, King 40
Mark, Gospel of 21, 29–30, 35–9, 41–4, 46–8, 50–6
Martin, George R.R. 69
Martyrdom of Blessed Peter of the Holy Trinity (Pseudo-Linus) 154
Mary, Gospel of 46, 135n118
Mary Magdalene 35, 38–9, 42–7, 49, 142
Mary Sue characters 49
Matthew, Gospel of 51n137, 53–4, 108, 137–8, 157–9
Matthews, Shelly 19
McDonald, Lee 69
McKee, Alan 150
Melusina (author) 161
Messianic Secret 53
metal music 82
Metzger, Bruce 35–6, 37
Meyer, Marvin 43
Millicent the cat (*Star Wars*) 140–2, 155
Miracle and Mission: The Authentication of Missionaries and Their Message in the Longer Ending of Mark (Kelhoffer) 47–8
miracles 47–8, 49–50, 146, 148–9, 153–4, 167
misogyny 44, 132, 135
Mittell, Jason 103–4
Moss, Candida 65
motivation to create 16–17, 30–1, 52n145, 62–3, 66, 117. *see also* fix-it fiction; political motivation; recontextualization
Mroczek, Eva 34, 72, 152
Muratorian Fragment 105–6
My Little Pony: Friendship is Magic 162
mythlogical creatures 144–6, 148

nativity scenes 142–3, 157–9, 160, 161, 163, 164–5

New Testament Apocrypha. *see* Apocrypha
nice 69
Nicklas, Tobias 4
noms de plume 66
non-canon 100, 103–5, 146–7, 155–6. *see also* headcanon
nostalgia 62–3, 71–7, 84n116, 85
novelty 62–3, 78–3, 84n116, 85

objectivity 172–4
objects of fandom 9–10
Old Testament Pseudepigrapha. *see* Pseudepigrapha
On Baptism (Tertullian) 19
Onesiphorus 156
Origen of Alexandria 48, 50, 55, 61n9, 101, 108–10, 158–60, 164
orthodoxy of belief 1, 2, 3–4, 55–6, 118, 131–2, 170–1
othering 98, 122, 128–30, 136
Otto, Jennifer 80n101
Ouspensky, Léonide 164

Pande, Rukmini 174
Pappas, Nickolas 81
parabiblical texts, a definition 22–4
paratext 66–8, 71, 76–7, 150n62
Parkhouse, Sarah 46, 135n118
Parks, Sara 44
Paul 18, 19–20, 47, 48n119, 106, 126, 156–7
Paul and Thecla 18, 19
payment 63–6
Pearson, Roberta 151, 155
personal involvement 171–4
Peter (apostle) 6, 45, 46, 80n101, 106, 153–4, 157
Peter, Gospel of 102–3, 105, 147–8
Peter, Revelation of 106
Petersen, Silke 134
Philip, Gospel of 45
Philo of Alexandria 80n101
Philumene 134
pilgrimages 151, 154–5, 160n113
Pistis Sophia 48
Playing Fans: Negotiating Fandom in the Digital Age (Booth) 62
political motivation 31, 32, 141, 143, 144, 147, 150, 166

Prescription Against Heretics (Tertullian) 132, 133–4
Pride and Prejudice archive 32
Primary World vs Secondary World 145, 148–9, 150, 167
problematic content 82, 141
professional status 16
prophecy 78–9
Pseudo-Gelasian decree 109–10
Pseudo-Matthew, Gospel of 158–9, 160
Pseudepigrapha, 12, 25, 163
  a definition 59
Pugh, Sheenagh 61–2

Ramey, Margaret 3
realism 88–92, 148–9, 167
received texts 105, 108, 111, 113, 153
Rechtgläubigkeit und Ketzerei im altesten Christentum (Orthodoxy and Heresy in Earliest Christianity) (Bauer) 117–18
recontextualization 52–4, 147
Reed, Annette 70
refocalization 43, 45, 142
repetition 119
resistive reading 81
retconning 78–80, 118
Revelation (of John) 106
Rice, Anne 1–6, 29–30, 59–60, 62, 66, 80n101, 87–89, 115–16, 138–9, 170–1
Richards, Denzell 151
Rodenbiker, Kelsie 23, 157
Rosland, Kristine Toft 12
Rowe, Kavin 173, 174
Rufinus 109–110

Satan 54
Schneemelcher, Wilhelm 141–2
Schröter, Jens 97, 103, 147
Scott, Suzanne 96, 127–128, 132–3, 135
scribes 65–6, 156
Secondary World vs Primary World 145, 148–9, 150, 167
secret knowledge 78
self-insertion fic 48–9, 51
semi-canon 104
Serapion of Antioch 102–3, 105
Shepherd of Hermas 106

Shoemaker, Stephen 33–4
slash fiction 82, 83
Smith, Geoffrey 124
snake-handling 47
Snyder, Julia 147
Spittler, Janet 11, 146, 149
Spurrill-Jones, Esther 115–16
Stanitek, George 67n33
Star Trek 9, 24, 49, 101
Star Wars 94–5, 96–7, 107–8, 110–11, 139–41, 142, 155–6
Star Wars Wikipedia page 110–11, 112
Stefaniw, Blossom 133
Stein, Robert 37
stereotypes of fans 124, 125, 131, 135, 171
The Story of Myth (Johnston) 144–5
storytelling 16, 18–19
storyworlds 93–4, 137–9, 143–50, 150–5, 155–66
Stratton, Kimberley 131
Stuart, Alasdair 161
subjectivity 172–4
Susanna, Book of 109
Swist, Jeremy 82

Tertullian 48, 50, 132, 133–5
Testament of Levi 73–4, 76–8
Testament of Reuben 68n41, 74, 75n78, 80
Testament of Simeon 77, 78–80, 81
Testaments of the Twelve Patriarchs 60, 67–74, 76–81, 83–5
text, a definition 150–1
The Text of the New Testament (Metzger & Ehrman) 37
Textual Commentary on the Greek New Testaments (Metzger) 35–6
Textual Poachers: Television Fans & Participatory Culture (Jenkins). *see* Jenkins, Henry
Textus Receptus. *see* Longer Ending
Theophilus of Antioch 48, 50
Thomas (apostle) 43

Thomas, Gospel of 45, 88, 145
Thomas, Paul 107–8, 110, 112
Tite, Philip 92
Tolkien, J.R.R. 24, 93, 145n36, 162n125
Tor.com 2
Traditions of the Bible: A Guide to the Bible As It Was at the Start of the Common Era (Kugel) 52–53
Transformative Works and Cultures 10, 12
translations 25–26, 35, 64, 74n74, 106, 109
transmedia 93–6, 104, 144, 148, 150–6, 161, 167
true crime community 130–131
Turk, Tisha 63–4
Tveit, Elaine 141
Twilight 20n95, 124, 125–30

Uhlenbruch, Frauke 40
useful canon 100–3, 106, 142, 147

Vaccaro Lewis, Jody 160n113
van Os, Bas 44
visual imagery 10, 153–4, 157–9, 161n113, 163, 164–5
von Harnack, Adolf 50

Warren, Meredith 12, 95, 122–3, 163
Wekker, Gloria 165–6
Willis, Ika 10–11
Windon, Brad 133
Wolf, Carissa 124
Wolf, Mark 148–9, 150, 155, 167
women 18–19, 49, 129, 131, 133–5. *see also* gendering fandom
women characters 43–4, 45–6, 74n75
world building. *see* storyworlds
Wright, N.T. 173–4

Young, Stephen 173

Zubernis, Lynn S. 9, 173
Zwarte Piet (Black Pete) 166

www.ingramcontent.com/pod-product-compliance
Lightning Source LLC
Chambersburg PA
CBHW051523230426
43668CB00012B/1724